FLUX

What Marketing Managers Need to Navigate the New Environment

Edited by
DAVID SOBERMAN AND DILIP SOMAN

With a foreword by Roger Martin

UNIVERSITY OF TORONTO PRESS
Toronto Buffalo London

© University of Toronto Press 2012
Rotman–UTP Publishing

University of Toronto Press
Toronto Buffalo London
www.utppublishing.com
Printed in Canada

ISBN 978-1-4426-4403-8

Printed on acid-free, 100% post-consumer recycled paper with vegetable-based inks.

Flux: What marketing managers need to navigate the new environment /
edited by David Soberman and Dilip Soman ; with foreword by
Roger Martin.

Includes bibliographical references and index.
ISBN 978-1-4426-4403-8

1. Marketing—Management.   2. Marketing—Decision making.
3. Consumer behavior.   I. Soberman, David Allan, 1960–   II. Soman, Dilip

HF5145.13.F58 2012   658.8   C2012-904873-9

University of Toronto Press acknowledges the financial assistance to its
publishing program of the Canada Council for the Arts and the Ontario
Arts Council.

 Canada Council   Conseil des Arts
for the Arts   du Canada    ONTARIO ARTS COUNCIL
CONSEIL DES ARTS DE L'ONTARIO

University of Toronto Press acknowledges the financial support of the
Government of Canada through the Canada Book Fund for its publishing
activities.

Contents

Part Three: Marketing Management to Engage

Foreword

While it is dangerous for a management school dean to show favouritism to one scholarly business discipline over another, I can claim that sentimentality drives me towards marketing. I have had the pleasure of working closely with senior management of Procter & Gamble since 1986, so marketing is very near and dear to my heart. Much has happened to the practice of marketing in the quarter-century that I have been involved there, so I am particularly pleased that the Rotman School marketing area has compiled this wonderful book, *Flux: What Marketing Managers Need to Navigate the New Environment*, which chronicles where we have come from, where we are today, and where we are going in marketing.

Flux takes the reader on a dazzling journey across the full sweep of marketing theory and practice, seen through the eyes of our gifted marketing professors. It has been a pleasure to watch our marketing area grow and prosper. Looking down the list of chapters, I can see only three professors who were here when I took over as dean; the other eleven are representative of the massive influx of marketing talent that has graced our school. At this point, our marketing area takes a back seat to no one.

It is a particular pleasure to see Delaine Hampton among the chapter authors. Delaine was a long-time thinking partner of mine at Proctor & Gamble and I was thrilled that she joined the Rotman School after her long and extremely successful career there. I always respected Delaine for creating a productive bridge between P&G and the academic marketing community – a model that I hope her successors at P&G follow and other companies would be wise to mimic.

In our many discussions about marketing during her time at P&G and since, one theme has consistently endured, and that is the convergence of marketing and strategy. If we go back to 1986, it was much easier to draw a bright boundary line between strategy and marketing. Strategy was about industry and competitive analysis and marketing was about the four Ps. I remember it well from business school a few years before!

Now I can't tell where strategy stops and marketing starts – or vice versa. Both are about creating a distinctive and powerful tie to the customer, and continuing to migrate and maintain that potent connection through the rapid and unpredictable changes in our modern global economy. Thus I see great wisdom in the three major sections of the book – the best new thinking on the changing landscape in which marketing takes place, the lessons from the latest in customer psychology, and the implications for marketing management.

Without a profound marketing strategy – if I can call it that – a firm is doomed to a miserable existence of price-pressure, customer-churn, and mediocrity. I think that any organization that wants to soar above that fate should absorb everything it can out of *Flux*.

I would like to thank all the authors for their contribution to this volume and in particular Professors Dilip Soman and David Soberman for their leadership role in editing it. It is truly a contribution to our knowledge in a critical business discipline.

Roger Martin
Dean
Rotman School of Management
University of Toronto

Introduction

The landscape on which firms interact with customers is in a state of flux. In the last few years, we have seen dramatic changes in the manner in which this interaction takes place. From the consumer's perspective, easy access to information has drastically changed the very nature of the purchasing behaviour. The traditional "store choice followed by brand choice" model has now given way to an "I know what I want and will seek it out" mentality, and in some cases even an "I know what I want and I'd like a seller who can help me customize it" mentality.

The nature of marketing communications has also changed. With the rise of social networking and the internet more generally, there is a lot more peer-to-peer communication, and consumers demand more interactivity. Given this easy access to information and ability to compare products, consumers are becoming savvier and more value conscious. They want the best value for every dollar they spend. The recent economic downturn has underscored this tendency. It has been argued, therefore, that consumers have become fickle towards brand equity, per se, unless it is matched by superior value delivery. Consequently, the traditional models of mass media and brand-building have eroded.

Things have also changed dramatically from the marketer's perspective. The cost of collecting, storing, and analysing consumer data is plummeting, and as a result it is easier to use consumer data to design customized marketing programs for different segments. Marketers are beginning to harness the power of social networks to create new-age, more contemporary brands and communication channels. Marketers have realized that brand-building is not enough – many strong brands are finding it difficult to compete in this new battlefield, the point of purchase! And given the growing power of both the retailer and the consumer in shaping brand equity, firms now need to wake up to the realization that the tight control they used to have on their brands may be loosening.

How does a firm respond to these challenges? How do they make the move from having customers who are satisfied to customers who are engaged? How do they draw from the latest research on the psychology and economics of consumer behaviour to better understand the new consumer? What specific guidelines can the latest academic research provide them as they start constructing a customer-focused enterprise?

Our colleagues at University of Toronto's Rotman School of Management are leading experts in marketing academia and have been building a portfolio of research that addresses precisely these questions. As an academic institution, we value rigorous academic research that stands to the highest quality of the peer-reviewed journal publishing process. As a business school, we value research that is applicable – research that informs the marketing manager in developing both short-term tactics as well as longer-term strategies for keeping the consumer engaged. Three key philosophical issues lie at the heart of our Rotman approach to marketing. First, we believe that marketing isn't a job that is restricted to the marketing department alone, but rather one that represents a business approach and a way of thinking about how a firm creates value for their customers and for themselves. Second, the only way to engage consumers is through a comprehensive 360-degree understanding of the consumer as a social animal. Third, technology and analytics are mere enablers of value creation. Without an understanding of consumers and their value drivers, these tools are of limited use.

This book is divided into three parts. In the first part, authors present the latest thinking on the changing landscape and what marketing managers need in order to navigate through the changes. In chapter 1, David Soberman addresses the role of a brand manager and provides guidance on how a manager should handle challenges like lack of good information (particularly key in a rapidly changing environment), politics, uncertainty, and fear of the unknown. These challenges are examined in the context of the planning process that is so essential to effective marketing. In chapter 2, David Dunne points out that if businesses in the past needed to take customer satisfaction into account, now they need to do much more to engage customers. There is now much more opportunity for customers to "talk back" to manufacturers, through blogs, Facebook, Twitter, and so on. Yet many marketers are not ready for this change and see this development as a threat. This chapter provides guidelines for how managers could (and should) embrace these changes successfully. In chapter 3, Sridhar Moorthy uses a number of cases in conjunction with a synthesis of psychology- and economics-based research to arrive at an integrated paradigm for thinking about branding strategy. Key to his framework is the recognition that brands are essentially ways to communicate with consumers, and they do so in multiple ways. And in chapter 4, Avi Goldfarb presents his research on the evolution of the internet and goes on to talk more generally about its effect on the field of marketing and, more specifically, on revenue models and models of advertising.

The second part of the book will move on to an analysis of the customer through several lenses. Given that the paradigm of marketing has shifted to one of engagement, it is critically important for managers to get a comprehensive 360-degree view of the consumer – a view that is informed not just by traditional market research, but also by all the relevant social sciences. In chapter 5, Andy Mitchell discusses models of persuasion to guide the manager on developing marketing communications programs. These models help the manager design advertising and measure its effectiveness using both old and new media. In chapter 6, Claire Tsai views consumers through the lens of behavioural economics. Her research shows that in many situations, people ultimately choose products that they do not enjoy as much as the ones they rejected. This clearly has implications for satisfaction, and hence this chapter explains (and prescribes a solution for) why products that sell well might not sustain in the long run.

In chapter 7, Andrew Ching presents a review of research based on the econometric models of forward-looking consumers. This quantitative lens helps the manager to understand customer behaviour better over time. Examples include the tendency to stockpile when products are on sale and the learning strategies that customers use following the introduction of a new product. The theme of forward-looking customers is further developed by Ron Borkovsky in chapter 8. This chapter discusses how firms need to think about marketing management decisions given the long-term effects that many decisions have. A key message of this chapter is that firms cannot afford to focus on the short-term impact of their decisions even when consumers themselves are myopic with their decision-making. The danger of not being forward-looking is demonstrated by a number of stories that highlight the inertia that is associated with many strategic decisions made by brand managers.

Chapters 9 and 10 use different elements in the "behavioural economics" lens. In chapter 9, Min Zhao discusses the role of visualization on consumer choice and in particular their decision to adopt new products. Her research provides insight into the marketing manager on behavioural strategies and tactics that can facilitate and accelerate the adoption of really new products. And in chapter 10, Nina Mazar dives deeply into the role that morality plays in purchasing decisions. Immoral behaviour has effects that are both local (e.g., customers cheat and that may cost the firm) and global (e.g., a social welfare problem).

The third part of the book contains five chapters that provide prescriptive advice and analyse elements of the marketing mix that have grown in importance in the new tomorrow. In chapter 11, Mengze Shi studies the management of consumer incentives and prescribes how managers should best tackle decisions about whether and how to promote products through incentives. Given the omnipresence of loyalty programs and contests, this chapter provides insight to managers on how to improve the effectiveness of these activities.

In chapter 12, Dilip Soman studies situations in which consumers have to wait. Drawing from his research in the area of social psychology and behavioural economics, he outlines a series of "wait management" strategies. In chapter 13, Pankaj Aggarwal challenges the belief that relationship-building and brand-building are different and distinct approaches to marketing, and presents his research showing the nexus between the two by using the metaphor of brands-as-people in a consumer-brand context. In chapter 14, Aparna Labroo studies altruism and giving behaviour. She not only elaborates on reasons why people behave altruistically, but also discusses a set of strategies and interventions that can get people to give more.

The final chapter in the book integrates and synthesizes the contents of this volume. It is a call to action for practising marketers, academics, and students of marketing to put the ideas and insights of this book to use as soon as possible. Its author, Delaine Hampton, draws on twenty-five years of experience supporting marketing innovation at P&G to show how this can be done: start with research findings, aim them at real problems, develop supporting tools and techniques, and finally help managers integrate these into the daily activities of their organizations. The need and the opportunity are obvious; the pace of change in today's marketplace demands much faster accommodation of new realities for consumers, marketers, retailers, and manufacturers. Marketers will be more agile with brand-building and serving consumers if they adopt the knowledge shared in this book, but this will not happen naturally or quickly. Much closer engagement between academics, marketers, and other specialists is needed. The final chapter uses cases and stories from P&G to identify how all the participants can co-operate to achieve better uptake of emerging knowledge. Based on her experience, Delaine presents direct challenges to all players.

Academics need to think in terms of solutions to problems that managers have and actively promote the application of their research. Practitioners and academics speak different languages and operate with different goals and rewards. Academics should not assume that marketing managers will notice new research or see the useful implications for research findings if they do notice. Academics are familiar with the science and need to help imagine how their findings might improve marketing success. Ongoing partnership between academics and practising marketers will create more relevant research and wiser experimentation. It will also break down the communication barriers that make academic journals impenetrable to the typical marketing manager, and make the daily challenges of marketing seem messy and un-researchable to academics.

Practitioners should consider academic research as a potential source of inspiration for new marketing practice. Typically, when faced with a challenging business problem, marketers do not turn to academia for answers. Yet the need for systematic and disciplined experimentation is greatest when conditions appear most chaotic. The complexity of new marketing channels and the failure of old methods to achieve the same results as they did in the past often leads organizations into reactionary experimentation. Even with intense pressure "to do something" in the face of new challenges, the best marketers will resist the "shotgun approach." Instead, they will structure their new marketing efforts so that they simultaneously learn about the specific experiment and deepen their overall understanding of consumer decision-making. Academics really can help design the right series of tests and experiments to guide productive learning and channel resources effectively; practitioners should be cultivating relationships with academics to learn jointly what succeeds in the new market environment.

Marketing Specialists are needed to turn knowledge into application products. This "productization" of research involves building concrete tools, methods, models, or guiding frameworks that allow people to work with the new concepts and theories. The final chapter begins with a detailed case study of how research on consumer choices and trade-off behaviours from the 1960s and 1970s was used to create new product forecasting models in the late 1970s and early 1980s. It shares an insider's view of how these tools were first considered and then eventually adopted by P&G in the early 1990s. Change is a very human process involving politics, career uncertainty, and challenges to existing competencies. This case reinforces the need for internal champions to motivate experimentation and document success. It demonstrates the value of "Market Makers," intermediaries who create demand for the new models and help organizations adapt the learning to their particular culture and work processes. Market Makers can be consultants, in-house experts, commercial market research experts, or entrepreneurial academics. Involving these experts and intermediaries early will accelerate the transformation of knowledge into practice.

Using a practitioner's lens, Delaine points out which ideas in this book are "Solution Ready" and which require "Productizing" to encourage implementation. Marketers will know what to do with the insights on brand relationship-building, ways to curb dishonest consumer behaviours, uses for new media channels, and ways to manage phone queues and wait times. These are aimed at challenges that are top-of-mind for many marketers today. However, they will have a much harder time sorting through all the psychological influences and biases affecting consumer choices that are presented in this book. How will managers know which influences are most important in their particular situation? Diagnostic tools and templates that help marketers navigate the myriad of possible influences would greatly assist implementation and ongoing learning.

Even though the advice and suggestions found in the final chapter are strongly influenced by packaged goods marketing, they are meant to stimulate thinking and conversations among many types of marketing professionals, academics, and students of marketing. The authors urge readers to engage by posing questions and sharing the experiences in their organizations. The most important message of the last chapter is that academics, marketers, and other specialists need to learn to work better together to refresh and reshape marketing practice in our ever-changing landscape.

We are confident that readers will finish this book feeling that they have added a tool or two to their marketing toolkit. If you have comments to make, examples to offer, or discussions to engage in, please email us at flux@rotman.utoronto.ca or find us at @FluxRotman.

Happy reading!
David Soberman and Dilip Soman
Toronto, December 2012

FLUX
What Marketing Managers Need to Navigate
the New Environment

PART ONE

The Changing Landscape

1 The Challenge of Today's Marketing Environment

DAVID SOBERMAN

In most organizations, the brand manager is a decision-maker who has plenty of responsibility for business performance but little authority to order people to implement policies. Beyond the basic dilemma of responsibility without authority, today's brand manager faces changes that are revolutionary in nature. Many categories are in a constant state of flux (from electronics to services), and this slows the organization's ability to react. Moreover, change is also affecting all activities that fall within the purview of the marketing manager, including research activities, data analysis, media strategy, and distribution. I start off the chapter by first reviewing the basic process that the brand manager employs to manage brands. Second, I discuss the work environment of the brand manager and highlight structural characteristics of the brand management environment that make effective marketing difficult. I then discuss some of the changes that are making the life of the brand manager increasingly difficult. Finally, I conclude with prescriptions based on simple ideas that will help the aspiring brand manager to deal better with today's environment.

The Process of Brand Management

Figure 1.1 represents the process that a brand manager goes through in order to manage a business. The process is comprised of two sides, the first being the Determinative Side of marketing (essentially the creation of strategy) and the second being the Implementation Side of marketing (essentially the execution of strategy).[1]

The four steps of the Determinative Side have a significant effect on what the brand manager *should* do to generate the raw material that she needs to make good decisions.

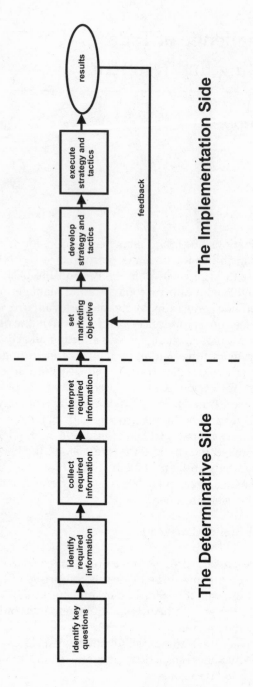

Figure 1.1 The Marketing Process Employed by Brand Managers

The Determinative Side of Marketing

The following are the four steps that comprise the Determinative Side of marketing.

THE IDENTIFICATION OF "KEY QUESTIONS"

In this step, the manager asks questions about her business on three levels. The first level is to identify consumer perceptions and feelings regarding the product or service that might affect consumer behaviour over the long term.

The second level is to fully analyse all competitive products and to understand why some competitive products are selling well and others are not. Today, with the emphasis on customer orientation, managers spend time trying to understand customers. This can make it difficult to commission in-depth market research studies on competitive products.

An anecdote from Renault demonstrates that the costs to understand the competition fully are far from negligible. At Renault's Technocenter in Guyancourt, France, more than 150 engineers and technicians work in a separate department called "competitive intelligence." People in this department rent and purchase competitive cars as soon as they are available. To understand these products, they are completely dismantled and often destroyed. But the information gathered by this department is critical in guiding the development of future models, and it reduces the likelihood that the competition offers features that are unavailable on Renaults.

The third level is to allow the brand manager the time to look for analogies in related or even unrelated product categories. Managers need to take the time and resources to examine their businesses on these three levels to identify the key questions that will affect their businesses.

IDENTIFICATION OF INFORMATION NEEDED TO ANSWER KEY QUESTIONS

In order for the brand manager to develop an effective plan, she needs to obtain answers to the questions she has identified. This implies the translation of these questions into market research. In addition, the manager needs to prioritize the questions because it is unlikely that every question can be answered.

COLLECTION OF INFORMATION

Over the last fifty years, one of the most important advances in marketing management has been the development of varied and rich techniques to collect information. Techniques such as conjoint analysis, usage and attitude surveys, multidimensional scaling, semantic scaling, focus groups, discriminant analysis, factor analysis, cluster analysis, and laddering comprise but a partial list of market research techniques that marketers use to obtain information. However, these techniques do not represent multiple paths to obtain the same information. They are designed to collect answers to different types of questions as shown below based on market research in the pharmaceutical industry.

Standard Questions that Marketers Need Answered	The Required Market Research Approach
Which doctors systematically prescribe Lilly versus the competitor's products?	Cross-sectional usage survey
How do patients think about erectile dysfunction treatments?	Multi-dimensional scaling
We are planning to discontinue two models of insulin pens. How do we know this won't cause mass switching to distributor brands?	Focus group (disaster check)
It'll cost £65 per month per patient to offer a once-a-day version of the product. Is it worth it?	Conjoint analysis
My product has twice the level of healthy cholesterol versus the competitor but consumers don't seem to care.	Semantic scales (are the perceptions different?) and conjoint analysis (do they care?)
Our product efficacy is significantly better than the generic product but doctors keep prescribing the generic version.	Conjoint analysis (is efficacy important?)

In order to get answers to questions effectively and efficiently, it is important that managers utilize the optimal methodology for the questions they have. When the optimal methodologies are not used, money is wasted and fewer questions are answered.

SYNTHESIS OF INFORMATION TO ANSWER QUESTIONS
Once market research has been commissioned to obtain answers to key questions, the next step is a presentation of the research findings by the market research agency. Usually, a presentation is made to a cross section of people within the firm. The marketing manager then uses the findings as a basis to set objectives and develop strategies for the business in question.

The Implementation Side of Marketing

The Implementation Side of marketing is more straightforward. It entails preparing a formal plan that is presented to top management.

SETTING OBJECTIVES

Generally, marketing plans start with a commitment to achieve a specific numerical objective in terms of sales, market share, and/or profit. In a well-run company, the objective is set in conjunction with the manager's superiors and is based on current performance, expectations of market growth, and a number of projections about specific occurrences that might affect the business.

OVERALL POSITIONING

The brand manager then formulates an overall strategy for the business that includes specifying the target market and the positioning of the business. Positioning involves the choice of a perceptual position for the brand that will be communicated to the segment that was chosen at the targeting stage. In multi-product marketing, each brand has a position. This refers to the way that the brand is intended to be perceived compared to other brands in the same category. The dimensions that are important within a category can be performance related (for example, durability), economic (for example, cost per day or price), or emotional (for example, nurturing versus aggressive, stylish versus conservative). The objective is to choose a position that is appealing to as many people in the target segment as possible.

DETAILED MARKETING STRATEGIES

The next stage in the Implementation Side of marketing is detailed planning. Basically, it involves translating the positioning of each brand into actions. A useful tool in marketing is to think of execution in terms of the "4 P's": price, promotion (including advertising), product, and place (sales and distribution). The challenge for the brand manager is to translate a brand's positioning into a series of actions that are consistent with that positioning. Given a target market, the objective is to create a marketing program that executes the positioning for a maximum number of people within the target segment.

EXECUTION

Of all the steps in Figure 1.1, execution is the one that takes the longest, because once a plan is approved, the marketing manager spends the rest of the year (until the next planning process starts again) executing the plan.

That completes the description of the marketing process. I now discuss how the office environment of the brand manager makes the brand manager's job so challenging.

The Decision Environment for Brand Managers

The goal of this section is to highlight the "built-in" characteristics of the brand manager's environment that make effective marketing difficult.[2]

Time Pressure

One of the most important characteristics of the marketing environment is time pressure. In fact, the planning process itself is a major source of time pressure. In a standard marketing environment, a manager needs to develop an action plan quickly and then prepare justification for what she wants to do. A study conducted by Accenture indicated that the average time it takes a company to create and launch a marketing campaign is two and a half months. Moreover, 58 per cent of the executives surveyed stated that a key objective is to shorten this time.[3] In almost any market, the development of a careful plan requires at least six months (if not an entire year), yet corporations do not build sufficient time into their planning cycle. In addition, brand managers need to demonstrate competence and the ability to get things done: they are under a constant process of personnel evaluation.

This situation means that brand managers have a strong incentive to trade off their time in favour of what needs to be accomplished now versus allocating time to strategic thinking that addresses the long term. Moreover, these managers have to justify or rationalize the paths they think best to themselves as well as to their superiors. It is this need that leads managers to find rules of thumb or shortcuts to support action that seems reasonable. The two easiest paths for a mid-level manager looking to justify her action are to utilize what was learned during training sessions and to ask colleagues for advice.

Training

Every firm has a structured process for introducing new employees to the firm, and this often involves training and exercises. There is strong evidence to suggest that this process has impact on the values that employees think are important. In addition, training is both recent and more relevant for brand managers (who tend to be younger mid-level managers) than for managers who are senior and have been with the company for a longer time.

It seems evident that the training and socialization processes of the modern workplace have a significant impact on how managers make decisions. Oddly, this is an idea that has not received a lot of attention in the decision-making literature. Training and socialization are key factors in both the creation and maintenance of distinct corporate cultures, and the potential of culture to affect managerial decisions is well established.[4] In a marketing context, research has identified direct links between organizational culture and company performance; this provides strong evidence that culture influences the way in which individual managers make decisions.[5]

A review of training at many Fortune 500 companies shows that systematic competitor censuring is a standard part of company training. The demonization of Bill Gates at Sun Microsystems is highly publicized. There is also the example of a firm giving a "shoot-'em-up" computer game to their employees in which the objective is to destroy targets that are identified by competitors' names and logos. The portrayal of competitors as enemies is reinforced by senior management. The chipmaker Cyrix once placed Intel's tombstone in its lobby atrium, and the CEO of Cabletron allegedly concluded his pep talks to sales recruits by plunging a knife into a beach ball inscribed with a competitor's name. Similarly, the CEO of Pepboys used videotapes of burning and burying baseball caps inscribed with competitors' logos.

The pervasiveness of corporate culture that encourages the destruction of competitors may explain the frequency of strategies that are effective in the short term but detrimental to all industry competitors in the long term. For example, the price wars between Dutch supermarkets, initiated by Albert Heijn in 2003, led to an industry-wide loss of €700 million and 10,000 jobs.[6]

To evaluate the effect of competitor censuring training on the decision-making of managers, a series of experiments with real managers were conducted using actual company training materials.[7] These experiments show that competitor censuring has a significant effect on decision-making. In particular, the experiments show that managers are willing to sacrifice profit to beat competitors. The training also has a significant effect on how managers believe the competitor is likely to behave.

A secondary finding of these studies was the identification of an interesting link between decision-making and the years of experience as a manager. The more experience a manager has, the more profit she is willing to sacrifice to reduce competitor profits. In short, it seems that training based on competitor censuring, while very common, has a detrimental impact on the decision-making of brand managers.

Getting Advice from Colleagues

When brand managers are under pressure and there is no clear path of action, a natural recourse is to obtain guidance from managers who have been in similar situations.[8] In particular, managers obtain advice from experienced colleagues (sometimes even the boss who was promoted from the manager's current position). As a result, the quality of the manager's decision-making relies on the quality of the advice she gets from colleagues.

An interesting question is whether a marketing manager who has access to advice from colleagues is likely to perform better when making marketing decisions. To investigate this issue, a series of experiments were conducted using the process of intergenerational games from experimental economics. The experiments were based on managers making a series of decisions in a competitive advertising game. The structure involved successive generations of managers playing the same game: the first generation received no advice, but the second generation of managers received advice from the first generation. In addition, the first generation of managers was incentivized to provide good advice to the second generation: the first generation received a payoff that was based on the performance of the second generation as well as their own. Nevertheless, the second generation performed significantly worse in terms of profit performance than the first generation: the only difference between the two generations was that the second generation received "helpful" advice from the first generation of subjects! Note that every generation played against a pre-programmed competitor whose decision-making was held constant across generations.

The deteriorating performance is explained first by a natural competitive "gene" that managers seem to possess. It seems that many marketing managers simply like competition and place high importance on winning. This often leads to decision-making that is not in the best interest of the firm (perhaps training reinforces these tendencies).

In addition, the path by which advice leads to deteriorating performance is important. The results of our experiments suggest that managers who receive advice perform worse because they do not take the time to determine how to play the game (or manage) optimally. In fact, in the experiments, the subjects in the "second generation" took aggressive decisions much sooner than the generation that did not receive advice. In a sense, advice appears to give managers a false sense of security.

It may be that the experiments understate the gravity of this problem. The most experienced managers at any level are often those whose career path has plateaued.[9] Managers often reach a point where they are too comfortable (or too old) to deal with the upheaval of changing jobs, too competent to be terminated but not sufficiently ambitious or capable to be promoted. As a result, there are many mid-level managers who have been in their positions for a long time: the de facto experts on the markets for which they are responsible. These *plateaued* managers are often important sources of advice for new managers.

Familiarity with Market Research

The third step of the Determinative Side of marketing entails the manager getting answers to a set of key questions for her business. Market research is generally commissioned to outside agencies, but this is not without risk. Finding a good market research company is not easy (it is not a licensed profession), and the issue of choosing the market research technique is often delegated to the agency.

While not optimal, delegating the choice of market research technique may not be a bad thing. Marketing managers often do not have technical expertise about the different market research methodologies that can be used to learn about customers and competitors. In a survey of experienced marketers attending an executive program in the fall of 2005, less than 50 per cent of the managers were able to identify the appropriate type of market research that should be used for at least 50 per cent of the questions that a manager might need answered with regards to a business in both the B2B and B2C context (see Figure 1.2).

This lack of basic knowledge poses major problems for firms. An essential responsibility for the brand manager is understanding customer needs. As a result, brand managers should be familiar with the standard tools that are used to understand customer needs. The lower the level of understanding in this area, the higher the likelihood of fundamental errors.

In addition, when the design of market research is delegated to an outside firm, the brand manager effectively delegates key thinking to

Figure 1.2 Marketing Research Technique Knowledge (Experienced Marketers)

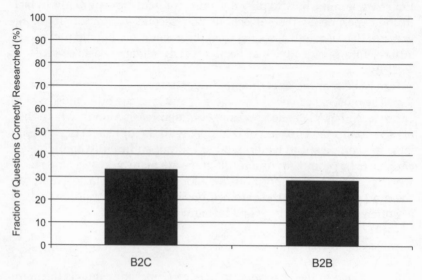

a third party. The danger of this practice is amplified by the fact that market research companies may not be entirely objective. Each agency specializes in certain research methodologies. Not surprisingly, they prefer to conduct research in their specialty area, which may not be the best approach. Some firms may attempt to sidestep this issue by delegating the management of market research to an outside consultancy. However, even this approach has risks. There is no guarantee that consultants are better informed about market research techniques than the people they are advising.

Interpreting Market Research

Invariably, market research results are shown in the form of a presentation by the market research agency. Written reports are provided, but the primary feedback channel is typically a formal presentation. There are potential problems with this practice.

First, when reviewing the findings from market research studies, managers often attend to information that is consistent with their pre-existing view of the world. Research has shown that one of the most serious obstacles to using market research effectively is a form of hindsight bias, whereby the reaction of managers to research is that "the research is telling us things we know already."[10] This reaction, which is quite natural, prevents managers from recognizing those sections of the research study where the findings contradict or challenge their pre-existing beliefs about the market.

Building on this idea is the reality that a significant fraction of market research is used for advocacy purposes within the organization; that is, the research is used to generate results that support a strategic decision or direction that has already been taken. The importance of "internal selling" (and the consequent need to provide facts and support for a given strategy) cannot be understated. Nevertheless, the goal of market research must always be to learn. Any time market research is designed to prove something, as opposed to learn, the likelihood of biased and/or misleading results is significantly higher.

A second problem concerns the forum for market research presentations. Often these presentations are not just attended by brand managers and their peers, but by senior people and vice-presidents of business units. As a result, these presentations become quite political. Managers are reluctant to admit that they are surprised in front of senior people. This, too, presents a significant hurdle to effective execution of the Determinative Side of marketing.

Summary

To summarize, the work environment of the brand manager is full of traps and pressure, all of which add challenges to the brand manager's job. Over and above these challenges, the brand manager must also deal with colossal change in the external world. Understanding or knowledge of how to deal with these changes is relatively absent in many organizations.

The Changing World and How This Adds to the Challenge of Brand Management

Increased Consumer Heterogeneity

The evolution of society away from the standard nuclear family (such as the Cleavers of the 1960s TV series *Leave It to Beaver*) to diverse household structures (like the household of Charlie Harper in the TV series *Two and a Half Men*), as well as the information revolution, have led to a society that is becoming more heterogeneous. In North American society, for example, the fraction of homes that are single-person households or same-sex two-person households is much higher, and technology has created varied work arrangements for people (including working from home). This presents a tremendous challenge for brand managers.[11] Marketing is predicated on the grouping of people into like-minded segments with similar needs, the idea being that firms orient themselves to serve one or more of the segments profitably by tailoring a product/service package. For this approach to be effective, segments must be large enough to warrant a customized offering, and a brand must serve enough segments to be profitable in a global sense. In this context, the effect of increased heterogeneity is serious for the following reasons:

- Increased heterogeneity means that there are more distinct segments. As a result, it is difficult to provide a tailored offering to each segment.
- It is increasingly difficult to identify the needs of each segment, since the splintering of society also makes finding people representative of each segment difficult.
- Finally, the needs of the segments, given the greater overall heterogeneity in society, will be broader and more differentiated.

A successful brand manager needs to understand the new heterogeneity that characterizes so many markets. The starting point for this understanding is to identify the basic needs that a product or service addresses. For example, smartphones allow people to communicate in various ways, to search for information, to send information to others, to entertain themselves (or others), to make a fashion statement, and to fulfill needs that may be met by other products (alarm clocks, watches, and portable music players). This list is certainly not comprehensive, but it highlights a possibility for segmentation as a function of the combination of needs that are being met by different groups of people. This process is more complicated than in the past, because there are many products that meet multiple needs, and people use these products in different ways.[12] This understanding then forms a basis for designing an approach to the market that recognizes the new heterogeneity. This is easier said than done!

Increased Consumer Expectations

A second change relates to the expectation that people are now develop-ing in terms of demanding products that are tailored to their individual needs. Firms like Dell ("made to measure" computers) and Panasonic ("made to measure" bicycles) create a Prisoners' Dilemma for all manu-facturers. In the past, consumers focused on offerings that provided good value for the price paid. This in large part explains the popularity of products from the Volkswagen to McDonald's. Customers knew that they were getting a standardized product that was essentially identi-cal to the product bought by both the customer served before and the customers served after the focal customer. Dell and Panasonic obtained a short-term advantage over the competition by providing customized service; however, the long-term impact of firms like Dell is to raise the expectations of consumers for customized products and services across multiple categories. Successful brand managers need to recognize this change in customer expectations and think creatively about how even the most mundane of categories can move away from the typical one-size-fits-all approach to serving markets. A further aspect to this move towards mass customization is that firms now have the ability to im-plement changes more quickly than in the past, due to improved in-formation systems and flexible manufacturing techniques. A manager that does not recognize the importance of reacting quickly to market changes will find that performance deteriorates more rapidly than in the past.

Media Fragmentation

Media fragmentation has made it difficult to cost-effectively inform a mass audience about one's products and services. While consumers now have increasingly diverse habits with regards to media, television, radio, and print remain the primary communication vehicles. But even these are not what they used to be.[13] For example, newspapers were always the quintessential local medium. No longer. It is common to see business people reading the *Wall Street Journal* and the *Financial Times* as they ride to work on the TTC in Toronto, the RATP in Paris, or the MRT in Singapore.

Television was always the quintessential national medium. No lon-ger. Not only are there scores of local stations (often serving immigrant communities in cities such as Toronto and New York, in languages such as Mandarin, Italian, and Arabic), but people around the globe watch CNN, ESPN, and HBO via satellite in homes, hotels, and bars. Alternatively, people keep up to date by watching live broadcasts on tablets in trains with WiFi capability.

Targeted mailings, telemarketing, video streaming, and SMS messaging play an important role in the marketing of many products, and out-of-home advertising (billboards, posters, and transit) has experienced a resurgence in recent years because of digital technology. A further complexity that needs to figure in the communication plans for most products and services is marketing on the World Wide Web and through social networks. Growth in this area, driven by organizations such as Google and Facebook, is double digit.[14]

How can firms manage communication activity to ensure that it is not lost in the sea of messages and noise that confronts today's consumer? The quality of communication and the ability to create a perceptual relationship with consumers is a key factor that determines success or failure. While fragmentation is a challenge, the splintering of the media has also created significant opportunities for brand managers, as explained in the following section.

Growth in the Quality and Targetability of Media

Two critical changes in the last twenty years have been (a) major improvements in the quality and quantity of consumer information (due to information technology) and (b) the growth of targeted media vehicles. The growth of targeted media has been driven by the fragmentation of existing media and a multitude of new advertising media (the internet, satellite shopping channels, and infomercials).

Traditionally, the objective in media planning was to minimize wasted advertising by reducing the quantity of advertising sent to consumers who were not interested in the product category. For example, consider the challenge of effective media buying in the United States beer market. In the past, this amounted to maximizing the amount of advertising sent to adult males and minimizing the amount sent elsewhere. Typically this was achieved through heavy buying of sports programming. Until recently, most models of informative advertising were based on the assumption that firms within a category have similar targets for their media.[15]

Today, media planning entails detailed objectives with narrower consumer segments. To be specific, marketing managers can target segments as a function of their pre-existing dispositions to buy one product or another. Recent research also shows that an important side benefit of targeted advertising is a reduction of price competition.[16] A firm accomplishes this by targeting heavier advertising to consumers who are strongly predisposed to buy its product at the expense of advertising targeted to consumers who are less committed in their brand preferences. Basically, firms reduce the fraction of comparison shoppers who are reached with advertising in order to reduce price competition. When a smaller fraction of the total market engages in comparison shopping, fewer price comparisons are made. This reduces the incentive of the firms to reduce price.

In addition, targeted advertising means that consumers who have a strong pre-disposition to a firm's product are targeted by that firm. After seeing the advertising, these consumers are almost certain to buy and are willing to pay high prices.

The targeting of advertising messages means advertising can be used by firms to *create differentiation* between competing offers. For marketers, this is a boon. Many marketing initiatives such as new distribution channels, better after-sales service, and additional product features only provide a temporary advantage within a market. Once the competition adopts similar initiatives, the profits of all firms are lower and the initiatives simply increase the cost of doing business.[17] In contrast, the targeting of media spending to create differentiation (as described above) is a win-win situation for all firms. It allows firms to reduce the degree to which they compete with each other (without breaking any laws!). And today, as long as the manager knows how to reach his target with advertising, the benefits of targeting have never been higher.

The move away from thirty-second spots on network TV to alternative media options, such as media packages, cable, and specialty channels, also has major implications for marketers.

Category Exclusivity, an Endemic Characteristic of Media Properties, Is Beneficial for All Competitors

Marketers often bid substantial sums in order to be the official or exclusive product of a media property. Clearly, exclusivity is attractive to the winning bidder because major events often lead to significant boosts in awareness for official sponsors.[18] But exclusivity also means that media activity creates greater consumer heterogeneity: the groups of consumers that are being informed about competing brands are independent and have less overlap. In fact, many explanations for prices that exceed "competitive levels" entail this type of "imperfect" information among consumers.[19] In sum, exclusivity helps all brands in the category, not just the exclusive sponsor; the owners of media properties do marketers a great service by offering exclusivity.

Many Non-Traditional Components Are Included in Media Packages

In the past, thirty-second spots were purchased at rates based on the demand for media and the nature of the audience. Marketers could compare the performance of a plan proposed by their advertising agency to industry norms. Now, many media packages include items like supers, rink or field board signage, product placements, and the like. These components clearly have value, but how much? A key challenge for marketers is to figure out what these components are worth. Misestimated values for media packages will lead to under or over bidding for media properties and this can be deadly in a tough market.

A Set of Prescriptions for Brand Managers: How to Get More from Your Marketing Effort!

The following are a set of prescriptions that can assist brand managers (and the marketing function) to deal with their challenging work environment and the dramatic changes that are taking place both in the outside world and technologically within the work environment.

1. Re-evaluate the Planning Process

Organizations need to re-evaluate the mantra of reducing the length of the planning cycle for marketing programs. As discussed earlier, excessive time pressure precludes managers from having the opportunity to engage in exploratory analysis about their business, their customers, and their competitors. The pressure of the marketplace means that punctuality is important, but the planning process of a company needs to find the right balance between thinking and polishing. As highlighted in the following industry example, it is possible to make planning more efficient but still allow time for managers to engage in exploratory thinking.

Since the early 1990s, Renault has reduced the time from conception to production of a new car model from fifty-six to twenty-two months (among the shortest in the industry). This has been achieved through extensive reengineering of vehicle development at a "state of the art" Technocenter at Guyancourt (opened in 1998). However, the acceleration of the development process has not been done at the expense of reducing the time designers have to develop the right models with the right features. Additional time has been built into the process to allow designers to understand fully trends in industrial design in unrelated product categories as well as throughout the auto industry. Such "out of box" thinking has been instrumental in the development of path-breaking models such as the Renault Twingo (a trendsetter in the small car category), the Renault Scenic (the pioneer of the Monospace category), and the Renault Megane (a family car with a look and appeal that is causing significant problems for competitors such as Peugeot and Volkswagen).

A first step to allow greater exploratory analysis is to reduce the formality of marketing plan presentations. In many companies, these presentations are attended by senior management and much of what is discussed is already a *fait accompli*.

A second step is to build a step into the planning process before the development of detailed marketing plans. This step should be a free-flowing session that gathers input from assorted personnel who are involved with the business. In addition, it is critical that such sessions have a broad horizontal scope (cross-functional) and flat vertical scope.

An effective example of how an exploratory step can be structured into the planning process is taken from Eli Lilly, the pharmaceutical manufacturer. Known as the archetype process, the process involves a "Brand Council" and places strong emphasis on thinking about products that are either innovative, second and better, or an improvement on an existing pharmaceutical. In addition, the Brand Council is primarily a lateral team that cuts across functions and countries. Eli Lilly has used this approach to maximize creativity and sharing in managing international blockbusters such as Prozac, Gemzar, and Zprexa. These "councils" are unique because they are horizontal in nature and do not have a formal leader. Lilly has found that this minimizes politics in the management of brands while allowing a high degree of creativity and sharing of best practices across geographic regions and functional areas.

In sum, to fight against time pressure, firms need to consciously ensure that brand managers have the time and support to think creatively about their business.

2. Reorient the Message of Training

Firms need to re-evaluate the orientation of their training for mid- and entry-level marketing managers. Most firms place too much emphasis on beating the competition and not enough emphasis on identifying strategies designed to maximize profitability. Before designing training modules, firms should think about the values that will be instilled in new hires and the potentially negative attendant effects. An example of how non-conventional approaches to training can pay off comes from the unrelated field of professional hockey. Peter Laviolette, formerly of the Carolina Hurricanes, took an unconventional approach to preparing his team for the Stanley Cup play-offs. As opposed to the standard "bash the opponent" approach of most professional hockey coaches, Laviolette built a harmonious dressing room attitude "through a series of team-building exercises that included events from obstacle course competitions to family outings."[20]

3. Strategize to Increase the Transfer of Good Advice

Unfortunately, the transfer of poor advice between employees cannot be avoided without completely eliminating contact between employees. As a result, companies need strategies that maximize the quality of advice that is transferred between employees: companies need to develop sources of expertise at each level within the organization. However, employees who are too good to fire but cannot be promoted must not be allowed to stagnate. Lateral moves or the practice of moving mid-level managers to different businesses (cross pollination) are recommended given the prevalence of advice-giving within organizations. Perhaps rearranging the deck chairs is a good idea as long as you are not on the *Titanic*. The experiments discussed earlier also highlight a potential cost of long-term employment. This is important given conventional wisdom, which holds that the impact of loyalty and long-term employment is unequivocally positive.[21]

4. Raise the Level of In-House Market Research Expertise

Firms should carefully evaluate the level of market research expertise possessed in-house. In particular, entry- and mid-level managers should be educated in the most common market research methodologies and the types of questions that each is best at answering. When brand managers have a high degree of understanding in this area, the likelihood of fundamental errors in the design of market research studies is reduced. In addition, the low level of market research understanding within organizations provides a strong argument for in-house experts that can provide guidance to marketing managers.

5. Alter Market Research Presentation Protocol

To improve the processing of market research within marketing departments, the presentation of the findings is critical. In particular, our earlier discussion provides a strong argument for multiple presentations within the company so that each managerial level is exposed to the findings individually.

A second practice that firms should adopt is to have managers predict the outcomes of research before the findings are presented. For example, the presenter should ask all attendees to guess the answers to the twenty most important questions addressed by the research. This practice focuses the attention of the manager on the differences between the findings and the manager's beliefs and highlights the value of the research to the manager. This idea is not new but a variation of the recommendation of Barraba and Zaltman on how market research agencies should present their findings to emphasize the value of the research and their work.[22] Barraba and Zaltman suggest that this is an effective procedure to limit the problem of managers (a) focusing on findings that confirm existing beliefs and (b) ignoring findings that are inconsistent with their beliefs. When managers predict important data, it is straightforward for them to identify the areas where their beliefs are significantly discrepant from the research findings: areas where the manager would have made decisions based on beliefs that were incorrect were she to have proceeded without the new information.

6. Obtain Better Information

In some sense, the changes in the market mean that brand managers need to obtain better information on their customers. John Hagel (the former leader of McKinsey & Co.'s global electronic commerce practice) mentions that information has been the key driver of negotiating power in economics, and firms will need better information to counter consumers who are better informed than ever before.[23]

A key source of valuable information for brand managers are databases compiled by market research firms on the behaviour and consumption habits of consumers. These databases contain individual-level information on millions of consumers that can be used to form groups of high potential buyers for targeted marketing efforts. This is the primary activity of companies such as ICOM, Experian, Acxiom, and Donelley Marketing. For example, Experian is the only market research company in the United States that has an extensive database on the credit worthiness and financial status of individuals. Donelley Marketing is the only research company that possesses information on the characteristics of firms and individuals based on their involvement in Yellow Pages telephone listings. It is straightforward to see how this information might be valuable for a firm that wants to increase the impact of its marketing effort.

A successful brand manager will not just be obliged to obtain better information on her customers: she will have to develop effective strategies to use the information. This involves difficult decisions including choices that go beyond issues of customized manufacturing and/or service. Brand managers need to develop a basis for knowing which customers not to serve, which customers to serve, and what aspects of their product or service to customize for those customers that are worth serving.

Some companies learn this the hard way. Dell, the famous "made to measure" computer manufacturer, has a business model of using instantly accessible customer information records to assist in taking direct orders from customers to build customized PCs with the latest peripherals. But in the early 1990s, this model of distribution meant that Dell did not distribute in standard retail stores where the vast majority of PCs were being sold. To address this limitation, Dell entered into agreements with several retailers in 1991 and launched two lines, Dimension and Precision, that were manufactured with a limited set of pre-determined configurations.[24]

However, the Dell manufacturing approach was not designed for mass production and the lower margins meant that Dell lost money.[25] In addition, the retail channel did not allow Dell to utilize its major innovation, "mass customization," for which it was generally able to charge a 15 per cent price premium. By 1994, Dell withdrew from the retail channel and refocused on its direct channels. This was a costly mistake for Dell, yet Dell has subsequently prospered, mainly because the direct market for PCs was larger than originally anticipated.

Through this experience, Dell learned that it was probably not the ideal company to serve the segment of small businesses and individuals who wished to shop for PCs in a showroom setting. One of the most difficult decisions that a firm must make is saying "no" to certain customers who ultimately may prove to be unprofitable.[26]

Of course, the PC market and Dell have evolved significantly in the last twenty years. Now there is a significant market for Dell with consumers who wish to buy predetermined configurations in the retail environment. As a result, Dell computers are once again being sold through retailers such as Best Buy and Future Shop.

7. Beware the Danger Areas

Earlier I highlighted some of the positive but challenging aspects of marketing created by increased complexity and media fragmentation. It is also useful to underline two areas where marketers must exercise care with their new-found capabilities.

8. Respect Privacy

The technological changes discussed earlier have the potential to bring benefits to consumers and firms. However, because tremendous quantities of information are used and processed, the consuming public has significant concern about the invasion of privacy through the unsolicited exchange or analysis of data.[27] Misuse of information, such as the resale of customer lists by marketers, can result in negative customer reaction, and in extreme cases, legal action. In addition, many electronic services make it possible for firms to monitor the behaviour of consumers without their consent. Not surprisingly, there has been a significant increase in the regulation of firms with regard to the use and provision of customer information. It is relatively easy for an uninformed brand manager to "cross the line" and implement activities that contravene either guidelines or regulations.[28] A key challenge for brand managers is to learn how to use consumer-specific information to deliver high value to consumers without violating their privacy.

9. Uphold Ethical Standards

According to a special report in the *Economist*, the average consumer sees more than 3,000 commercials per day.[29] Not surprisingly, many consumers feel that their lives are constantly invaded by companies trying to sell them things. A typical example of this is the telemarketer who always phones at dinnertime because he/she knows that the target is likely to be at home. A secondary effect of media fragmentation is that companies can now hone in on consumers when they are most vulnerable to the company's pitch (through timing or the occasion that the message is delivered). In fact, companies sometimes have the ability to convince people to do things that are not in their best interest. There are cases of telemarketers targeting senior citizens who may be particularly vulnerable to aggressive sales pitches due to infirmity or loneliness. In the past, this was less of a problem because telemarketers phoned random numbers within an area code to conduct their campaigns. Today, however, telemarketers can target specific demographic groups by linking databases to electronic phone directories.

Clearly, there should be limits on the types of marketing initiatives that brand managers employ. For example, citizens should not find that the only way to avoid the harassment of frequent telemarketing is to take unlisted phone numbers. Today, the capability that firms have to convince people to buy things is high. It is important that this capability be balanced by ethical concerns for protecting consumers from activities that are either intrusive or potentially fraudulent.

A Prescription to Get More from Marketing

Brand management is characterized by unrealistic time pressure, politics, a lack of resources, and the need to be a jack of all trades. No wonder marketing often "underperforms." To get more from marketing:

- Build TIME into the planning process, and to get IDEAS, look outside the company and outside the category.
- Train managers to make profit, NOT to beat competitors.
- Make sure marketing managers gain cross-functional and cross-category experience over their career path.
- Don't be afraid to ask questions that the company has already answered.
- Make sure somebody in the organization knows how to get answers to questions with the right kind of research.
- Use market research to learn, NOT to confirm.

REFERENCES

1 The figure is intended to be representative of a comprehensive process (and not definitive). Many authors discuss a similar process with a slightly different number of steps that are sometimes named differently. For example, see Philip Kotler, *Marketing Management*, Millennium Edition (Upper Saddle River, NJ: Prentice-Hall International, 2000), 63–94.
2 These ideas are explored in Ajay Kalra and David A. Soberman, "The Forgotten Side of Marketing," *Journal of Brand Management* 17, no. 1 (2010): 301–14.
3 From "Sixty Eight Percent of Executives Unable to Measure Marketing Campaign Return On Investment, Says Accenture Study," *Business Wire*, 7 November 2001, 1.
4 G.J. Badovik and S.E. Beatty, "Shared Organisational Values: Measurement and Impact Upon Strategic Marketing Implementation," *Journal of the Academy of Marketing Science* 15, no. 1 (1987): 19–26.
5 These issues are discussed in R. Deshpandé, J.U. Farley, and F.E. Webster, "Corporate Culture, Customer Orientation and Innovativeness in Japanese Firms: A Quadrad Analysis," *Journal of Marketing* 57 (1993): 23–7; Frederick E. Webster, *Marketing Driven Management: Using the New Marketing Concept to Create a Customer-Oriented Company* (New York: John Wiley, 1994); and P.C. Wright and G.D. Geroy, "Experience, Judgement, and Intuition: Qualitative Data-Gathering Methods as Aids to Strategic Planning," *Leadership and Organizational Development Journal* 12, no. 3 (1991): 2–32.
6 This is discussed in "Dutch Supermarket Price War Has Many Losers and Only a Few Winners," *Agence France Presse*, 25 October 2004.
7 Ajay Kalra and David A. Soberman, "The Curse of Competitiveness – How Advice from Experienced Colleagues and Training Can Hurt Marketing Profitability," *Journal of Marketing* 72, no. 3 (2008): 32–47.
8 A. Schotter and B. Sopher, "Advice and Behavior in Inter-Generational Ultimatum Games: An Experimental Approach," *Games and Economic Behavior* 58, no. 2 (2007): 365–93; A. Schotter, and B. Sopher, "Social Learning and Convention Creation in Inter-Generational Games: An Experimental Study," *Journal of Political Economy* 111, no. 3 (2003): 498–529.
9 The Peter Principle is a theory developed by Laurence J. Peter whereby managers rise to a level within an organization just above their competence level and then stay there for the rest of their careers. On the one hand, organizations restrict promotion to employees only after they have demonstrated competence at their current level. On the other hand, the theory implies that there are a significant fraction of incompetent

managers at every level within an organization. See Laurence J. Peter and R. Hull, *The Peter Principle: Why Things Always Go Wrong* (New York: Morrow and Company, 1969).

10 The mechanism by which pre-existing attitudes affect the interpretation of new information is discussed by R.H. Fazio,"How Do Attitudes Guide Behaviour," in R. Sorrentino and E. Tory Higgins, eds., *Handbook of Motivation and Cognition* (New York: Guildford Press, 1986), 204–43. Further discussion of this issue in the context of market research presentations is found in V.B. Barraba and G. Zaltman, *Hearing the Voice of the Market* (Cambridge, MA: Harvard Business School Press, 1991), 118–19.

11 This basic change in market structure is discussed in David A. Soberman, "It's a Whole New Ball Game," *European Management Journal* 17, no. 3 (1999): 290–5.

12 The author recalls a colleague enamoured with his new iPhone not because of its styling or browsing capabilities but because of its GPS application that has allowed him to dispose of an expensive and unreliable navigation system on his fourteen-metre racing sloop.

13 The challenge of media fragmentation is discussed in David A. Soberman, "Marketers Set Their Sights on Consumers," *Financial Times*, 11 August 2004, 7.

14 See "Billboard Boom," *Economist*, 23 April 2011, 71.

15 See for example, Gérard R. Butters, "Equilibrium Distributions of Sales and Advertising Prices," *Review of Economics and Statistics* 44 (1977): 465–91, and Gene M. Grossman and Carl Shapiro, "Informative Advertising with Differentiated Products," *Review of Economics Studies* 51 (1984): 63–81.

16 Ganesh K. Iyer, David A. Soberman, and J. Miguel Villas-Boas, "The Targeting of Advertising," *Marketing Science* 24, no. 3 (2005): 461–76.

17 See, for example, Benjamin Hermalin, "Notes in Microeconomics" (University of California, Berkeley, 1993, mimeographed); and Cabral Luis and J. Miguel Villas-Boas "Bertrand Supertraps," *Management Science* 51, no. 4 (2004): 599–613.

18 This issue is explored in Anthony Dukes and Esther Gal-Or, "Negotiations and Exclusivity Contracts for Advertising," *Marketing Science* 22, no. 2 (2003): 222–45.

19 David M. Grether and Charles R. Plott, "The Effects of Market Practices in Oligopolistic Markets: An Experimental Examination of the Ethyl Case," *Economic Inquiry* 22 (1984): 479–507.

20 "Laviolette Lifts Bargaining Position," *USA Today*, 9 June 2006, 9c.

21 This argument is presented in F.F. Reicheld, *The Loyalty Effect* (Cambridge, MA: Harvard Business School Press, 1996).

22 Please refer to V.B. Barraba and G. Zaltman, *Hearing the Voice of the Market* (Cambridge, MA: Harvard Business School Press, 1991), 118–19.

23 From David Bank, "According to John Hagel, the Web is Revolutionizing Business," *Wall Street Journal Europe*, 7 December 1998, 14.

24 Based on publicly available information and on Das Narayandas and V. Katsuri Rangan, *Dell Computer Corporation*, Case 9-596-058 (Boston, MA: Harvard Business School, 1995).

25 Andrew E. Serwer, "Michael Dell Turns the PC World Inside Out," *Fortune*, 8 September 1997, accessed 25 April 2012 from http://money.cnn.com/magazines/fortune/fortune_archive/1997/09/08/230827/index.htm

26 Frederick F. Reicheld, *The Loyalty Effect* (Boston, MA: Harvard Business School Press, 1996), 63–90.

27 Huaiqing Wang, Mathew Lee, and Chen Wang, "Consumer Privacy Concerns about Internet Marketing," *Communications of the ACM* 41, no. 3 (1998): 63–70.

28 Avi Goldfarb and Catherine E. Tucker, "Privacy Regulation and Online Advertising," *Management Science* 57, no. 1 (2011): 57–71.

29 "The Harder Hard Sell," in "Special Report: The Future of Advertising," *Economist*, 26 June 2004, 69–71.

2 Losing Control and Loving It

DAVID DUNNE

Flux Becomes Flood

In March 2008, Dave Carroll, a musician from Halifax, Canada, and his band, the Sons of Maxwell, travelled from Halifax to Nebraska via O'Hare airport in Chicago. What happened on the journey became the subject of outrage, embarrassment, and amusement, and transformed Carroll from country singer to customer service guru.

In Carroll's own words, what happened was as follows:

> In the spring of 2008, Sons of Maxwell were traveling to Nebraska for a one-week tour and my Taylor guitar was witnessed being thrown by United Airlines baggage handlers in Chicago. I discovered later that the $3500 guitar was severely damaged. They didn't deny the experience occurred but for nine months the various people I communicated with put the responsibility for dealing with the damage on everyone other than themselves and finally said they would do nothing to compensate me for my loss. So I promised the last person to finally say "no" to compensation (Ms. Irlweg) that I would write and produce three songs about my experience with United Airlines and make videos for each to be viewed online by anyone in the world.[1]

Carroll's three promised videos were subsequently posted to the web. The first was posted on 6 July 2009 and by the end of that day had received 150,000 hits. By 9 July, the number of hits reached 500,000, and by 21 August, 5 million. The song hit number one on the iTunes Music Store in the week following its release; Carroll's videos and United's embarrassment received widespread exposure in mainstream media and were the subject of thousands of tweets, Facebook comments, and blog posts. The United Kingdom's *Daily Mail* claimed that United lost 10 per cent of its share value, or $180 million, as a result of the ad.[2]

United apologized to Carroll and offered him $1,200 in flight vouchers, which he declined, suggesting that the airline give the money to charity. Ultimately, United donated $3,000 to the Thelonious Monk Institute of Jazz as a "gesture of goodwill." Bob Taylor, owner of Taylor Guitars, immediately offered Carroll two guitars and other props for his second video.

In December 2009, *Time* magazine named "United Breaks Guitars" number seven on their list of the Top Ten Viral Videos of 2009. Following the incident, Carroll was in great demand as a musician and a speaker on customer service. His website (http://www.davecarrollmusic .com/) offered for sale T-shirts printed with "United Breaks Guitars" and a "Dave Carroll Travellers Edition" hardshell guitar case by Calton.

In turning his misfortune to advantage, Carroll undermined the United brand and created a brand of his own; his ability to accomplish this caught United and many other marketers by surprise. It offered a glimpse into Web 2.0: a future in which marketers, long accustomed to controlling the message projected by their brands, need to negotiate this control with consumers. Challenging as this is, some marketers have succeeded in this new environment, creating a level of consumer engagement heretofore unknown.

Flux is defined by *Merriam-Webster Dictionary* as "a continuous moving on or passing by (as of a stream)."[3] Yet the new environment resembles a rushing river more than a stream: not just flux, but flood. Web 2.0 is not just a new advertising medium. The new communications environment's social consequences include the Wikileaks scandal of late 2010 and uprisings in the Middle East. Just as the social discourse has shifted, the discourse between advertisers and consumers has fundamentally changed. As a result, marketers need to shift from controlling the message to engaging in a dialogue with consumers.

In the discussion that follows, I will trace the implications of Web 2.0 for marketing, suggest strategies for succeeding in this new environment, and discuss how some marketers have created value for their brands by engaging consumers both online and offline.

How Web 1.0 Changed Marketing

The early emergence of the internet moved advertising away from a model in which consumers were largely involuntarily exposed to messages through interruption of TV and radio programs and browsing of print vehicles.[4] In traditional media, advertising was accepted as a means of financing entertainment, but often resented by consumers as an interruption. Advertisers' primary goal was to deliver a clear and memorable message to a passive audience, sufficiently well for them to include the brand in their consideration set,[5] and to retain enduring brand associations.

To accomplish this, marketers focused on understanding what might attract and hold target consumers' attention, delivering timely messages when consumers were considering purchase or consumption, and resonating with their needs and desires.

Yet while consumers were passive, they were not captive. TV commercial breaks were treated as an opportunity to "tune out" in various ways, through inattention or by physically leaving the room. In an attempt to measure this, A.C. Nielsen installed "people meters" in homes to identify how many people were in the room when a commercial aired, but these could only measure physical presence, not attention.

As recording technology developed, consumers developed other, more sophisticated, ways to avoid advertising by "zipping" (fast-forwarding) through commercials and "zapping" (deleting) them. In response, advertisers developed short commercials and banners that were on-screen during some programs. Advertising became a game of leapfrog in which consumers developed ways of avoiding advertising and advertisers attempted to prevent them from doing so.

In some cases, however, consumers were willing and even eager to view advertising. For high-involvement products such as automobiles, consumers actively sought information in print advertising; many commercials, such as Apple's *1984* launch teaser for the Macintosh computer and Nike's "Just Do It" campaign, garnered a high degree of consumer engagement through traditional media and developed strong brand values.

The initial emergence of the internet as what is now known as Web 1.0 did not fundamentally change the relationship between advertisers and their audiences. The internet was essentially a search medium, not unlike print, with, as Avi Goldfarb points out in chapter 4, greatly reduced search costs. Nevertheless, consumers were unlikely to find an advertiser's website through random surfing, instead clicking through from search sites such as Yahoo! and Google. Online advertising was generally not sufficient to get consumers' attention on its own, and needed to be supplemented with traditional "awareness" media such as TV. The idea of "Integrated Marketing Communications," or the co-ordination of messages across a variety of media, was born.

In retrospect, however, the early days of the internet foreshadowed the emergence of active consumers who, as the internet's popularity increased, were increasingly able to choose what advertising they would and would not expose themselves to. Advertisers responded by developing campaigns that got consumers talking.

BMW was a pioneer in the world of Integrated Marketing Communications. For the launch of the Z-3 in 1996, the company combined traditional media with event marketing and support of the James Bond film *Goldeneye*; in 2001, BMW developed a series of short films, *The Hire*, directed by acclaimed Hollywood directors and posted them on its website to attract traffic. Other advertisers such as Red Bull, Starbucks, and the movie *The Blair Witch Project* eschewed mass media in favour of non-traditional campaigns, online and offline, that built awareness by stoking word-of-mouth communications between consumers.

Offline, mass media did not expire with the emergence of the internet. On the contrary, offline media were seen, and continue to be seen, as a complement to online vehicles. Such media could still be used in creative ways, such as catching consumers off guard by surprising them at work and at play, and engaging them with games.[6] But as channels proliferated and audiences fragmented, the costs of communicating a single message to a mass audience through traditional media became prohibitive.

Web 1.0 brought a shift, but a subtle one: from controlling the message, marketers were pushed to provide the information consumers wanted. Yet the centre of this communication was the brand, not the consumer. The marketer's focus was on what the brand needed to communicate, not what the audience needed or wanted to hear. This was about to change.

How Web 2.0 Shifted the Paradigm

The beginnings of the two pillars of Web 2.0, Facebook and YouTube, are both the stuff of legend, and some controversy.

In 2004, a fresh-faced nineteen-year-old Harvard student, Mark Zuckerberg, wrote Facemash, the predecessor to Facebook. The Facemash site used photos hacked from the sites of Harvard dormitories and asked users to choose the "hotter" person. The site attracted 22,000 views in its first twenty-four hours online and was shut down by Harvard administration. In February 2004, inspired by an editorial in *The Harvard Crimson* about the Facemash incident, Zuckerberg launched what later became Facebook. The company was incorporated in the summer of 2004. Yet Facebook's origins were the subject of dispute and bitter lawsuits: in 2008, Zuckerberg settled with the Winklevoss twins for $65 million in a dispute over his alleged plagiarism of the original idea, and for an undisclosed amount with former partner Eduardo Saverin.

As of 2011, Facebook had over 750 million users, sharing more than 30 billion pieces of content each month.[7] More than 250 million users access Facebook through mobile devices, and these users are twice as active as non-mobile users.

YouTube, the legend goes, all started with a dinner party.[8] Chad Hurley, a pallid fine arts graduate and former PayPal employee in his mid-twenties, and his friend Steve Chen became frustrated with the difficulty they were having in sharing videos of a dinner party with friends online. The site they developed for this purpose eventually became YouTube. And, like Facebook, the origins of YouTube became mired in dispute: a third PayPal employee, Jawed Karim, later claimed that his contribution was not acknowledged.

The idea morphed into a video dating site, then into an online auction site. But when the site was launched in May 2005 as a beta test, it became clear that users were posting whatever they liked.* Sequoia Capital invested $11.5 million in the start-up after its full launch in November 2005, and by July 2006, 65,000 videos were being uploaded per day, of everything from grandmothers to stand-up comics. And advertising, real or fake.

At 62 per cent participation among American adults, online video watching on YouTube and similar sites now outranks social networking (46 per cent), podcast downloading (19 per cent), and Twitter (11 per cent). While young adults lead online video viewing with 90 per cent participation, usage is growing steadily in other age groups.[9]

Web 2.0 is defined by these two capabilities: easy sharing and inexpensive, easy creation. Whereas advertisers were the sole creators and disseminators of commercial content in traditional media and in Web 1.0, this exclusivity can no longer be taken for granted. Consumers have become active content-creators and content-sharers. As Dave Carroll showed, this gives individual consumers the power to make or break brands – an uncomfortable state of affairs for marketers accustomed to

---

* Not including pornography, which was self-policed by users and removed.

controlling the message, but an exciting one for consumers who resent the influence of advertising in their lives.

One important form of protest is parody, or fake, advertising. From the early days of advertising, it has been the butt of jokes in print, radio, and TV; advertisers themselves sometimes took this as an opportunity to jab their competitors' products. One of the more famous advertising personalities, the Energizer Bunny, was launched in a parody commercial in which the bunny was being filmed in a TV commercial and ran amok through a series of film sets for commercials.[10]

Advertisers have historically tolerated these parodies, either because taking legal action is expensive and risky, or because they reason that the extra exposure, even as a parody, is harmless and perhaps even beneficial to their brand. With the rise in popularity of YouTube and similar sites, however, consumers have gained the ability to develop their own parodies. Actions by advertisers to block such parodies are now likely to be seen as an abuse of commercial power, and advertisers are essentially powerless to prevent them.

In 2008, 10 per cent of ads on YouTube were parody ads. Most widely parodied was the "Mac vs. PC" campaign for Apple, occupying three of the top five (according to number of unique viewings) parodies on YouTube (see Table 2.1).

Yet in exchange for this loss of control, marketers have gained a great opportunity. The effect of "word-of-mouth" advertising, where consumers pass information or impressions about a brand to others, has long been recognized in marketing. The growth of Web 2.0 means that such communication can now be instantaneous, visual, and disseminated to large numbers of potential consumers; those who receive the message can respond, allowing great opportunities for a conversation to emerge about the brand, for consumers to become deeply engaged with it, and for advertisers to receive and respond to feedback.

Table 2.1 Top Five Parody Ads on YouTube (2008)

Rank	Description
1	South Park Mac vs. PC, a parody of the Apple Mac vs. PC commercials
2	Vote Different, a parody of the Apple 1984 ad featuring Hillary Clinton
3	Powerthirst, a spoof on ubiquitous commercials for energy drinks
4	Marvel vs. DC, a parody of Apple vs. Mac using Spiderman (Marvel Comics) and Superman (DC Comics)
5	Gates vs. Jobs, a parody of Mac vs. PC using Bill Gates and Steve Jobs

The Death of STP

These changes are sparking a revolution in marketing, one casualty of which is its fundamental concept, STP.

Marketing strategy development has classically been based on analysing the "three Cs" (customers, competition, and company) to develop "STP" (segmentation, targeting, positioning) and "four P's" (product, price, promotion, place). Web 2.0 has an important impact at all levels of this model, not merely on promotion. The strategic core of this model, STP, is now open to serious question. The impact of the changes on the classical model is summarized in Table 2.2 and discussed below.

Segmentation

As David Soberman points out in chapter 1, consumers have become more heterogeneous and, as a result, the task of segmentation has become more challenging; but marketers need to go much further and rethink the concept of segmentation itself.

With the power of social networking and sharing, the consumer is not just an independent, individual economic agent, but one who influences, and is heavily influenced by, his/her peers. In addition to analysing individual decision-making, marketers need to pay enhanced attention to how the experience of the brand is shared with others. This goes beyond the idea of segmentation, or clustering consumers into groups with shared attributes, to learning how consumers – either within a segment or across segments – interact with each other.

Traditional segmentation according to demographic, behavioural, and psychographic variables pays scant attention to the *affective* links between consumers that describe the tribes they belong to.[11] Consumers need to be considered as communities or tribes, not merely individuals. Brand managers need to get in touch with the personal and social context in which the consumer lives, both online and offline.

As an example, while Harley-Davidson motorcycle owners can be described in demographic terms (e.g., men over forty), what is more important than demographic characteristics are the social links that exist between owners through Harley Owners Groups (HOGs). Harley-Davidson cares deeply about what its owners are saying to each other, who is saying it, and where and how they are saying it, to the extent that it supports HOG events and facilitates a password-protected HOG website.

Table 2.2 STP and Web 2.0

	Classical Model	World of Web 2.0	Where to Look	What to Measure
Segment	• Demographic • Behavioural • Psychographic	• Influence • Opinion • Leadership	• Tweets • Blogs • Social networks • Virtual lives	• Breadth of network • Quality of network • Creativity • Web expertise • Engagement • Tribal interaction • Tribal values
Target	• Competitive advantage • Segment attractiveness	• Tribes not segments • Engagement with the brand • Degree of influence	• Tribe sites • Events • Blogs	• Consumer-consumer influence • Tribe membership • Tribe trajectory • Keywords
Position	• Marketing warfare • 360° brand	• Influence, not control • Provide information • Facilitate discussion	• Blogs, postings, and chats	• Patterns and trends in consumer-consumer discourse • Pain points • Consumer workarounds

Yet because influences may come from a variety of directions, consumers' contexts may cut across traditional segments. In the world of Web 2.0, it is more important to think about what influence consumers have on each other than what demographic segment they belong to. New variables such as creativity, web competence, and propensity to tweet or blog need to be considered.

By treating customers as a set of homogeneous groups, traditional ways of analysing segments can distance a manager from consumers and their lives. Web 2.0, on the other hand, creates a need for deep understanding. To put this in concrete terms: in the world of classic marketing, a brand manager in consumer products would routinely analyse Nielsen data on market share and distribution, usage and attitude data on segment characteristics, and perhaps focus group or survey data on responses to advertising. In the world of Web 2.0, he/she needs to think about tweets, blogs, online networks, and virtual lives, looking at key influencers, the breadth and quality of their networks, and engagement with the brand. To understand this, he/she will need to use insight-based research tools such as observation and depth interviews in addition to online data and traditional research.

Targeting

One classical model of target market selection is the "9-box" matrix adapted from GE/McKinsey (see Table 2.3),[12] which considers the segment's attractiveness as measured by size, growth, profit margins, and so on, and the company's (potential) competitive advantage through product fit with the segment, brand loyalty, access to distribution channels, and so on.

In a world of hypercompetition and fragmentation, and where influence matters more than segment membership, it is important not just to measure and evaluate segments but to consider how each segment may influence others. So we are concerned not just with our position in the matrix, but how the brand moves through it: how consumers in one segment may look to others for guidance on what to consume and how to consume it. One group's workaround may spark the ingenuity of another group and create new uses or usage occasions.

Table 2.3 Adaptation of GE/McKinsey Matrix to Market Segment Evaluation

Segment Attractiveness	Competitive Position		
	Strong	**Medium**	**Weak**
High	Desirable potential target: protect	Desirable potential target: invest to build	Build selectively: specialize, overcome weaknesses
Medium	Build selectively	Manage for earnings: protect and invest	Limited expansion of harvest: minimize investment and risk; focus operations
Low	Protect and refocus: defend strengths, look for profit opportunities	Protect but minimize investment	Divest: cut fixed costs, sell

Positioning

Whereas Web 1.0 essentially provided marketers with another medium with which to communicate a tightly controlled message, user-generated content takes this control out of marketers' hands. Combined with rapid sharing of content through social networks, parody brand advertising can be disseminated instantaneously. Marketers can now participate in a conversation about their brands, and perhaps influence it, but they can no longer direct it as in the past.

Web 2.0 fundamentally changes the relationship between marketers and consumers, but this change has been coming for some time. As early as 1996, one researcher discussed "postmodern" marketing, before the growth of Web 2.0:

> In postmodern marketing, the consumer is not just a passive target for image marketing but an active link in the continual production of meanings. He calls for an experience-based marketing that emphasizes interactivity, connectivity and creativity.[13]

The ability of consumers to communicate rapidly in Web 2.0 puts this movement into hyperdrive. And it raises the question of whether the concept of positioning, a pillar of traditional marketing, continues to be tenable.

In the classic model, "Positioning is not what you do to a product. Positioning is what you *do to the mind of a prospect*. That is, you position the product in the mind of the prospect" (emphasis added).[14] It is usually considered the foundation of marketing strategy, and all elements of the mix are expected to conform to it.

This is a pretty deterministic approach. While marketers are quite aware that there can be a big difference between a statement of the *intended* message and the message that is actually received by consumers, the concept of positioning tends to assume that the advertiser is in the driver's seat – that he/she "does something to" the mind of the prospect.

Now the advertiser is no longer the driver, but another passenger. In this situation, positioning becomes a statement not of intent but of *hope* for the end result of an open conversation between advertisers and consumers, and between consumers and consumers – a conversation that may lead anywhere, but that the advertiser can only influence.

Loss of control also calls into question the wisdom that brand owners need to direct every touch point consumers have with their brand: the well-known "360° brand" model. That they should be concerned about and aware of how consumers interact with the brand is beyond question, but deft responses to consumers' postings will be more productive than attempts at rigid message control.

However, the advertiser's new role provides new opportunities. By engaging actively with consumers online, it is possible to develop a much deeper understanding of the issues consumers face: difficulties they encounter using the product, workarounds, and customization. Harley-Davidson, for example, benefits greatly by understanding how its HOG members customize their bikes. This understanding can become the basis of product improvements and communications.

Old ways of segmenting and targeting are no longer viable; the core concept of positioning is called into question: is there anything left of marketing as we know it? There is an upside: some marketers have embraced the world of Web 2.0 and leveraged it to develop a level of engagement that is rare for mass-marketed brands. I discuss one case, where a marketer enhanced a traditional advertising campaign with grass-roots activity, in the next section.

The Real World of Real Beauty: Dove[15]

In early 2004, Unilever launched Dove's Campaign for Real Beauty (CRB). CRB was a global campaign, developed in London, Dusseldorf, Chicago, and Toronto, which struck a chord with women around the world. In contrast to most personal care advertising, CRB emphasized women's "real" beauty and showed realistic images of women instead of idealized models.

Towards the end of 2004, the Dove Self-Esteem Fund was created globally to educate and inspire girls about a wider definition of beauty. In Canada, Unilever and its agency focused heavily on this element of the campaign. Global research indicated that an alarming number of girls suffered from low self-esteem; 92 per cent expressed a desire to change at least one aspect of their appearance.

A particularly important insight in Unilever's research gave rise to the Self-Esteem Fund: girlfriends and mothers had a greater influence on their daughters' self-esteem than either the media or celebrities. To quote from the research:

Our study shows that girlfriends at 34% and mothers at 27% are the earliest and most powerful influencers on a girl's feelings about her appearance, ahead of the media at 19% (including television, magazines and internet), or celebrities at 10%. Younger women (ages 15–17) were even more likely to name girlfriends at 41% and moms at 30% as primary shapers of attitudes surrounding beauty and body image.

Unilever sponsored self-esteem workshops for little girls and their mothers. In support of this initiative, the company produced three commercials for dissemination in traditional and online media. In January 2005, "Little Girls" was aired: the sixty-second television commercial juxtaposed the beauty of many different types of little girls against their issues, such as "thinks she's fat," "hates her freckles," or "wishes she were blonde." The commercial then closed with an invitation to tell these girls that their perceptions are wrong.

"Little Girls" ran alongside global advertising for specific products in the Dove range until January 2006. To drive workshop enrollment, Unilever and its agency created two viral films to tackle self-esteem from different angles: "Daughters" and "Evolution." "Daughters" profiled girls and young women speaking frankly about the impact that beauty culture was having on them, while "Evolution" (http://www.youtube.com/watch?v=iYhCn0jf46U) showed the transformation of an ordinary, attractive woman into a billboard model through the application of make-up, retouching, and Photoshop. It closed with the statement: "No wonder our perception of beauty is so distorted."

Unilever used the web exclusively to disseminate these last two films: on the Campaign for Real Beauty site (http://www.dove.ca/en/default.aspx#/cfrb/), as an email link to Unilever subscribers, and on Google Videos and YouTube. The films broke on 5 September and 16 October 2006, respectively.

Through 2005 and 2006, the Dove brand used both traditional media, such as TV, print, and out-of-home (e.g., billboards, transit ads), and non-traditional media. While product-based advertising for the varieties in the range was carried throughout both years in television, out-of-home, and print, the Canadian work supporting the Dove Self-Esteem Fund used appointment television* and the web.

---

* Television programming for which one sets aside time to watch, either live or on videotape. Specific TV programs are purchased specifically for the target audience, in contrast to a traditional media buy, which attempts to deliver the lowest cost per audience rating.

The Dove campaign created huge momentum online, especially around the "Evolution" film, which generated passionate discussion and many parodies. "Daughters" and "Evolution" were not shown in conventional media and received no media support. "Evolution" received over 2 million views and twenty-two postings after two weeks on YouTube. For ten days, it topped the charts of linked-to-brand videos on both Blogpulse and Technorati; as of December 2010, "Evolution" had been uniquely viewed 41 million times and was ranked sixth on *Advertising Age*'s list of the top ten viral ads of all time.[16] Every workshop across Canada was sold out after the launch.

Unilever also exceeded its goal of touching the lives of young girls, measured as at least one hour of interaction with a Dove Self-Esteem program: with 55,000 such touch points, the goal of 30,000 lives touched by 2008 was exceeded by 2006.

Reporting on the campaign to Unilever in October 2006, Nielsen BuzzMetrics commented as follows:

> Little in the history of Unilever tracking has done as much for Unilever buzz as the Dove Campaign for Real Beauty and now the Dove "Evolution" ad . . . the effects of the video are far-reaching in Consumer Generated Media as it helps to engage general consumers in Unilever and consumer packaged goods dialogue, opens new possibilities . . . and enlightens consumers who aren't wed to a cause.

Although Unilever did not provide media support to "Evolution," the company estimated the PR and media coverage arising from the film to be worth U.S.$150,000,000; the brand was featured on every popular talk show in the United States, with talk show host Rosie O'Donnell commenting, "I'm going to use Dove from now on because of that ad."

"Evolution" and other Dove videos were widely parodied, a testament to the campaign's impact; however, many of the parodies did not contribute to the brand's image and may even have damaged it. For example, one video contrasts the Dove ads to another Unilever product, Axe, which portrays women in a very different light (http://www.youtube.com/watch?v=SwDEF-w4rJk). Unilever did not attempt to shut these parodies down but instead appears to have accepted them as an inevitability.

A McLuhan Moment

Few could have predicted, a few years ago, that the web would turn marketing on its head. But Marshall McLuhan (1911–80) did.

McLuhan's most famous aphorism, "The medium is the message," coined well before Web 2.0,[17] referred to the fact that a medium influences society by virtue not just of the content it carries, but because of the characteristics of the medium itself. As an example, fast access to information creates an expectation that supply chains will improve and that goods and services will become more readily available: the medium influences expectations, which in turn influence behaviour.

McLuhan would have felt vindicated by Web 2.0. His other observation (he made many) that "we shape our tools and thereafter our tools shape us" has never seemed more real. While the emergence of Web 2.0 can be seen as an evolution from the reality that preceded it – as it did not involve the invention of any new technology – its impact has been revolutionary.

For some time now, agencies and their clients have merged the processes of creative and media development, and Web 2.0 integrates them even more closely. Creativity is just as likely to be applied to developing online events and engagement as it is to art and copy for TV, print, and radio. The message depends on the medium, and the medium truly is the message.

Thus Web 2.0 exposes a world of indeterminacy and apparent chaos, in which the distinction between "content" and "communication" is meaningless and ideas can flow in any direction: a postmodern world in which the deterministic models that form the foundation of marketing itself are questioned. Think about the following table (Table 2.4), which one researcher used to represent modern and postmodern thought.[18] Ask yourself: which of these represents the reality of the context consumers live in? Which represents the worldview of most marketing managers?

Marketing was built in the TV age around a model of one-way mass communication. As communications media became more fragmented, marketers had to adapt to smaller, more diverse audiences: this stretched the traditional model, as one message was no longer appropriate to all groups. But the development of user-created content has strained it to the breaking point. Modern marketing attempts to impose predictability on an unpredictable, postmodern world. In an attempt to understand consumers better, we aggregate them into segments; yet, as Dave Carroll showed, individual consumers can turn a brand on its head. The act of segmentation has the effect of distancing us from individual consumers, when we need to get closer to them.

Above all, postmodern marketing is concerned with the *creation of meaning*; consumers no longer consume products, but the symbolic

Table 2.4 The Modern and Postmodern

Modern	Postmodern
Order/control	Disorder/chaos
Certainty/determinacy	Ambiguity/indeterminacy
Fordism*/factory	Post-Fordism+/office
Content/depth	Style/surface
Progress/tomorrow	Stasis/today
Homogeneity/consensus	Heterogeneity/plurality
Hierarchy/adulthood	Equality/youth
Existence/reality	Performance/imitation
Deliberate/outer-directed	Playful/self-centred
Contemplation/metaphysics	Participation/parody
Congruity/design	Incongruity/chance

* Mass production
+ Computer-aided customization

meanings associated with those products. Who better to create meaning than consumers themselves? Consumers' meanings relate to both individuality and membership of tribes. For Harley-Davidson, it is not the technical specifications about the bike that matter, but the set of personal meanings and social connections it creates: America, freedom, rebellion, machismo, and so on. By supporting HOGs, Harley-Davidson is providing a frame for the creation of social meaning.

For Pankaj Aggarwal's colleague in chapter 13, Apple was more than an easy-to-use computer: it was a person, who embodied meanings of coolness, creativity, and individuality. Apple reinforces its meanings both through its mass advertising and through relentless introduction of new products, high-touch retail stores, and user seminars – but it is not Apple that creates these meanings; it is consumers themselves.

Web 2.0 is the perfect vehicle for the creation of meaning by consumers through engagement with the brand and connection with others. Tribes are formed online, their values expressed, their membership defined. The role of marketers is not to form these tribes or impose meanings on them, as this will only be resisted by consumers, but to provide a frame, suggest possible meanings, and respond creatively to consumers' own creative interpretations.

Thriving in Web 2.0: Lose, Monitor, Engage

Web 2.0 presents marketers with a dilemma. On the one hand, being talked about, shared, and parodied on the internet brings attention to the brand; on the other, it may not be the kind of attention the brand wants.

Yet to quote Oscar Wilde, "The only thing worse than being talked about is not being talked about." Dove is not alone in harnessing Web 2.0: other advertisers, such as T-Mobile and Old Spice, have seen their videos widely shared and parodied. Those who have thrived in Web 2.0 have exposed themselves to the risk that their brand will be damaged by the exposure. Yet the experience of some marketers demonstrates the power of video sharing to create a level of brand engagement beyond anything that was dreamed of in the past.

Some have used the web creatively to generate coverage beyond the scope of traditional media. In Italy, Heineken created a spoof concert (http://www.youtube.com/watch?v=iK-deK6B9g4), where target consumers' girlfriends and bosses were recruited to pressure them to attend a classical concert that conflicted with a major football match.

Smaller brands with insufficient budgets for mainstream media have developed online videos and seen them widely shared, such as Andes Beer's "Teletransporter" campaign (http://www.youtube.com/watch?v=7WWwbBFrrSI) in which sound booths were installed in bars and the target consumers (young men) would use these to convince their girlfriends that they were at work, at a wedding, or at a funeral instead of at the pub.

Other brands have actively brought users into the marketing process. In Canada, Doritos invited consumers to make their own ads for a hitherto unnamed new flavour, through TV ads and its website, http://www.youtube.com/user/doritosguru. The site received over 1.5 million unique visits, over 2,000 approved submissions, and over 30,000 fans on Facebook.

How, then, to maximize the benefit to the brand and minimize the risk of damage? Marketers would do well to *lose* the illusion of control, *monitor* activity on Web 2.0, and *engage* with tribes of consumers.

Lose the Illusion of Control

In the world of Web 2.0, brands have become community property. Advertisers (contrary to mythology) never could control what consumers thought; nowadays, they cannot even control what they hear or see about the brand. The message can be influenced from any direction: target consumers, non-consumers, competitors, happy or disgruntled employees, distributors, and more.

Ogilvy & Mather, one of the world's largest advertising agencies, uses a model of "360 Degree Brand Stewardship"® to manage its clients' brands.[19] The model's underlying thesis is that consumers encounter a brand at several "touch points" and these touch points must be managed effectively. At one time, this might have been seen as a need to communicate a single, coherent message at all touch points, and indeed, advertisers might have had a chance of succeeding. But in the world of Web 2.0, its meaning has shifted: advertisers need to be acutely aware of the brand's essence and understand these touch points, but recognize that they can only be influenced, not controlled. Ogilvy & Mather is Unilever's global agency on the Dove brand.

Losing the illusion of control does not mean giving up. The brand's owner is more than just one more voice: by virtue of his knowledge and understanding of the brand and of consumers, he punches above his weight and can propose and frame discussions, provide information, and reinforce desired meanings.

Monitor Web 2.0

The example of Dave Carroll and United Airlines was one of many situations in which companies' reputations have been damaged through web activity. The web has few boundaries; it is instantaneous, anonymous, and – perhaps most damaging of all – permanent. Emails, blogs, and shared videos can last forever and be revived at any time. Information, true or not, circulates rapidly through user networks.

What determines whether a rumour will spread or wither on the vine? Several factors appear to be at work:[20]

CREDIBILITY

A rumour that is plausible seems to be distributed faster and last longer. Dave Carroll's experience with United Airlines resonated with travellers who have had their bags mishandled, and seemed to be the type of thing that could happen to anyone.

SEVERITY

Information about risks that are perceived to be more severe will spread more quickly. One email that wrongly associated tampons with asbestos has been circulating for at least ten years. The rumour has long been refuted by the FDA.

SALIENCE

If the rumour is likely to affect a large number of people, it will spread quickly and be sustained over time. The tampon rumour has arguably lasted so long because of its potentially widespread effects.

By being aware of emerging rumours and negative information about the brand, a marketer can take steps to provide an alternative version quickly, before the rumour spreads too far (although it should be recognized that it may do so anyway).

The first step to dealing such a rumour is to be aware of it. In some industries, there are specific sites that need to be monitored constantly, such as http://www.tripadvisor.com in the travel industry. There are also sites that provide a home for issues arising in any industry, such as "Sucks 500.com" (http://www.newsucks500.com/), which was established to house complaints against Fortune 500 companies and provides a forum for users to post complaints about companies, brands, politicians, issues, and so on. Individual blogs, sharing, and mashups can be monitored through one of the many web crawling services available that monitor activity around specific brands.

But it would be a mistake to view monitoring of Web 2.0 as a completely defensive activity. Discussions on the web – whether positive or negative, based on truth or falsehood – give a sense of the zeitgeist and how attitudes to the brand are shifting; how tribal communities are forming and unforming; where there are pain points and pleasure points in the brand experience; and workarounds or innovations users undertake on their own, that might be the basis of the brand's next move. So monitoring needs to be done with a curious mindset that seeks to understand the discussion, as opposed to one that immediately jumps to defend the brand.

Engage Consumers

Web 2.0 is about capturing consumers' interest for a time – sometimes fleetingly, but sometimes on a sustained basis, as in the case of Dove's Self-Esteem Fund, which continued over a period of several years. This is distinct from traditional approaches of market segmentation and relationship marketing: marketers need to think about tribes and create viral value that will be shared.

THINK TRIBES, NOT SEGMENTS

Tribal marketing is not new, but Web 2.0 provides new opportunities to nurture and engage with brand tribes: consumers are now clustering into "e-tribes,"[21] online groups who have interests in common and who establish their own membership, cultural meanings, and identities.

Segments are typically constructed from demographic or behavioural indicators. As an example, consumers are often segmented on the basis of their loyalty, as measured by share of requirements, retention, and so on. But tribes are communities, not segments: while consumers in the same segment are not assumed to interact with each other, tribe members do, and it is from this interaction that marketers can develop a deep understanding of the discourse about their brand. Indeed, as Mengze Shi points out in chapter 11, marketers can use this understanding to influence the structure of social networks – that is, e-tribes – and their behaviour through the use of incentives.

Vans, a manufacturer of shoes for skateboarders, BMXers, and snowboarders, supports its tribe through sponsorship of skate parks, concerts, and venues for boarders to meet and interact. Through Vans Customs on its website, the company allows tribe members to log on and design their own pair of Vans slip-on, mid-cut, or high-top shoes. This in turn creates the ability for Vans to enter a dialogue with them and moderate discussions between users.

Create Viral Value

Advertising Age monitors the most-shared ten videos of each week through its partner, viralvideos.com (http://www.visiblemeasures.com/adage). The videos are fascinating viewing, and as of 9 May 2011, included spoofs of news events such as the wedding of Prince William and Kate Middleton in April 2011 (T-Mobile), digitally manipulated footage of babies seemingly doing calisthenics (Evian), a child's experience with a new car (VW Passat – first shown during the 2011 Super Bowl), a stand-up comic sleeping in Macy's window for a week (Downy), and a demonstration of a blender liquidizing an iPad (Blendtec).

In short, the videos that are shared are entertaining, by being funny, cute, clever, and original. Often, the videos rely on a high level of technical sophistication, as in the case of Dove "Evolution" or Evian "Live Young." The videos ranged in length from thirty seconds to two minutes forty-one seconds.

Advertising that seeks to persuade without entertaining will simply be ignored in this medium. Among all widely-shared videos, it is interesting to note what is *not* there: a heavy degree of brand sell. The brand identification of these videos is usually quite subtle and often consists only of a brief credit at the end. This is particularly remarkable given that advertisers such as Unilever and Procter & Gamble, with long histories of aggressively persuasive advertising, have developed a strong track record in video sharing – no doubt the result of much internal discussion and angst.

In many ways, Web 2.0 returns us to the foundations of marketing: understand your customers and develop actively engaged relationships with them. For marketers who live in the past, the loss of control is scary; for those who embrace the new environment, the potential benefits are huge, as Dave Carroll can attest. United may have broken his guitar, but it made his brand fly.

A Prescription for Thriving in the New Communications Environment
Given the revolution in social media and communication, the brand is no longer the sole driver of communication. To thrive in this environment, the manager needs to:

- LOSE the illusion of control. Branding is now a constantly renegotiated set of relationships with customers. Lead the discussion, but don't control it.
- MONITOR how your brand is being discussed on Web 2.0. Respond genuinely and proactively.
- ENGAGE your customers through transparent, honest, quick, and action-oriented communication. Relate to them as people, and not as targets of persuasive campaigns.

REFERENCES

1 Dave Carroll, "United Breaks Guitars," accessed 5 January 2010 from
   http://www.davecarrollmusic.com/story/united-breaks-guitars.
   Video 1: http://www.youtube.com/watch?v=5YGc4zOqozo
   Video 2: http://www.youtube.com/
   watch?v=h-UoERHaSQg&feature=channel
   Video 3: http://www.youtube.com/watch?v=P45E0uGVyeg
2 "The Sweet Music of Revenge: Singer Pens YouTube Hit after United Airlines Breaks His Guitar ... and Shares Plunge 10%," Eddie Wrenn, *Daily*

Mail, 24 July 2009, accessed 11 January 2010 from http://www.dailymail.co.uk/news/article-1201671/Singer-Dave-Carroll-pens-YouTube-hit-United-Airlines-breaks-guitar--shares-plunge-10.html. The claim was disputed by other authors.

3 *Merriam-Webster Online Dictionary*, accessed 23 October 2011 from http://www.merriam-webster.com/dictionary/flux.

4 Seth Godin, *Permission Marketing: Turning Strangers into Friends, and Friends Into Customers* (New York: Simon and Schuster, 1999).

5 E. DuPlessis, *The Advertised Mind: Groundbreaking Insights into How Our Brains Respond to Advertising* (Philadelphia: Millward Brown/Kogan Page, 2008).

6 P. Nunes and J. Merrihue, "The Continuing Power of Mass Advertising," *Sloan Management Review* 48, no. 2 (2007): 63–71.

7 "Company Info/Fact Sheet," *Facebook Newsroom*, accessed 25 July 2011 from http://www.facebook.com/press/info.php?statistics; and "Goldman to Cleints: Facebook Has 600 Million Users," Tech and Gadgets, *msnbc.com*, accessed 25 July 2011 from http://www.msnbc.msn.com/id/40929239/ns/technology_and_science-tech_and_gadgets/.

8 J. Cloud, "The Gurus of YouTube," *Time*, 16 December 2006, accessed 25 July 2011 from http://www.time.com/time/magazine/article/0,9171,1570795,00.html.

9 Mary Madden, "The Audience for Online Video-Sharing Sites Shoots Up," *Pew Internet* (Washington, DC: Pew Research Center, 2009), accessed 6 May 2011 from http://pewinternet.org/~/media/Files/Reports/2009/The-Audience-for-Online-Video-Sharing-Sites-Shoots-Up.pdf.

10 P. Berthon, L. Pitt, and C. Campbell, "Ad Lib: When Customers Create the Ad," *California Management Review* 50, no. 4 (2008): 6–30.

11 B. Cova and V. Cova, "Tribal Marketing: The Tribalisation of Society and its Impact on the Conduct of Marketing," *European Journal of Marketing* 36, nos. 5/6 (2002): 595–620.

12 K. Coyne, "Enduring Ideas: The GE–McKinsey Nine-box Matrix," *The McKinsey Quarterly* (2008), accessed 14 May 2011 from https://www.mckinseyquarterly.com/Enduring_ideas_The_GE-McKinsey_nine-box_matrix_2198.

13 B. Cova, "The Postmodern Explained to Managers: Implications for Marketing," *Business Horizons* 39 (1996): 15–23.

14 Al Ries and Jack Trout, *Positioning: The Battle for Your Mind* (New York: McGraw-Hill, 2000).

15 David Dunne, "Supporting the Dove Self-Esteem Fund," case study (2009). Available from author.

16 Michael Learmonth, "The Top 10 Viral Ads of All Time," *AdAge Digital* (2010), accessed 6 May 2011 from http://adage.com/article/the-viral-video-chart/digital-marketing-top-10-viral-ads-time/145673/ . The methodology combines data from brand-driven seeded video placements with results from community-driven viral video placements such as spoofs, parodies, and mashups.

17 Marshall McLuhan, *Understanding Media: The Extensions of Man* (New York: McGraw-Hill, 1964).

18 S. Brown, "Postmodern Marketing?" *European Journal of Marketing* 27, no. 4 (1993): 19–34.

19 Ogilvy & Mather internal handbook cited in K. Keller, *Strategic Brand Management: Building, Managing and Measuring Brand Equity* (Upper Saddle River, NJ: Pearson Education, 2008), 350–1.

20 P. Blackshaw and K. Iyer, "Rumors and Issues on the Internet: Using the Web to manage reputations and Crises . . . Before It's Too Late," an Intelliseek White Paper, Cincinnati, Ohio, 2003, accessed 10 May 2011 from http://www.brandchannel.com/images/Papers/222_RumorsIssues.pdf.

21 R. Kozinets,"E-Tribalized Marketing? The Strategic Implications of Virtual Communities of Consumption," *European Journal of Marketing* 17, no. 3 (1998): 252–64.

3 Brand Extension Strategy: An Integrative Framework

SRIDHAR MOORTHY

In the last ten years or so, the marketing environment has changed profoundly. One big change is the establishment and growth of the internet, which has changed the advertising media landscape, creating new media while simultaneously weakening old media such as television and newspapers. Consumer behaviour has changed concomitantly: more people are spending more time online, choosing to get their news and entertainment there, interacting with other consumers, and, in general, getting much of their information about products and services from independent third parties, instead of from the marketers themselves. For manufacturers, another source of concern has been the simultaneous growth of big retailers, with brands of their own, and the wherewithal to leverage them in conjunction with point-of-purchase data to dictate terms to the manufacturers. The brand manager's job, never easy, has become even more challenging. To navigate this difficult terrain, brand managers must have a comprehensive up-to-date understanding of brands and branding strategy. In this chapter I focus on a particular aspect of branding strategy: brand extension strategy.

Most new products are brand extensions – new applications of existing brands.[1] Examples include Arm & Hammer, a baking soda, a toothpaste, detergent, and cat litter; and Sony, a brand name created for transistor radios and extended to televisions, computers, cameras, and many other categories. And then there is Virgin, a brand so ubiquitous that *The Observer* observes that it is possible to lead "a Virgin life":

> You can eat Virgin food in a Virgin hotel; drink Virgin cola; wear Virgin clothes and cosmetics; use a Virgin mobile; surf the Virgin.net; use Virgin

condoms; go to a Virgin doctor; buy a car through Virgin with money from your Virgin account; get married with Virgin brides; buy your house with a Virgin mortgage; listen to Virgin radio; see Virgin-funded films in a Virgin cinema; work out in a Virgin Active gym; play Virgin video games as you go on holiday on a Virgin train or plane, stopping only to buy your Virgin vodka in duty free. (*Observer*, 15 October 2000)

New brands are comparatively rare. But they are seen from time to time – often from the same companies that pursue brand extensions in other parts of their business. For example, in the 1980s, the three major Japanese companies in the North American automobile market – Toyota, Honda, and Nissan – each chose to create entirely new brands of cars and trucks – Lexus, Acura, and Infiniti, respectively – even though they already had, and continue to have, their corporate brands on many models of cars and trucks. In the packaged goods industry, Procter & Gamble is renowned for its "house of brands" strategy. It has distinctive brands in each category – Tide in detergent, Pampers in diapers, Crest in toothpaste, to name just a few – and even multiple brands within categories (for instance, Tide is accompanied by Bold, Cheer, and Dash).

Why do firms extend their brands? Why do firms introduce new brands instead of extending their existing brands? What circumstances determine which is the better strategy? How far can a brand extension strategy go? These are important questions – arguably among the most important in all of marketing. So it is not surprising to find a large literature in marketing dedicated to answering them. Typing "brand extension" into Google Scholar yields over half a million references!

Volume of research has not equated to clarity of understanding, however. A marketing manager looking for guidance in the academic literature is more likely than not to end up confused rather than enlightened. Consider, for example, the two classic papers in the field – Wernerfelt[2] and Aaker and Keller.[3] On cursory examination they do not even appear to be about the same topic. Digging deeper, a semblance of similarity of concerns may reveal itself, but the methodology and conclusions are quite different. Aaker and Keller's work, a survey of consumers asking them to evaluate the merits of different hypothetical brand extensions by real brands, finds that those evaluations depend on how well the old and new applications of the brands "fit." Wernerfelt's paper, on the other hand, argues that it is possible for consumers to evaluate brand extensions favourably even in the absence of anything resembling fit.

In this chapter I offer a new framework for thinking about branding strategy that synthesizes these disparate perspectives. Key to my framework is the recognition that brands are essentially ways to communicate with consumers, and they do so in multiple ways. The different strands of the academic literature, with their seemingly contradictory prescriptions, are really looking at different facets of brands. Some concerns raised in the literature cease to be concerns away from the modelling world, in the real world.

I begin by discussing the conventional wisdom on branding strategy, and argue that it faces many challenges in explaining the success and failure of real-world brand extensions. Theoretical and empirical research in marketing has attempted to refine the conventional wisdom to accommodate these challenges, but not wholly successfully. Hopefully, my integrated framework will serve as a one-stop shop for the practicing manager seeking guidance on brand extension strategy.

The Conventional Wisdom

Why extend a brand? The textbook answer is that it takes the risk out of new product introduction, by allowing the new product to free-ride on the equity already established in the brand. As Richard Branson, well-known architect of the Virgin brand, puts it: "Consumers understand that all the values that apply to one product – good service, style, quality, value and fair dealing – apply to the others" (*Time*, 24 June 1996). By contrast, new products under new brands are an unknown quantity, and it will take time and money to establish them. Without a track record, consumers will hesitate to try them, especially when established alternatives are available. As compensation for bearing additional risk, the firm may have to sweeten the pot via lower prices, but this will hurt its bottom line, especially if incumbents match those prices.

In short, introducing a new product under a new brand name is risky, costly, and time-consuming. While no general estimates are available for how long it takes to establish a new brand, we do have some idea about the out-of-pocket costs. According to Keller,[4]

From a marketing communications perspective, one obvious advantage of introducing a new product as a brand extension is that the introductory campaign does not have to create awareness of both the brand and the new product but instead can concentrate on only the new product itself

... Several research studies document this extension benefit. One study of 98 consumer brands in 11 markets found that successful brand extensions spent less on advertising than did comparable new-name entries. Another comprehensive study found similar results, indicating that the average advertising-to-sales ratio for brand extensions was 10 percent, compared with 19 percent for new brands ... it has been estimated that a firm can save 40 percent to 80 percent on the estimated $30 million to $50 million it can cost to launch a new supermarket product nationally in the United States.

Tauber's[5] estimates are perhaps even more extreme: he estimates the cost of establishing a new brand at $150 million (circa 1988), three times the cost of introducing a brand extension.

This logic for brand extension, pushed to the extreme, leads to a single brand for the entire company. The firm becomes a "branded house." Companies with well-known corporate brands such as Sony, Apple, and GE bear testimony to the practical viability of this approach.

Complicating the picture, however, is the recognition that this is not the only branding strategy out there. As I noted earlier, companies like P&G pursue a "houses of brands" strategy: in each category they have a different brand, and sometimes, multiple brands within categories. Why create a new brand when there is an opportunity to extend a brand? While many reasons can be given, the main justification is that sometimes a new product needs a fresh start. And when might a new product need a fresh start? When the firm deems it necessary to market the new product with a new "strategy" – a strategy different from the strategies behind existing brands in the firm's portfolio. This was the case in the Acura, Infiniti, and Lexus examples given earlier. Honda, Nissan, and Toyota each wanted a new car line to compete in the "luxury" segment of the market. This was a new segment for these companies: while consumers thought well of their corporate brands, they were perceived mainly as well-made, utilitarian cars, not luxury cars. Given the strategy shift, these auto makers were willing to swallow the cost of creating a new brand in order to have the freedom to position it differently.

Challenging the Conventional Wisdom

The idea that brand equity can be leveraged in a new brand extension rests on the presumption that consumers will evaluate new brand extensions on the basis of how they perceive the brand. But is that necessarily so? To what extent does brand equity transfer to a new product from existing products bearing the brand name? Consider the following. At a macro level, we know that not all brand extensions succeed; in fact, a majority of them fail. Well-known examples of brand extension failures include Roots Air, the Jaguar X-Type, and Virgin Brides. In each case, at the time these products were introduced, the parent brands were strong. In fact, it was the strength of the brands that motivated the extension. Yet the goodwill embedded in the brands was apparently not enough to make the extensions succeed. What failed here? Was it that brand equity didn't transfer at all to the new extension, or was it that the new extensions failed in spite of the transfer? Many new brands fail as well, so the relevant question is whether brand extensions are more likely to succeed than new brands. But on this score as well, we get negative answers. Reddy, Holak, and Bhat[6] observe that "the failure rates of extensions approach the rates of failure of new brand introductions." Sullivan's[7] data corroborates. The implication is that the main raison d'être for a brand extension – its alleged ability to inherit brand equity – either doesn't happen at all, or if it does, is not strong enough to materially alter the new product's prospects.

Academic research has also examined the brand equity transfer property at the micro level. Broadly speaking, the literature is divided into two subliteratures, one using economics and game theory models, exemplified by Wernerfelt,[2] and another using social psychology models ("the behavioral literature"), exemplified by Aaker and Keller.[3] Historically, these literatures have proceeded independently, with nary an acknowledgment of the other. Whereas the behavioural literature is largely based on laboratory experiments involving student subjects, the economics/game theory literature is largely theoretical, probing the firm's rationality in extending the brand, and the consumer's rationality in inferring anything from it. It may be hard to see much common ground between these paradigms. Yet I plan to do just that in this presentation. Before I do that, though, I will lay out the main messages of these subliteratures.

Behavioural Frameworks

Aaker and Keller[3] asked consumers to evaluate a number of hypothetical brand extensions of well-known brand names. They found that there was no main effect of perceived quality of the brand on attitudes towards the extension. In other words, there was "no direct link from perceived quality of the brand to the attitude toward the extension" – contradicting the conventional wisdom. There was an interaction effect, though. The extension was evaluated highly only when the brand was perceived as high quality *and* there was "fit" between the old and new applications – either substitutability in demand or complementarity in demand. For instance, Crest mouthwash was evaluated favourably, but not Crest shaving cream; a Häagen-Dazs candy bar was evaluated favourably, but not Häagen-Dazs cottage cheese.

Later research has expanded on the notion of fit. Besides substitutability and complementarity in demand, fit is now conceptualized as a broader notion encompassing ideas of "concept consistency,"[8] "technological complementarity," and "relevance of brand-specific associations in the extension application."[9] Technological complementarity is a supply-side notion; it speaks to production considerations. There is technological fit, for instance, when Heineken beer extends to light beer, but not when it extends to wine: production processes are quite different for beer and wine. Concept consistency continues to be a demand-side notion, but on a higher, more abstract plane than demand substitutability or demand complementarity. Two applications of a brand may be concept consistent without being substitutes or complements. For instance, the brand Rolex is concept-consistent when it extends from watches to bracelets and rings, but not when it extends to stop-watches and calculators, the reason being that it is Rolex's "prestige" that is being extended, and this concept is relevant in hedonistic applications, but not in utilitarian applications. Broniarczyk and Alba[9] build on this idea to arrive at the more general notion of "brand-specific associations." Successful brands exude unique associations – the things that give these brands their distinct identities. For instance, Close-Up is associated with "breath freshening" and Crest is associated with "dental protection." It is a small leap from this to then argue that brands extend well to applications where their unique associations have relevance. For instance, in Broniarczyk and Alba's data, Close-Up extends better to breath mints than Crest even though, in their original category of toothpaste, Crest is rated higher than Close-Up.

With fit as a mediating variable, it is no longer automatic that brand extensions inherit brand equity from the parent brand. This may explain why some brand extensions succeed and others fail. For instance, by this reckoning, Crystal Pepsi's failure may now be pinned on the poor fit between "a clear cola" and the traditional caramel-coloured drink, characteristic of both Pepsi, the brand, and colas, the category. Similarly, Clorox's "bleachness" translates well to toilet bowl cleaner, but not to laundry detergent, and this may explain the success of the former and the failure of the latter.

However, fit can go only so far. The Virgin brand is a poster child for these difficulties. It is hard to see how fit, or lack thereof, can be the story behind the success of Virgin Money on the one hand and the failure of Virgin Cola on the other. Arguably, Virgin's youthful image doesn't translate well in the former application, but it does in the latter application. Yet the results are the opposite of what you would expect.

It is harder still to be proactive with the fit concept. The multiple criteria underlying "fit" often contradict each other. For example, Heineken popcorn may be a good fit with Heineken beer on demand complementarity grounds, but a poor fit on technological grounds. Second, brands often acquire and radiate many concepts in each application, and a brand extension may be concept-consistent in one but concept-inconsistent in another. For example, Arm & Hammer has successfully extended itself from baking soda to laundry detergent, and to cat litter. While the deodorizing properties of baking soda are concept-consistent in the detergent and cat litter applications, these applications also generate other concepts, such as "things you don't put in your mouth," that are concept-inconsistent in the original food application.

More significantly, however, the biggest knock on the behavioural theories is that they ignore the firm and its motivations. As such, these theories have nothing to say about the following conundrum underlying many brand extensions. Products are generally experience goods, so when consumers buy a new brand extension, they do not have much information about it, other than that it is an extension of a brand they know and probably like. They could simply assume that they *will* also like the new brand extension. But if they do, firms may have an incentive to take advantage of this belief, passing off inferior extensions as the real thing – especially since extending a brand is less costly than creating a new brand. And if they do, will consumers be justified in holding on to their prior beliefs?

Economics/Game-Theory Frameworks

If the behavioural literature more or less ignores the conundrum, the economics/game-theory literature is fairly obsessed with it. It offers two broad approaches to deal with it, the "signalling approach" and the "moral hazard approach." What these approaches have in common is the idea that branding, brand equity, and the brand extension decision itself all have meaning only in the context of experience goods – products whose key attributes are experiential, maybe even "credence"; certainly not observed before purchase, but maybe observed after purchase, perhaps noisily. Where they differ is the function they attribute to brand extension. In the signalling framework, exemplified by Wernerfelt[2] and Cabral,[10] the firm is portrayed as making a brand extension decision on a new product whose quality is already set at the time of the brand extension decision. Of course, consumers do not know what that quality is, but the firm does. The brand extension decision becomes an opportunity to provide information to consumers about the new product's quality. In contrast, in the moral hazard literature, exemplified by Hakenes and Pietz[11] and Cabral,[12] the firm is portrayed as choosing product quality for old and new products – over many periods – following the brand extension decision. The function of brand extension becomes one of providing assurance to consumers that high quality will be maintained on each and every purchase occasion.

In the signalling approach, the key question is, are there reasons to expect that only a firm with good quality products would extend the brand? The answer is yes, and what sustains this answer is the possibility of collateral damage to other products under the same brand should the new extension fail to perform up to expectations. The collateral damage angle is important because on the new product itself, the incentives to uphold consumer expectations are the same, regardless of whether it is a brand extension or a new brand. In addition, the risk of collateral damage has to be on existing brand extensions, not future extensions, because a new brand risks collateral damage on (its) future extensions as well.

Compelling as this argument is, modelling it is not straightforward, as I have discussed elsewhere.[13] I do not want to regurgitate the technicalities of that discussion here, but would like to highlight two issues that arise in that discussion. The signalling argument relies on brand being the gatekeeper controlling the adverse belief spillovers from one extension to another. This is an assumption. Its importance is understood by asking the following question: what would happen if, instead of introducing a new brand extension, the firm were to introduce a new brand, and it failed? The signalling argument presumes that collateral damage is avoided in that instance. Consumers' beliefs about a brand stay within the brand – they do not cross brand boundaries even if a common firm underlies the multiple brands. For low-involvement categories this seems reasonable – consumers are generally brand-oriented for such products. For high-involvement categories, however, one might expect consumers to be more willing to research the corporate origin of a brand, and hence more willing to ascribe the problems associated with a brand as a firm-wide problem, affecting all its brands. That would make the collateral damage justification for brand extension harder to sustain.

Fortunately, the only empirical study speaking to this issue that we are aware of does not find evidence of spillovers crossing brand boundaries. Sullivan[14] investigates the collateral damage to the Audi brand that resulted when one of its models, the Audi 5000, became the subject of rumors about "sudden acceleration" in 1986. She finds that other Audi models suffered, but not VW or Porsche, even though all three brands belong to the same corporate parent. However, the same sort of analysis on the more recent troubles at Toyota and Lexus might yield a different result.

Another important issue is the role played by other products under the brand name. Their risk of collateral damage effectively supports the transfer of brand equity to the new extension. The larger the number of such "hostages," the stronger the signal, presumably. This suggests that the best time to introduce a brand extension is at the beginning, when the brand is most vulnerable – when its reputation hasn't solidified to the point where it can't be held hostage. That is, brand extension must coincide with brand creation. In reality, this is almost never the case: brand extensions are typically introduced only after a brand is well-established. For instance, Roots Air was introduced in 2001, nearly twenty years after Roots itself. It is not surprising that Roots Air's failure hardly made a dent on Roots sales. Under these circumstances, should consumers have approached Roots Air with positive quality expectations?

The moral hazard subgenre of the literature approaches the question of brand equity transfer slightly differently – but, as it turns out, only slightly differently. The key difference is that now the firm is seen as choosing quality after the brand extension decision, rather than it being a given at the time of the brand extension decision. First, in terms of formulation, having quality chosen rather than being an endowment of the firm seems more realistic. Second, the order – brand extension first, quality choice later – is also realistic if quality choice is thought of as "quality maintenance." After all, quality maintenance is also a decision – the decision not to degrade quality. In other words, every brand extension decision is followed by a series of period-by-period quality maintenance decisions. The term "moral hazard" comes from the fact that "trusting" the brand extension exposes the consumer to the "hazard" that the firm may take advantage of the trust and lower quality to save costs.

Since the brand extension decision precedes the quality decisions in the moral hazard framework, there is nothing to be read from the brand extension decision. Still, brand extension can support or hinder particular outcomes in the quality choice phase. Specifically, brand extension allows the consumer to connect the performances of multiple products, and hold the entire brand accountable for delivering quality. In particular, she can withhold purchases of one or all brand extensions should she conclude that any of them has lowered its quality. Both draconian and lenient "punishments" are possible. For example, a draconian punishment regimen would be that *one* failure of *any* brand extension results in zero future sales of the entire brand; a lenient standard would be that all brand extensions have to fail simultaneously for one to lose sales. Optimal consumer response is a trade-off between setting too harsh a standard of performance that a firm cannot possibly fulfill versus setting it so leniently that firms are tempted to "cheat."

As might be evident from this discussion, the signalling and moral hazard approaches have much in common. In fact, the core mechanism sustaining brand extension's connection to quality is quite similar in the two models: "adverse belief spillovers" in one, "cross-product punishments" in the other. Note, too, that both approaches rely substantially on the assumption that choosing a new brand allows a firm to isolate the new product from other products produced by the firm and escape "spillovers."

Ultimately, these theoretical models must confront empirical reality. Will consumers' beliefs spill over from one brand extension to another? Will consumers punish one brand extension for the transgressions of another? The behavioural literature suggests that these things may not happen generally. We must take a different approach to conceptualizing brand extensions. This is what I do next.

Brand Extension as Communication

I believe that the key to developing a unified perspective from these disparate strands of research is to recognize that brand extension is basically an act of communication. By extending a brand into a new product, a firm seeks to communicate that the new product has the same "values" as the brand applied to it. But the proof of the pudding is in the eating; "seeking" is not "achieving." The consumer is willing to accept the "sought" message provisionally, but if the extension does not live up to it, then the reality is what governs, not the aspiration. Central to this conceptualization is the notion of brand as both repository of information and communication tool. When a brand is being built, the repository is being stocked; as soon as the repository has something in it, the brand has the power to communicate. Both are changing in real time, the mediator being "brand performance," broadly conceptualized as encompassing *every* act of the brand – the conventional ones of providing satisfaction on every trial of every product in the brand family, as well as the "brand extension act" itself. In other words, repeated non-performance of brand extensions will exact a toll on what the brand communicates.

In the brand-building phase, a brand absorbs information from the two things to which it is attached: (1) the product(s) that carry the brand name, and (2) the marketing associated with the brand. From the first it gets information about the products offered under the brand – their "search and experience attributes"[15] – and their track record in fulfilling consumers' expectations. From marketing, the brand gets awareness, familiarity, imagery associations, brand personality, and so on. For instance, the brand McDonald's is attached to the products and services provided at McDonald's restaurants – hamburgers, fries, salads, and so on – as well as its "quick service" philosophy. It is also attached to a long history of advertising campaigns – such as the "I'm Lovin' It" ad campaign, the Ronald McDonald character, and the "golden arches" – that have imbued the brand with a "kid-friendly, fun" brand personality.

A brand may or may not communicate all that it has absorbed. Its ability to communicate is limited to what is identity-defining, the common elements or themes that exist in all the pieces of information that the brand has absorbed. If there are no such common elements, the brand doesn't have an identity. If a brand has no identity, it doesn't communicate anything.

A brand potentially has a marketing-based identity and a product-based identity, but it might have one and not the other, and, of course, it might have neither. For instance, if one thinks about the Virgin brand, its identity is largely marketing-based – the products themselves are

Figure 3.1 Brand Effects

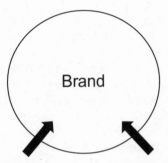

Brand

Marketing–based effects:
Awareness, familiarity,
imagery-based associations,
brand personality

Product-based effects:
Search attributes and
history of performance on
experience attributes

so diverse that it is hard to expect a common essence to come out of them. It derives its identity from the image of its founder, Sir Richard Branson, including the history of irreverent advertising associated with previous incarnations of the Virgin brand, its youthful brand personality, and so on. However, it is easy to think of examples of brands that have no marketing-based identity. These are brands, such as 7-Up, that have been associated with so many different marketing messages over their histories that no common theme or message has solidified to give the brand a marketing-based identity. However, these same brands might well have a well-defined product-based identity based on the common characteristics underlying their products. For instance, 7-Up has a product-based identity as a "lemon-lime" drink.

Marketing- and product-based identities can be developed more or less independently. This comes from a basic tenet of marketing– that product puts few, if any, restrictions on the marketing associated with it, and that marketing can "position" physically identical products distinctly. For example, in Allison and Uhl's famous taste-test experiments,[16] consumers rated several brands of beer about equally in a blind taste test when no brand identification was present, but when the same beers were presented and tasted with their brand identifications, the consumers' evaluations changed, and they began to see differences among them. Marketing folklore is replete with stories of brands being positioned differently at different times even though the product itself never changed.

When a new brand extension is introduced, awareness and familiarity are assured for the new product. In fact, the new extension's presence on the shelves and its marketing will only reinforce the brand's awareness and familiarity. The marketing-based identity also carries over as long as the new product or its marketing does not get in the way. Interference from product, however, is unlikely. As noted earlier, products are mostly orthogonal to the imagery pinned on them, and in the rare cases where they aren't, well, those are exactly the cases where management should be thinking about a new brand. For instance, we have noted the many diverse categories to which the Virgin brand has been extended successfully. But we can easily imagine the sort of categories Virgin should not pursue. For instance, Virgin dentures would be a poor extension on marketing grounds; the user base for dentures conflicts with Virgin's brand identity. The many cases of poor fit identified in the behavioural literature reviewed earlier speak to cases such as these. In each of those cases, a new brand is the obvious solution.

If the new extension's marketing campaign introduces imagery discordant with the brand's received imagery, then it will hinder the uptake of the brand's marketing-based identity and potentially dilute the brand's image in return. For instance, if Virgin Mobile's advertising campaign featured older-looking business people in suits communicating on BlackBerrys, that would introduce discordant notes with received Virgin imagery, limiting the uptake of the latter, as well as causing potential dilution of Virgin brand's image. (To what extent each of these things happens depends on the strength and clarity of Virgin's marketing-based brand identity pitted against the strength and clarity of the new extension's campaign.) To avoid this sort of mistake, management must truly understand what the brand's image is – what its key associations are, and what its personality is. While this is easier said than done, it is doable. An array of marketing research tools, ranging from focus groups to quantitative techniques like conjoint analysis, are available to diagnose a brand's image. Once management understands the brand's image, avoiding campaigns that conflict with it becomes a matter of sorting through different executions to pick the one that is most consistent with the brand's image. Fortunately, there is likely to be no cost implication in making this choice: right and wrong executions cost the same. For example, in the Virgin Mobile example, instead of using older people in business suits speaking on BlackBerrys, the ad agency could use teenagers speaking on iPhones.

Assuming management is successful in avoiding these pitfalls, the remaining question is whether the new product will benefit from the transfer of marketing-based brand equity from an existing brand. The key consideration is whether the brand associations transferred will be relevant in the new application. If the answer is no, a new brand might be the answer.

A brand's product-based brand identity is more likely to come from the experience attributes characterizing its product line, such as quality, than from its search attributes. One reason is that it is hard to share search attributes when the brand is extended across categories – Honda lawnmowers must necessarily have different search attributes than Honda cars. Experience attributes like quality and reliability, however, transcend categories and can be the basis of a brand's product-based identity. Another reason it is hard to carve out a brand identity on the basis of search attributes is that those attributes are the very attributes on which a differentiated product line is created within a brand – even a brand limited to a given category. For example, line extensions are often differentiated by their search attributes: ingredients, size, colour, and product form (powder versus liquid for Tide detergent, for example).

But hard does not mean impossible, and it is possible for a brand to have a search attributes-based brand identity, such as a brand identity based on the products' distinctive "look and design." For example, the BMW automobile product line ranges from two-seater coupes to five-passenger SUVs. So search attributes like size cannot work as a brand identity element. However, all the BMW models pull off a distinctive look characterized by the distinctive kidney-shaped grille treatment in the front. In this case, of course, another aspect of the brand's product-based brand identity is the sporty driving experience, which is an experience attribute.

Whatever the basis for a brand's product-based identity, the presumption is that the new extension will deliver on that identity. If it doesn't, a dilution of brand identity and/or reputation will surely follow. How serious that proves to be will vary from case to case. If it is a case of a brand extension not delivering on its search attribute-based brand identity, then it will probably not be so serious. The consumer can see that the new product does not conform to the brand's identity and can choose whether to buy it or not. And any dilution of brand identity will have limited impact if consumers can see that the other products under the brand maintain the brand identity. For instance, even though consumers did not respond to the concept of a clear cola in Crystal Pepsi, its downfall had negligible impact on the brand. On the other hand, when a brand extension does not deliver on its experience attribute-based brand identity, then the consequences are necessarily more serious. This is because there is always uncertainty about experience attributes on the next purchase, regardless of how many times a consumer has bought a brand before. A loss of brand reputation can prove catastrophic if the brand plays in categories where it has close substitutes. Such was the case of Schlitz in the mid-1970s, when an ill-fated attempt at cutting costs by downgrading ingredients ultimately led to the failure of the entire company. In most cases, a reputation for delivering on an experience attributes-based brand identity is sufficiently valuable that a firm would want to preserve it, thereby assuring consumers that their next consumption of the brand will be like their last.

A new brand is the answer if the firm wants to communicate a different strategic direction with a new product – a brand identity different from the existing brands available in the firm's portfolio. This might have been the reasoning behind Toyota, Nissan, and Honda creating Lexus, Infiniti, and Acura, respectively. It might also have been the reason behind BMW's decision to keep its acquired MINI brand as a distinct brand, and not fold it into the BMW product line. The VW Phaeton, however, represents a case of a brand stretched too far. VW's marketing-based identity wasn't able to accommodate a car priced in the upper reaches of the car stratosphere – comparable to BMW 7-Series, the Mercedes S-Class, and VW's own Audi A8.

Conclusion

Brand extension can be a remarkably efficient way to communicate an identity for a new product right from the get-go. Still, it is important to keep in mind that brand extension is not a panacea guaranteeing new product success. Communication is one ingredient for new product success, but not the only one. A brand extension may fail because there are other deficiencies in the offering. The product may be inappropriate for the intended market, the pricing may be too high or too low, and the distribution may be inadequate. This product would have failed even under a new brand. The fault is either in the business case itself, or in the way it has been implemented – the branding decision has nothing to do with it.

In developing a branding strategy for a new product, brand extension ought to be on the table as the default first option, if for no other reason than its incontrovertible advantages are so large that in most cases they are sufficient to carry the day. First is the cost saving – it costs many times more to develop a new brand than to extend a brand. Second is the awareness and recognition the new product gains from the brand extension. This benefit can be substantial for any product, but for low-involvement products it might be decisive. For such products, research has shown that awareness and familiarity may be sufficient for consumers to like the new product, and ultimately to choose it.[17]

Whether brand extension can go further depends on how the firm's brand assets match up to the strategic requirements imposed by the product and its competitive environment. For instance, if the product is in a low-involvement category, success may depend more on creating a distinctive marketing-based identity than on product differentiation. If the marketing manager has the good fortune to have in his portfolio a brand with a marketing-based identity that is relevant in the product's category, and distinctive enough from a competitive standpoint, then extending the brand to the new product is optimal. If the new product is in a high-involvement category, then product differentiation is more of a strategic imperative, and the relevant consideration becomes whether to fit the product to the brand or the brand to the product. The manager scans his brand portfolio for extension candidates that can provide the necessary differentiation through their product-based brand identities. Assuming such a brand exists, now it becomes a juggling act of trying to decide whether it is worth it to develop the new product to conform to the brand's product-based identity or give the new product a free hand to develop its own competitive differentiation, and coining a new brand identity in the process.

A Prescription for Managing Brands in an Era of Customer Power
Brand managers need to cope simultaneously with the new media landscape, the growth of consumer-generated content, and growing retailer clout. To get the most from their brands, managers should:

- UNDERSTAND the source of their brand's appeal and ensure that their "new media" actions remain true to this appeal.
- BALANCE the benefits of extending the brand with the risks of brand dilution. Extension is good as long as the new products are true to the original promise.
- USE brand assets well, instead of just hoarding them.

REFERENCES

1 Some people distinguish between line and brand extensions, the former referring to extensions within a category – to new models, flavours, sizes, and so on – and the latter referring to extensions across categories. I do not make this distinction.

2 B. Wernerfelt, "Umbrella Branding as a Signal of New Product Quality: An Example of Signalling by Posting a Bond," *The RAND Journal of Economics* 19, no. 3 (1988): 458–66.

3 D.A. Aaker and K.L. Keller, "Consumer Evaluations of Brand Extensions," *Journal of Marketing* 54, no. 1 (1990): 27–41.

4 K.L. Keller, *Strategic Brand Management: Building, Measuring and Managing Brand Equity* (Upper Saddle River, NJ: Prentice Hall, 2008), 498.

5 E.M. Tauber, "Brand Leverage: Strategy for Growth in a Cost-Control World," *Journal of Advertising Research* 28, no. 4 (1988): 26–30.

6 S.K. Reddy, S.L. Holak, and S. Bhat, "To Extend or Not to Extend: Success Determinants of Line Extensions," *Journal of Marketing Research* 31 (1994): 243–62.

7 M. Sullivan,"Brand Extensions: When to Use Them," *Management Science* 38 (1992), 793–806.

8 C.W. Park, S. Milberg, and R. Lawson, "Evaluation of Brand Extensions: The Role of Product Feature Similarity and Brand Concept Consistency," *The Journal of Consumer Research* 18, no. 2 (1991): 185–93.

9 Susan M. Broniarczyk and Joseph W. Alba, "The Importance of the Brand in Brand Extension," Special Issue of *Journal of Marketing Research* 31, no. 2 (1994): 214–28.

10 L.M.B. Cabral, "Stretching Firm and Brand Reputation," *The RAND Journal of Economics* 31, no. 4 (2000): 658–73.

11 H. Hakenes and M. Peitz, "Umbrella Branding and the Provision of Quality," *International Journal of Industrial Organization* 26 (2008): 546–56.

12 L.M.B. Cabral, "Umbrella Branding with Imperfect Observability and Moral Hazard," *International Journal of Industrial Organization* 27, no. 2 (2009): 206–13.

13 S. Moorthy,"Can Brand Extension Signal Product Quality?" working paper, Rotman School of Management, University of Toronto, 2011.

14 M. Sullivan,"Measuring Image Spillovers in Umbrella-Branded Products," *The Journal of Business* 63, no. 3 (1990): 309–29.

15 Products generally have both search and experience attributes. The former are those that appear on the surface of the product, and can be seen before buying the product. The latter can be seen only after buying and using the product. For example, in a car, colour, size, design, and features –

front-wheel drive or rear-wheel drive, two-door or four-door, and so on – are all search attributes. On the other hand, how well the car drives under different conditions, the usability of its controls, reliability, and so on, can only be ascertained after the consumer has bought the product and used it for some time. Similarly, in a restaurant, location and menu are typically search attributes, whereas quality of food and service are experience attributes.

16 Ralph I. Allison and Kenneth P. Uhl, "Influence of Beer Brand Identification on Taste Perception," *Journal of Marketing Research* 1, no. 3 (1964): 36–9.
17 Wayne D. Hoyer and Steven P. Brown, "Effects of Brand Awareness on Choice for a Common, Repeat-Purchase Product," *Journal of Consumer Research* 17, no. 2 (1990): 141–59.

4 What Makes the Internet Different?

AVI GOLDFARB

Businesses today face a rapidly changing and competitive marketplace. Perhaps the most important change over the past twenty years is the arrival of the internet and the digital economy. Since the internet's origins in the late 1960s and its commercialization in the 1990s, people increasingly spend many hours online every week, or even every day. Well over half of North American households have broadband internet at home, and many of these also access the internet through a mobile device. If marketers do not incorporate insights into how the internet impacts marketing efforts, they will fall behind.

How can we understand the changes associated with new communications technology? As with any technology, it is important to understand what has changed, and it is equally important to understand what has not changed. Are there costs that are lower for consumers? Are there costs that are lower for sellers? Are there new consumer benefits from the new technology? Are there new opportunities for companies for the new technology?

The internet provides many such changes. Perhaps the three most important relate to changes in search costs, changes in the role of geographic proximity, and changes in the availability and use of data. In other words, the internet makes it easier to search for things, it allows people to connect with others anywhere in the world, and it makes it easier to use quantitative data to optimize operations and product offerings. In this chapter, I will discuss each of these in turn, emphasizing what has changed as well as what has not. I conclude with some suggestions of effective management responses to these trends.

Search Costs

Search costs are the costs of looking for information.[1] This means that every information gathering activity involves at least some search costs. Job seekers incur search costs in finding vacancies that they can fill. Single men and women incur search costs in finding mates. And shoppers incur search costs in finding the products they want.

These searches are multidimensional.[2] In looking for a job, wages matter. But so do hours, type of work, benefits, the characteristics of potential coworkers, and dozens of other factors. In dating, the dimensions of search range from looks, education, and age to nuances of personality. In shopping, price, quality, and product features all matter.

These dimensions of search can be classified into three categories: search, experience, and credence attributes. Search attributes are attributes that can be understood during the search process, before the choice is made. For example, salary in jobs, looks in dating, and product colour in shopping are all search attributes. Experience attributes are attributes that can only be understood after the choice is made. Movies are a great example of a product whose primary attributes are experience attributes: until you see the movie, you don't know whether you like it. Credence attributes are attributes that, even after the choice is made, may not be well understood. Even after visiting a dentist for years, you do not really know whether you have fewer cavities than you would at another dentist. While some attributes of dentists are search attributes (location) and experience attributes (whether you experience pain, and how much, during a visit), the primary reason for visiting a dentist is a credence attribute. You cannot really know if your money was better spent elsewhere.

What does that have to do with online behaviour? In general, it is easier to search for things online than offline.[3] You can compare prices without leaving your house, at any time of day or night. This is much easier than driving from store to store or even using the phone to gather prices. Furthermore, you can easily compare many product features online.

But there are some attributes that cannot easily be assessed online. If you are buying clothes, it is easy to learn and compare prices, colours, and perhaps styles. These are search attributes that can easily be described in an online setting. It is much harder to assess whether a particular pair of pants will fit without actually trying them on. Therefore, while price and colour become very easy to compare, fit moves from being a search attribute to an experience attribute. Offline, before purchase you know if a pair of pants will fit because you can try them on. Online, you cannot know until after purchase.

The online channel therefore reduces the cost of search, but not in the same way for all attributes. Consider a consumer searching for a new camera at an online retailer. There are many things that the consumer might consider: price, resolution, shutter speed, colour, size, durability, and so on. Except durability, each of these is a search attribute that can easily be communicated and compared online: "The silver 14 mega- pixel Canon camera costs $X while the orange 10 megapixel Olympus camera costs $Y."

The easy price comparison suggests that price competition will be fiercer online than offline. At the same time, the easy resolution com- parison suggests competition on resolution will be fiercer online. The only attribute that will experience no clear change in the level of com- petition is durability, because it cannot easily be compared. In general, online markets mean fierce competition in search attributes.

Managers, however, have some control over the ease of comparison. While all search attributes are easier to compare online, website design can influence which attributes are most salient. If your company beats the competition in price, then you want to make that as clear and salient as possible in describing the product on your website. In contrast, if your company has high resolution cameras that fit easily into a pocket, those are the search attributes that should be most prominent on the website.

As another example of how the online setting changes the relative weight of various attributes in a search, consider dating. What are the relevant attributes for finding a mate? Compatibility? Personality? Sense of humour? But how do you assess those before the first date? In a bar or club, the most relevant search attribute is looks (including gender and perceived age). Looks are perhaps the only salient attribute. Compatibility, sense of humour, and so on become known over time. Traditional matchmakers might focus more on family history, educa- tion, and their intuition on compatibility. Online, other attributes be- come focal. Yes, a profile picture means that looks are a salient attribute, but often profile pictures are only seen after an initial screen on educa- tion, age, home address, and income. Online dating therefore makes income and education particularly salient attributes in the search pro- cess.[4] Interestingly, some online dating companies, such as eHarmony, have attempted to differentiate themselves by trying to convert the experience attribute of compatibility into a search attribute through psychographic profiling.

Another consequence of low search costs online is the availability of products in the "long tail."[5] The long tail refers to the set of products that individually do not have high sales but in aggregate represent a large potential marketing opportunity. The online setting is particularly suited to selling products in the tail of the distribution (such as *Diamonds Are Forever, Computers Are Not* – a favourite of mine that ranks around 3 millionth on Amazon). Such products were almost never found in offline retailers. Anderson notes that the typical Barnes & Noble carries tens of thousands of items, while the typical online retailer can hold millions (and potentially more if the goods can be distributed digitally – without shipping a physical item). Items in the tail are frequently available online because of low inventory costs (warehouse space and digital storage are cheaper than retail space) and low search costs. In a physical store, it is challenging for people to find the exact rare item they want. Online, it is easy. Apple's iTunes enables people to search for particular songs and find them in seconds, no matter how obscure. For those of us who remember visiting Tower Records and other offline music stores, finding the right item (even if the item was known in advance) could take an afternoon of searching, and even then the search could fail.

Partly in response to this ability of end consumers to find items in the long tail, there has been a dramatic rise in "user generated content" – products created by consumers for potentially widespread consumption. YouTube videos, consumer-suggested prototypes, and a myriad of blogs are all examples of a wave of consumer creativity. One of the key enablers of this creativity is the ability of others to find "long tail" content through low search costs.

Overall, low search costs online mean that competition is fierce for both niche and popular products. This is especially true because prices are particularly easy to search online. At the same time, these search costs can be managed. First, it is important to understand which aspects of searching are easier online (and which, like the fit of a pair of pants, may even be more difficult). Second, it is important to recognize that the relative salience of the various attributes on a website is a managerial decision. Websites can be designed to make it easy for consumers to compare your strengths but harder to compare your weaknesses against your competitor's characteristics.

Data

In essence, computers do three things: they calculate, they remember, and they communicate. These functions are sometimes respectively called processing, storage, and input/output. When assessing the impact of any new information and communication technology, a key consideration is which of these functions is most affected.

The internet has meant that many aspects of commercial activity are intermediated by computers. The online setting makes it relatively inexpensive for consumers to communicate with businesses electronically. Recent improvements in computer memory and speed mean that it is also inexpensive to store information about these transactions and to analyze the resulting data. Therefore, digitization makes the collection, storage, and analysis of information relatively inexpensive. Because everything that happens online is, by definition, digital, it is easy for computers to observe, store, and analyze such activity.

One of the largest opportunities, and most difficult challenges, of managing in the online space is responding to this deluge of data. When making important decisions in the absence of data, companies rely on Highly Paid People's Opinions (known as HiPPOs in the industry). Data reduces the importance of the experience and intuition of HiPPOs in determining tactical decisions.[6] Online data provides rich information that can help identify product improvements, new opportunities, and areas of weakness that might have otherwise slipped the attention of the key decision-makers.

For example, online data facilitates the creation of an effective "spell-check." If something is spelled incorrectly in one search, people usually correct the spelling in a subsequent search. Search engines can therefore guess what was meant rather than what was typed. They use data on past searches to give results based on what the user meant rather than what the user typed.

Data can also be used to improve website design. By observing which pages lead to sales and which do not, website managers can try to direct traffic to the stronger pages and improve the design of the weaker pages.

The online setting also creates control over what each individual user sees. Specifically, because each user sees a webpage based on a specific individual request to the website's server, companies have the ability to vary the content shown at the individual level. Clearly, this facilitates targeting specific information to specific customers. This is useful for several reasons, including developing recommendation systems, targeting and measuring advertising, and using experiments to do marketing research.

Companies are increasingly using online data to recommend purchases to their customers. Perhaps most familiar are Amazon's "People who bought this also bought" recommendations. Netflix collects information on user ratings and then uses sophisticated algorithms to recommend movies to its customers. These algorithms all rely on data. The more companies know about what consumers choose and like, the more companies are able to determine what consumers will like in the future. People who buy the sixth Harry Potter book are likely to buy the seventh. They are apparently also likely to buy *The Chronicles of Narnia* and books by Rick Riordan. With more data, such recommendations are possible even for obscure books. Buyers of *Mostly Harmless Econometrics* are also likely to buy *Counterfactuals and Causal Interference.* Neither of these books is in the top 5,000 in sales, but by collecting and storing data, Amazon can usefully recommend books in a highly targeted way. The ability to vary content at the individual level enables firms to send individually customized recommendations based on rich data. Like reduced search costs, this facilitates profitability selling in the "long tail" of items that are relatively unpopular.

The ability to target specific information to specific customers is particularly useful for online advertising. Broadly, this ability, combined with inexpensive data collection and storage, means that online advertising is distinct from offline advertising in two fundamental ways: targeting and measurability.[7]

Advertisements are said to be targeted when they are shown to a particular subset of potential viewers. Most ads are targeted to some degree, both online and offline. Television advertisers target to particular demographics based on the audience of the programs: for example, they may target teenagers on MTV and women on the Oprah Winfrey Network. Online targeting options are much richer. First, online advertisers can use demographics just like offline advertisers. The difference is that now the demographic information could include all data entered on Facebook, including exact age, gender, education, location, and even preferences for particular celebrities. Second, advertisers can use contextual targeting in which the ad is matched to the content it is displayed beside, just as car advertisements are common on the Speed Network. Again, however, the targeting options are more varied. Third, advertisers can use behavioural targeting, using prior clickstream data to determine whether a particular user is a good match for an ad. For example, a user who has bought certain types of electronics in the past may be a good target for an ad for the latest gadget.

One type of behavioural targeting that is becoming increasingly common is retargeting. In retargeting, an online ad is shown to a user who searched for (or saw) a particular kind of content. For example, if a user searched for "new cars" in the last few days, advertisers can target them on multiple websites with ads for new cars. Retargeting has been shown to be especially effective when information on past searches (and surfing behaviour) can be used to better inform a current search by a customer who is actively involved in the category.[8]

In addition to the opportunities for targeting, online advertising is more measurable than offline advertising. Measuring the effectiveness of traditional advertising is hard because it is difficult to causally link an ad view with a purchase. There are two challenges with this. First, it is hard to link the people who see ads (and the people who do not) with relevant actions such as purchases. Second, it is hard to ensure that any observed correlation is not spurious. In particular, it could be that the type of person who sees the ad is more likely to buy anyway. For example, sports fans may be more likely to see beer advertising than others, but they may also be more likely to buy beer for reasons that are not a result of having seen an ad.

Online, both of these weaknesses are mitigated. Most simply, some online advertising is often priced per click, meaning that advertisers only pay for ads that lead to an action. Furthermore, the digital nature of online advertising means that individual responses to ads are recorded as part of the log files of a website. Advertisers can therefore observe ad exposure of an individual, and then through tools such as cookies, link the ad exposure to actual online purchases. Furthermore, the online setting permits randomized field tests. One group of web users can be exposed to an ad while another is exposed to an alternative stimulus (such as an ad for an unrelated product). The advertiser can then compare the behaviour of users who saw the ad with the behaviour of those who did not. If users who saw the ad are more likely to purchase than the randomly assigned group who saw an alternative ad, then that increase in purchase likelihood can be causally attributed to the ad. In other words, experiments allow for causal interpretation of effects.

This idea applies more broadly than online advertising. The combination of data storage and the ability to vary the content shown at the individual level makes it relatively straightforward to run experiments. Experiments are therefore increasingly part of the toolkit of successful web companies.[9] Google, Amazon, and many others each run thousands of experiments every year. The experiments tweak website design, algorithms, and marketing communications. Why experiments? Because experiments are the best tool for allowing a company to determine causality. Called "A/B tests" in the industry, experiments typically provide a clear way for determining the optimal tactics: Should the website have a red background or a blue background? Should the ad be in the middle or on the left? Which search algorithm maximizes user click rates? Which kinds of users respond well to graphical information (and which kinds respond to text)?

There are several important points of caution in using data. For example, suppose a newspaper is interested in determining what to place most prominently on the home page. It could use data to pick the most clicked items in the most prominent positions. Overwhelmingly, however, in the short run, the most clicked items will relate to celebrity gossip and similar categories. If the newspaper is trying to differentiate itself in the long run based on a particular point of view, then focusing on clicks alone will make it look like all other similar newspapers. In other words, if all websites ordered information based on the most popular items, then there might be little differentiation between websites. And this could hurt the websites in the long run given that, as discussed above, search costs are especially low in the online setting. In addition, collection and use of data can raise privacy concerns. It is important to consider how consumers and governments will perceive the use of data. Is it manipulative or does it help the end users to receive better service or a better product?[10]

Geography

Generally, distance does not affect the speed of online communication. An email sent from less than a mile away does not take noticeably longer to arrive than one sent from 3,000 miles away. This understanding led Frances Cairncross to declare "The Death of Distance" and Thomas Friedman to declare "The World Is Flat."[11] Overall, they argue that the internet makes geographic isolation irrelevant.

At the same time, while online activity appears to occur in cyberspace, the users generating the activity live offline. Therefore, the offline context will have an influence on online behaviour. Broadly, there are three types of reasons why geography matters to online behaviour. First, the internet (and what is offered) has different characteristics across locations. Second, while the internet does lead to a fall in communication costs, this matters differently across locations. Third, and similarly, a fall in distribution costs has different effects across locations.

These suggest several ways in which we expect to see geographically correlated behaviours. Broadband speeds vary across locations and therefore people in such locations will be able to perform higher bandwidth activities online. Larger cities have more local content offered, from local news and sports to information about local amenities. Preferences are spatially correlated: the visitors to the *Toronto Star*'s website are disproportionately from the Toronto area, and fans of Woody Allen movies disproportionately live in New York. Social networks are local: while the internet facilitates round-the-world connections, most email comes from within a mile of where you live and work. Finally, offline options change what you value online. All else equal, people with many local booksellers buy fewer books on Amazon. People who live in a location with many parents of young children can buy all their baby needs offline. In contrast, parents who live in a location with few other parents may buy some relatively rare items online.[12] Offline options therefore determine how people use the online channel. More generally, research has shown that "preference minorities," or people who are different from their surrounding community, get an especially large benefit from the online channel, because they can read news from far away, buy items they could not buy locally, or communicate with like-minded people in other locations.

This creates an opportunity for truly global brands. If a brand is relevant to people wherever they live, then reduced communication costs mean that the entire world is the potential market. At the same time, there is an opportunity for hyper-local brands. People still live offline, and want to know what is happening in their neighbourhood, including crime, schools, retail, real estate, and sports.

Overall, the characteristics of where you live and work affect what you do online, but not in the same ways that they affect offline behaviour. The key is to understand how a reduction in communication costs affects behaviour differently across locations.

The Mobile Internet

The above discussion highlights three ways in which internet marketing is different from offline marketing: search is easy for customers, data is prevalent, and the role of geography is diminished (though still substantial). In many ways the mobile internet is a simple extension of this. Data is even more prevalent and a search can be conducted whenever a potential consumer thinks of it. However, in two important ways, the mobile (smartphone) internet is different from the PC-based internet. First, the screen size is smaller. While searches can happen anywhere, the cost of any particular search rises substantially. Looking beyond the first two or three results is much harder on a mobile phone than on a personal computer and therefore the importance of showing up first in search results rises. With less "real estate," each square inch becomes more valuable. Consumers will search for less on any particular occasion. Second, geography matters more. User behaviour on the mobile internet is much more location-specific than behaviour on the PC-based internet. This is because behaviour on the mobile internet is often triggered by local cues such as "I need directions," "I want to find a good restaurant nearby," or "I want to know where to find the item in that advertisement." Therefore, in many ways, the mobile internet suggests behaviour that might look more like the pre-internet consumer: less search, more local.[13]

This has direct consequences for companies that plan to operate in the mobile space. First, less search means that it will be more difficult to get on the radar of most consumers. Second, less search also means that if you do get on the radar of many consumers, it will be harder for the competition to unseat you. Consumer attention on the mobile internet implies less competition and higher mark-ups than in the PC-based internet. Third, increased distance effects means that local retailers, restaurants, and other businesses have a particularly large amount to gain from marketing through the mobile internet. In contrast to the PC-based internet where marketing by offline retailers simply facilitated price comparisons, on the mobile internet, marketing by offline retailers could mean attracting customers exactly when they are most ready to accept marketing messages from your business.

The Social Internet

Easy search, prevalent data, and cheap communication have facilitated the development of a more social internet. Facebook and Twitter are increasingly important venues for online activity. Other social applications and websites are also growing, including Foursquare, Linked In, and others. These websites have been able to thrive for several reasons. Just as with other aspects of online activity, online social interactions can be understood by thinking through search, data, and geography.

Of these, the most important in the social media space is data. Facebook "knows" a lot about its users. It can therefore carefully target advertising to specific groups (e.g., graduates of the University of Toronto who like hockey). It can also use data to improve its operations by adjusting the website in general and the news feed in particular to better fit consumer tastes. It is data that allows these websites to build a business model and allows customers to sort through the mass of potential information. In other words, it is with data that social media facilitate search.

The search process is also important. Social media facilitate search in two ways. First, they allow people to find information based on what their "friends" are saying. Second, they sort even this information from friends by relevance to make the most useful items most salient. Social media therefore reduce the costs for their users to find the most relevant information. As University of Toronto strategy professor Joshua Gans has reported on his blog, the "news feed" is called that for a reason. Yes, it is the most directly relevant type of news – your friends' reports – but it is still news in a real sense. It is also other news as filtered by your friends' interests and postings. This news feed means that even people who never post online may visit social media sites regularly as "lurkers" who read and watch what their friends are saying.

Finally, geography matters in social media. Social media facilitate personally relevant information feeds that are not necessarily local. While it is true that most Facebook relationships are local – people are friends with people who live or work near them – social media makes it easy to receive information from people who are far away. Therefore, people no longer have to rely on local news sources and community papers to see the information most directly relevant to them. Social media allows people to follow their friends' activities, passively, even if those friends live thousands of miles away.

Effective management of social media involves using the rich available data to improve offerings, measurement, and targeting. An important use of this data is to facilitate search, allowing users to find the information they want as quickly as possible. In contrast to offline media, social media means this information can be deeply personal and relevant but still be about distant places and people.

This last point on personal data suggests one important challenge in effective marketing through social media: privacy. Users of social media often post very personal information to the network. As marketers, it is important to recognize that users do not want their most personal messages to be used as fodder for ad targeting. While it is tempting to respond to a comment about an upcoming vacation with an ad for cheap flights, it is also important to ensure that users see online ads as informative rather than manipulative. If ads are seen as manipulative through the inappropriate use of data, they can backfire and reduce consumer preferences for the product. Social media marketing is most successful when it informs in response to real needs without seeming manipulative.

Conclusions

This chapter has highlighted three important aspects of internet marketing: search, data, and geography. Search costs are lower in the online setting. This means that consumers find it easier to compare prices and some other attributes, intensifying competition. It also means that companies find it easier to identify products that match consumer needs, and consumers find it easier to identify products that appeal to them but are relatively obscure. In response to this, marketers can focus on attributes that are easy for consumers to understand in an online context.

Data is abundant in the online setting. This is an opportunity and a threat. The opportunity is that it enables firms to get the right information to the right person at the right time, through advertising, recommender systems, and other means. It also allows firms to experiment and measure the impact of different marketing and strategic choices. The threat is that the data can become overwhelming. There is so much of it that managers may lose the forest for the trees and end up spending all of their time organizing and cleaning data rather than learning from it. Effective management in this environment requires investing in an infrastructure for gathering data and undertaking analytics.

Communication costs matter less in the online setting. This means that firms are not protected by geographic boundaries. It also means that some geographic characteristics (such as social networks) end up having an important role online. Furthermore, it suggests opportunities to serve isolated segments that may not be satisfied with local choices.

Nearly twenty years after its privatization, we now understand several ways in which marketing through the internet is different from marketing in other settings. In this chapter, I have highlighted three of the most important: search, data, and geography.

A Prescription for Leveraging the Power of the Internet
The internet has fundamentally changed the marketing landscape by (a) making it easier to find information, (b) making abundant data available, and (c) reducing the role of distance. To leverage this asset, the manager needs to:

- FOCUS on attributes that are easy to understand in an online context.
- EMPHASIZE analytics and use data to inform marketing decisions.
- TARGET isolated groups that may be underserved by local choices.

REFERENCES

1 Yannis Bakos, "Reducing Buyer Search Costs: Implications for Electronic Marketplaces," *Management Science* 43 (1997): 1676–92.
2 John Lynch and Dan Ariely, "Wine Online: Search Costs Affect Competition on Price, Quality, and Distribution," *Marketing Science* 19, no. 83 (2000): 103.
3 This has been documented in many settings. For example, J. Brown and Austan Goolsbee, "Does the Internet Make Markets More Competitive? Evidence from the Life Insurance Industry," *Journal of Political Economy* 110 (2002): 481–507; Michael Baye, John Morgan, and Patrick Scholten, "Price Dispersion in the Small and the Large: Evidence from an Internet Price Comparison Site," *Journal of Industrial Economics* 52 (2004): 463–96; Michael Baye, Rupert Gatti, P. Kattuman, and John Morgan, "Clicks, Discontinuities, and Firm Demand Online," *Journal of Economics and Management Strategy* 18 (2009): 935–75; Erik Brynjolfsson, Y. Jeffrey Hu, and Duncan Simester, "Goodbye Pareto Principle, Hello Long Tail: The Effect of Search Costs on the Concentration of Product Sales,"*Management Science* (forthcoming).
4 Gunter J. Hitsch, Ali Hortacsu, and Dan Ariely, "What Makes You Click? – Mate Preferences in Online Dating," *Quantitative Marketing and Economics* 8 (2010): 393–427.
5 Chris Anderson, *The Long Tail* (New York: Hyperion, 2006).
6 Ron Kohavi, Roger Longbotham, Dan Sommerfield, and Randal Henne, "Controlled Experiments on the Web: Survey and Practical Guide," *Data Mining and Knowledge Discovery* 18 (2008): 140–81.
7 Avi Goldfarb and Catherine Tucker, "Online Advertising," *Advances in Computers,* Volume 81: *The Internet and Mobile Technology,* ed. Marvin V. Zelkowitz (Maryland Heights, MO: Academic Press, 2011), 289–315.
8 Anja Lambrecht and Catherine Tucker, "When Does Retargeting Work? Timing Information Specificity," working paper, Massachusetts Institute of Technology, Cambridge, MA, 2011.

9 Avi Goldfarb and Catherine Tucker, "Privacy and Innovation," in Josh Le-
   rner and Scott Stern, eds., *Innovation Policy and the Economy*, vol. 11 (forthcoming 2012); Asim Ansari and Carl Mela, "E-customization," *Journal of
   Marketing Research* 40 (2003): 131–45.
10 Avi Goldfarb and Catherine Tucker, "Online Display Advertising: Targeting and Obtrusiveness," *Marketing Science* 30 (2011): 389–404.
11 Frances Cairncross, *The Death of Distance* (Cambridge, MA: Harvard University Press, 1997); Thomas Friedman, *The World Is Flat* (New York: Farrar,
   Straus, and Giroux, 2005).
12 The ideas in the paragraph are derived from a wide literature. This includes Jeonghye Choi and David Bell, "Preference Minorities and the
   Internet," *Journal of Marketing Research* (forthcoming); Bernardo Blum and
   Avi Goldfarb, "Does the Internet Defy the Law of Gravity?" *Journal of International Economics* 70 (2006): 384–405; Ajay Agrawal and Avi Goldfarb,
   "Restructuring Research: Communication Costs and the Democratization
   of University Innovation," *American Economic Review* 98 (2008): 1578–90;
   Chris Forman, Anindya Ghose, and Avi Goldfarb, "Competition between
   Local and Electronic Markets: How the Benefit of Buying Online Depends
   on Where You Live," *Management Science* 55 (2009): 47–57; Todd Sinai and
   Joel Waldfogel, "Geography and the Internet: Is the Internet a Substitute or
   a Complement for Cities?" *Journal of Urban Economics* 56 (2004): 1–24.
13 Anindya Ghose, Avi Goldfarb, and Sang Pil Han, "How is the Mobile
   Internet Different? Search Costs and Local Activities," working paper, Rotman School of Management, University of Toronto, 2011.

PART TWO

Understanding to Engage:
Key Lessons from the Latest in the
Psychology and Economics of
Consumer Behaviour

5 Memory, Persuasion, and Decision-Making

ANDREW A. MITCHELL

Marketing communications programs have undergone major changes over the last ten years. A major part of this change has been due to use of the internet as a way to communicate with consumers. While the internet has frequently been thought of as an entirely new medium for communicating with consumers, we argue that the same basic principles are involved in developing effective persuasive messages, whether they are placed on the internet or in traditional media. Since exposure to an advertisement and its effect on a purchase decision typically occur at two different points in time, memory is necessarily involved. The effect of the advertisement depends on how exposure to it causes changes in memory and whether these changes will affect purchase decisions. These critical topics are discussed in this chapter in the context of developing a marketing communications program.

Developing a marketing communications program involves decisions concerning what to communicate, how to communicate, when to communicate, and where to communicate. In this chapter we discuss the factors that need to be considered in making these decisions and the relevant psychological theories that suggest how these decisions should be made. We focus only on advertising that involves payment for the placement of messages, while recognizing that there are other ways of communicating with consumers, such as through social networks.

We assume that the brand manager has analysed the market for the product or service to be advertised, has determined what he/she wants to communicate, and who should be exposed to the advertisements.

The purpose of the advertising may simply be to reinforce what consumers already know about the product, or it may be to provide new information about the product. The receivers of the message may already purchase and use the product, or the advertising may be directed at consumers who currently do not use the product, with the goal of getting them to try it. We also assume that the brand manager has a rough idea as to the budget that top management is willing to invest in advertising.

In the next section we discuss the relevant psychological theories that affect the development of a marketing communications program.

Psychological Theories

This section discusses current theories of memory, attitudes, the information acquisition process, the accessibility of information in memory, and how judgments and choices are made.

Memory

The standard model of memory is a spreading activation associative network model,[1] where concepts are represented by nodes in the network and associations between concepts are represented by links that vary in strength. Nodes become activated in memory when we think about the concept or when we encounter it in the environment. When a node becomes activated in memory, activation spreads through the links to activate related nodes depending on the strength of the link. The stronger the links, the more activation flows through the links. When activation in a particular node reaches a threshold level, the information in that node reaches conscious awareness. Consequently, when a node becomes activated in memory, some of the information linked to that node also becomes activated and some of this information will reach conscious awareness.

We may think about a brand as being a node in memory and the information that a consumer has about that brand as being linked to that node. Consequently, when we think about a brand or are exposed to information about a brand, information linked to that brand will also be activated; however, if there is considerable information linked to that brand, then only a subset of that information will reach conscious awareness. Learning information about a brand results in new links being formed between the brand and the new information.

Attitudes

Attitudes are a measure of how much someone likes or dislikes an object, person, or concept. They come in two flavours. Explicit attitudes are typically measured on scales and represent a conscious evaluation of the object or concept. In other words, when reporting your explicit attitude towards a brand, you may consciously think about the information associated with the brand and use this information to form your attitude, or you may already know your attitude and simply report it.

Implicit attitudes are the likes or dislikes of an object, person, or concept that immediately come to mind when you are exposed to the object, person, or representation of it.[2] For instance, observing a cockroach will immediately create a negative feeling in most of us and this will trigger an avoidance response. Objects that immediately create a positive feeling, like flowers, will trigger an approach response. Since implicit attitudes represent an immediate response to an object, they are typically assessed by measuring how quickly someone responds to positive and negative stimuli after the object or concept has been activated in memory.[3] What is especially important about implicit attitudes is that they are difficult to change. Simply presenting arguments as to why cockroaches are good will not change someone's implicit attitude towards them, but it may change their explicit attitude. In order to change an implicit attitude, multiple exposures of contrary information are required.[4] Finally, it should be noted that consumers may or may not have explicit or implicit attitudes towards a particular object or concept.

Attitudes may also be formed towards the advertisement. Previous research has shown that if consumers like the advertisement, they will form a positive attitude towards it, which will influence their attitude towards the brand being advertised.[5]

Information Acquisition Processes

When exposed to an advertisement, the advertisement must first attract and hold the consumers' attention. After the consumers' attention has been attracted, they may take either an active or a passive role in processing the information in the advertisement.[6] If they take an active role, they will consciously process the information and may elaborate on it by generating new thoughts. These new thoughts may involve forming inferences based on the information presented or by agreeing or disagreeing with the information. If consumers make inferences, these inferences will also be linked to the brand. If consumers agree with the presented information, this information will be linked to the brand node in memory; however, if they disagree with the information, it will not be linked to the brand node. For instance, an advertisement for an automobile may claim that it gets forty miles to the gallon; however, if the viewer consciously disagrees with this claim, it will not be linked to the brand node. Usually individuals only disagree and mentally argue against verbal information. They generally do not argue against visual information or sounds.

If consumers play a passive role while exposed to the advertisement, some of the information in the message will become linked to the brand node. This may happen at both a conscious and a non-conscious level. In other words, consumers may consciously process some information in the message (e.g., the headline in a print advertisement) and be aware of linkages being formed, or they may not be aware of linkages being formed. For instance, some visual images in the messages may communicate information about the brand, and although consumers are aware of the pictures, they may not realize that the pictures are affecting the associations linked to the brand. For instance, pictures of kittens in advertisements have been shown to affect the perception of the softness of facial tissues. Generally, a message must be seen a number of times before these non-conscious linkages are made.

A special case of the latter is what is called evaluative conditioning. Here valenced words or pictures of objects, such as images of flowers, may be included in an advertisement, and after a number of exposures these may influence the implicit attitude towards the advertised brand. If the valenced words or objects are positive, a positive implicit attitude of the brand will be formed. Figure 5.1 is an example of an advertisement that contains only a picture of a rose and a product. Since a rose represents a positive object to most people, exposure to this advertisement many times would create a positive implicit attitude towards the product.

Advertising that is distinctive is more likely to be recalled since consumers will focus their attention to it. Making an advertisement distinctive means that it must stand out in the environment. One way to make the advertisement distinctive is to include an attention-getting device. As we will discuss later, the use of an attention-getting device may be detrimental if it focuses attention away from the desired information in the message so it is not learned. Consequently, even though an advertisement is distinctive and recalled, if it does not communicate any new information to the consumer, it will not be persuasive. It is also possible that an advertisement that is not distinctive may be persuasive if con-

Figure 5.1 Issey Miyake

Source: Beauté Prestige International, Paris

sumers acquire new information from it, even though it is not recalled. Therefore, if an advertisement is recalled, it does not necessarily mean that it is persuasive.

Information Accessibility

At any given point in time, the information stored in memory will vary as to its accessibility. Some information is chronically accessible in memory, simply because we are frequently exposed to and use this information. Most North Americans can immediately respond to the question, "What is the capital of France?" However, they would require considerable thought to answer the question, "What is the capital of Romania?"

In addition, environmental factors also affect what information is accessible in memory. For instance, when you meet someone and enter into a conversation with him/her, you activate this person's node in memory, which activates the linked information about this person. This information allows you to determine what may or may not be appropriate to say. In addition, the topic of the conversation will also activate information in the memory that allows you to carry on the conversation.

The same thing happens when you are exposed to an advertisement. If you are able to identify the brand being advertised in the communication immediately, that brand node and the accessible information about the brand will be activated in memory. If the information in the advertisement is actively processed and inferences are formed, the new information will become linked to the brand and these linkages will be relatively strong.

If the individual passively processes the message, some of the verbal, visual, and auditory information in the advertisement may be linked to the brand node; however, these linkages will be relatively weak. These linkages will only occur if the individual identifies the brand being advertised. If a different brand is identified, the linkages will be made to this alternative brand. If no brand is identified, no linkages will be made. If your brand is not the dominant brand in the product category, your advertisement may activate the brand node of the dominant brand instead of your brand. This will cause the information in your advertisement to be linked to the dominant brand.

The accessibility of concepts such as brands depends on the frequency with which we think about them or encounter them in the environment. Every time we think about a brand or encounter the brand name in the environment, its accessibility increases. However, if we do not think about a brand or do not encounter it in the environment, its accessibility will gradually decay over time.

Perceptual Fluency

When we have been previously exposed to a word or picture, this familiarity allows us to process it faster the next time we see it. We are sensitive to this faster processing and use it to interpret our familiarity with the word or picture. We frequently use fluency to make judgments. For instance, fluent objects are generally liked more than objects that are not fluent. When exposed to numerous words or pictures, some of which we have seen before, the words or pictures that we have seen before are fluent and "stand out" in the environment.

Our attention is drawn to them and if we quickly make choices from the numerous words or pictures, we are more likely to choose the ones that are fluent.

Judgments and Choices

There are two critical aspects with respect to how judgments and choices are made. First, in some cases, judgments or choices seem to come to us with little thought, whereas in other cases we put in considerable thought when making a judgment or choice.

The second aspect is whether the judgment or choice is memory-based or stimulus-based. In the former case, the judgment or choice is based entirely on information stored in memory. When selecting a restaurant for dinner, we typically retrieve alternative restaurants from memory along with information about them and then use this information to make a choice. Stimulus-based choice occurs when we are selecting from a specific set of alternatives that are present in the environment. This may involve a list of alternatives or it may be a set of products on a shelf in a self-service store.

With memory-based choice, your brand name must be highly accessible in memory, so that when consumers think about a specific product category, your brand comes to mind. If it is not highly accessible, your brand will not be considered when making a purchase decision. This is also important if the choice is made from a list of alternatives. However, if the choice is made from a set of products on the shelf of a self-service store, your package must stand out from the alternatives on the shelf in order to be purchased. This means that the consumer must have a fluent mental representation of the package linked to the brand node in memory consistently; advertisements for products purchased in self-service stores should contain a picture of the package. With memory-based choice, the accessibility of the brand in memory will largely determine brand choice. With stimulus-based choice in a self-service outlet, the fluency of visual representation of the package will have an important influence on brand choice. When the consumer views the packages of the different brands in the product category, your package will "stand out" and be more likely to be chosen. If the choice process is made with considerable thought, the information stored in memory about the alternatives will determine choice; however, brand accessibility is still required for the brand to be considered.

We will now discuss the critical factors that affect the development of a marketing communication program.

Developing a Marketing Communications Program

When developing a marketing communications program, there are a number of factors that need to be taken into account. These include the characteristics of the consumer that you want to influence, your market position, size of the budget, and the purpose of the communication.

Characteristics of the Consumer

The most important characteristics are the consumer's knowledge of the relevant product category and their interest in obtaining information about the product or service. The first characteristic is important when the communication involves a technical product, such as a computer. These products have technical characteristics that only highly knowledgeable consumers understand, such as the number of megabytes of memory. A very knowledgeable consumer will understand how differing amounts of memory will affect what you can do with a computer. A less knowledgeable consumer will not understand this. They may know that more megabytes of memory is better, but they will not understand what they can do with a specific amount of memory. Consequently, if you provide only technical information in your communication, it will be useful for the highly knowledgeable consumer, but will be of little value to the less knowledgeable consumer.

Figure 5.2 is a recent advertisement for a laptop. The advertisement for the Sony laptop contains no technical information and only focuses on its lightness. Makers of personal computers today are aiming at a broader market that has little technical knowledge. This should be contrasted with advertisements for personal computers thirty years ago, which contained considerable technical information, when personal computers were only purchased by individuals who were very knowledgeable about them.

The second characteristic concerns the extent to which the consumer is interested in acquiring information about the product or service you are providing. Some consumers may have an inherent interest in the product category and are always interested in acquiring useful information about it. Other consumers who do not have this inherent interest may be planning to purchase a product from the product category and are interested in acquiring information. Consumers who want to

Figure 5.2 Sony: Light Like No Other

Source: Photo by Pier Nicola D'Amico

acquire information will pay close attention to your message and think carefully about it; however, you must make sure that the consumer understands the information that is presented. Consequently, you can provide a considerable amount of information in your advertisement. If they are not interested in acquiring information, they may attend to the advertisement, but they will not put much effort into processing the information in it.

Other Considerations

The other considerations include your market position, the size of your budget, and the purpose of the communication. Market position refers to whether you are the dominant brand in the product category. This is of concern because when consumers see an advertisement for a particular product category, they typically perceive it as a message for the dominant brand in the product category. If consumers do not immediately identify the brand being advertised, they are likely to activate the brand node of the dominant brand when processing the information in your message, and this information will be linked to the dominant brand instead of your brand. If you are not the dominant brand, then you must make sure that consumers immediately recognize that it is an advertisement for your brand.

The size of the budget obviously determines the number of advertisements that you can send to consumers. If you can only send a limited number of advertisements, you must make sure that consumers who are exposed to the advertisement are motivated to pay attention to it and to obtain information from it. If consumers are not intrinsically motivated to pay attention to the advertisement, an attention-getting device can be used, so they will attend to it and acquire the information that you wish to communicate. The attention-getting device should be designed so that it communicates the information you wish to communicate. If it does not, consumers may focus their attention on the attention-getting device and ignore the information that you want to communicate.

The final issue is the purpose of the communication. Here you may want to provide new information about your product or service, or you may simply want to remind consumers about your brand. In the latter case, the purpose of the message is to increase or maintain the accessibility of both the brand in memory as well as the most important information that you want your consumer to have about the brand. As long as the advertisement activates the brand node in memory, advertising exposure will increase the accessibility of the brand in memory and some of the information linked to it. Consequently, using billboards becomes a relatively inexpensive way to accomplish this. Alternatively, if you want consumers to obtain new information about your brand, the message must focus on providing this information and making sure that the consumer acquires it and links it to the brand node in memory.

Communication Process

The purpose of this section is to tie everything together by discussing the communication process. As we discussed previously, when consumers are exposed to an advertisement and pay attention to it, they may either actively process the message and form inferences and possibly agree or disagree with the content of the message, or they may passively process the message and acquire some information from it.[7] When consumers actively process the message, they will almost always form or change their explicit attitude towards the product or service being communicated.

When consumers passively process the message, they may form an explicit attitude towards the product or service; however, in most cases they will not. If they do form an explicit attitude towards it, it will be strongly influenced by visual aspects of the message, which do not require processing effort, and their attitude towards the advertisement. In order to acquire information about the product, they will probably need to be exposed to the message numerous times.

If consumers do not form an explicit attitude towards the product or service after seeing the advertisement, they may form a positive implicit attitude towards the product or service if they frequently see an advertisement that contains elements that are evaluated positively. When this occurs, the positive implicit attitude creates an approach tendency towards the product or service and increases the likelihood of the consumer purchasing it.[8] As discussed previously, a further advantage of creating a positive implicit attitude is that these attitudes are difficult to change.

General Strategies

Based on the discussion of the communication process, there are two general strategies that can be used. The first involves sending a limited number of messages. In order for this to be effective, this strategy requires the audience to be actively involved in attending to the message and obtaining information from it. This will occur if the audience is interested in acquiring information about the product or service. If they are not, there must be something in the message to grab their attention. This attention-getting device should identify the brand and communicate information about it. Otherwise, the attention-getting device may overwhelm the desired information to be communicated. This strategy obviously has risks.

Sometimes firms will use attention-getting devices that become the themes of their advertising. Here again the attention-getting device should also communicate the information about the product that the firm wishes to communicate. A good example is Mr. Clean, the magical genie who communicates strength, safety, and cleanliness. A bad example is the frogs that Budweiser used in their advertising a number of years ago. This was purely an attention-getting device that did not communicate anything about the product.

Humour can also be used as an attention-getting device. However, as with all attention-getting devices, the humour should also communicate the information that you wish to present. A good example of an advertisement that uses humour very effectively is a print advertisement for Listerine. The advertisement contains a picture of a pastor preaching in a church; however, all the parishioners are seated in the back rows of the church. Even though the advertisement contains no copy, the picture effectively communicates the dangers of bad breath with subtle humour.

The use of celebrities is also an attention-getting device. An example of a successful advertising campaign that effectively used celebrities is the Miller Lite "Great Taste . . . Less Filling!" campaign in the 1970s and 1980s that featured well-known sports figures. The use of the sports figures was to convince "Joe Six Pack" that you could drink Miller Lite and still be masculine. In general, celebrities can be used to communicate the type of people who use or consume the product, or suggest that the product has the same attributes as the celebrity. Advertisements for luxury watches frequently use celebrities. Figure 5.3 is an advertisement for Breitling watches that features John Travolta, who is also a professional pilot. The advertisement is communicating that since he is a professional pilot, he must rely on sophisticated instruments when flying and, therefore, has considerable knowledge about them. Based on this knowledge, he selects Breitling watches.

The use of celebrities as simply an attention-getting device will generally not be effective. An example of an ineffective celebrity advertisement is a print advertisement for Sharpie Pens that featured David Beckham. Here the attributes of David Beckham do not transfer to "pens," and the

Figure 5.3 Breitling Navitimer

Source: Breitling/Patricia von Ah

copy does not imply that he uses Sharpie Pens. Consequently, the use of David Beckham in the advertisement does not provide any information about the product. He is only used to grab the attention of the reader.

A recent celebrity advertisement that has developed considerable controversy was the introductory campaign for the Fiat 500 with Jennifer Lopez. It has been criticized because it contains no information about the product and just features Jennifer Lopez driving the car. On the other hand, it can be argued that the advertisement is simply communicating to the target audience that you can drive the Fiat 500 and be considered "with it."

Finally, it should be pointed out that there is always a danger in becoming too closely associated with a celebrity because they could become involved in image-damaging events. Accenture learned this with Tiger Woods, who was featured in their advertising campaign for many years to personify its claimed attributes of integrity and high performance. Unfortunately, these two attributes are no longer associated with him, given his marital troubles.

The alternative strategy is to send numerous messages to the consumer. This strategy assumes that the consumer is passive in processing the message, so numerous repetitions are required in order for the consumer to acquire the desired information.

Message Placement

Message placement has become more complicated with the increased use of the internet. In this section, we will discuss message placement in both the "old" and "new" media: the types of messages are the same and only their placement differs.

Alternative Media

The four alternative media are video, print, audio, and billboard. Videos in the "old" media are television advertisements, while in the "new" media they may be a "pop up" message or a message that precedes another video that has been accessed. Video has a number of advantages over the other media. First, it has both sight and sound, so it has the greatest impact in communicating information. Second, the use of sight and sound can be used to create an emotional reaction in the consumer. Its major disadvantages are that consumers watch television to see specific shows, not advertising. Therefore, television advertisements need to use attention-getting devices so that viewers will pay attention to the advertisement. In addition, since most videos are relatively short, there is only a limited amount of information that can be communicated.

Print is purely a visual medium which can contain both pictures and written information. Its primary advantage over the other media is the consumer can spend as much time with the advertisement as they desire. Consequently, if the consumer wants to acquire information, a print advertisement can contain a lot of information and the consumer will expend the time and effort to process the information. When directed at an audience that is very knowledgeable about the product category and is interested in acquiring information about it, print can be very effective.

If, however, the audience is not very interested in the product category, they will passively process the information in the advertisement. Consequently, only the pictures and possibly the headline in the message can be used to communicate information; however, attention-getting devices can be used to create more active processing of the advertisement.

Audio is primarily thought of as radio. It generally serves as background while the audience is doing something else (e.g., driving), and radio advertisements are short in duration. Consequently, audio advertisements are generally processed passively. It is, however, possible to have an attention-getting device in the message that will attract the listener's attention, so they will pay attention to the advertisement and acquire information from it.

Finally, billboards and other signage can be used to increase the accessibility of the brand name and the most important information about your brand. As long as consumers pay attention to the billboard or other signage, exposure to them will increase or maintain the accessibility of the brand name as well as communicate an important piece of information that you want linked to the brand name.

In summary, video messages are the most effective means for providing new information about your brand since they involves both sight and sound; however, since messages are generally of a short duration, only a limited amount of information can be communicated. Print can be very effective for communicating with highly knowledgeable and involved consumers since they can spend an unlimited amount of time with the message. Finally, billboards are primarily used to increase the accessibility of the brand and provide a copy point.

"New" and "Old" Media Differences

While the alternative media used with the "old" and "new" media are the same, with the possible exception of audio, there are a number of important differences between them. In addition, measures of the effectiveness of messages in the two media typically differ, when they really should not.

First, the audiences typically differ by age. Younger consumers have adopted the internet as their primary mode of acquiring information and their use of the "old" media has steadily declined. Second, internet users usually access the internet over their computers and are actively involved in searching for information. Consequently, they tend to be more actively involved with what they are doing and are more likely to actively process messages that they receive with the "new" media. Third, internet firms have more information about their users, so they are better able to target messages to consumers who are interested in a specific product category.

Finally, measures of the success of a message in the "new" media generally involve measures of "click-through"; however, the message itself will have an impact on the consumer in the same way that messages in the "old" media did. For example, we have shown that banner ads can increase the likelihood of someone purchasing the brand by simply increasing the accessibility of the brand.[9] Because of this, advertisements on the internet that allow for "click-through" can have both the effect from exposure to the advertisement and from the possibility of someone attaining additional information about the product or service from "click-through."

Message Design

Here we will discuss issues in message design with respect to the different types of media. We assume that the firm has decided what it wants to communicate and whether they want consumers to actively or passively process the message. In all cases, attention-getting devices will be required so that consumers will pay attention to the advertisement, unless he or she is intrinsically motivated to obtain information about the advertised product. As mentioned previously, if an attention-getting device is used, care must be taken to ensure that this device does not impede the learning of the information to be communicated. Attention-getting devices can be used in all the different types of media to increase attention to the advertisement and to induce more active processing of the information in the advertisement.

With video, there are a number of approaches, including "talking head," product demonstration, "slice-of-life," and visual scene. The "talking head" approach has someone presenting the message, a product demonstration illustrates product usage, "slice-of-life" is a vignette that involves people using or discussing the product, and a visual scene approach uses visuals to communicate information about the product. The "talking head" approach grabs the audiences' attention; however, it is susceptible to having the viewer disagree with the message and mentally argue against it. This can be partially alleviated by using a well-known and trusted spokesperson. A demonstration approach is useful if it can be demonstrated that your product performs better than a competitor, or if it may not be clear to the consumer how your product works. A "slice-of-life" approach minimizes the possibility of the consumer arguing against the message, but the audience must be able to follow the story in order to learn the message. Finally, the visual scene approach induces a purely passive processing orientation in the audience; however, it takes a number of exposures for the message to be learned, so this type of advertising requires a large media budget. The scenes that are used should either provide information about the product or service or should contain positively evaluated objects so evaluative conditioning occurs. In addition, individuals should form positive attitudes towards the advertisement.

As previously mentioned, radio, which uses audio messages, typically occurs while someone is doing something else (e.g., driving); therefore, their attention is directed elsewhere. This means that the message will be processed passively, unless there is some attention-getting device in the message.

With print, information can be communicated either visually or verbally. If consumers are interested in the product, they may be willing to expend the effort to read a considerable amount of verbal information. If they are not, they will simply skim the advertisement, so pictures and the headline must communicate the message that you want to communicate.

As mentioned previously, billboards are primarily used to maintain the accessibility of the brand and provide key information that you want the consumer to associate with the brand. If the product is typically purchased in a self-service store, it should also contain a picture of the product.

Measuring Advertising Effectiveness

While there are a number of procedures for measuring advertising effectiveness such as "day after recall test," "theater test," "starch scores," and so on, none of them provide an indication of whether consumers have acquired the information you wanted them to acquire or whether it increased the accessibility of the brand and the information associated with it. Techniques such as the lexical decision procedure can be used to measure the associations consumers have with a brand to determine whether advertising added the desired associations. If an evaluative conditioning approach is used in the advertisement, evaluative priming procedures can be used to determine if positive implicit attitudes were formed. Finally, if the goal of the advertising is just to maintain or increase the accessibility of the brand and key information, this can also be measured with a lexical decision procedure.

All of these procedures involve having the consumer react to stimuli which appear on a computer screen. With both the lexical decision procedure and evaluative priming, your brand name appears on the computer screen so quickly that it cannot be identified. After a short period of time a string of letters appears on the screen. With the lexical decision task, this string of letters may be a word or a non-word. If it is a word, the respondent hits a specific key on the keyboard, or another key if it's a non-word.

Evaluative priming uses a similar procedure. After the brand name appears on the screen subliminally, the consumer then responds to a valenced word that appears on the screen by indicating whether it is a positive or a negative word. If they respond faster to the positive word than the negative word, it indicates that the consumer has a positive implicit attitude. Finally, in order to measure the accessibility of a brand, the product category would subliminally appear on the computer screen and the consumer would respond to different brand names. The speed with which they respond to the brand names indicates their accessibility with respect to the product category.

In all these procedures, even though the consumer cannot identify the brand name or product category when it appears on the computer screen, it activates the brand or product category node in memory. Activation then spreads from the brand or product category node to related nodes in memory, so if they see a word that represents a node that is linked to the brand or product category node, they are able to respond to it faster than if the brand or product category node was not activated.[10] Comparing how quickly the consumer responds to a word when the brand node is activated than when it is not allows one to determine which associations are linked to brand nodes in memory.[11]

Conclusion

In this chapter we have used current psychological theories to provide guidance in developing marketing communication programs. These theories concern memory, attitudes, information acquisition, and

. judgments and choices. We have assumed that the firm knows what needs to be communicated and who should receive the messages.

We have discussed two types of processing that may occur while the consumer is exposed to the advertisement. With active processing, the consumer expends efforts in processing information from the advertisement. This means that they will acquire more information about the advertised product or service; however, they may also argue against the information in the advertisement which means that it will not be acquired. Consumers who have an inherent interest in the product category or who may be interested in making a purchase from the product category are most likely to engage in active processing. If the consumer would not normally actively process information from the advertisement, then an attention-getting device can be used, but this attention-getting device should also convey the information the firm wants to communicate or it may overwhelm the other information in the advertisement that you want the consumer to know.

In most cases, advertisements are passively processed. This means that very little information can be communicated in each advertisement, and numerous repetitions will be required to communicate the required information.

All advertising will have some impact on the consumer even if it only increases or maintains the accessibility of the brand in memory. It is very important to maintain high levels of brand accessibility since this will affect which brand individuals choose with both memory-based and stimulus-based choice.

Finally, whether the goal of advertising is to provide new information to the consumer about the brand or to just increase brand accessibility, procedures were discussed for measuring whether the advertising campaign was successful in accomplishing these goals.

A Prescription to Get More from Communications

Developing effective communication is perhaps the most critical task for the marketing manager and this task has gone through radical changes recently. Research from psychology indicates that managers need to:

- ADVERTISING has an effect at both a conscious and a non-conscious level.
- ATTENTION-GETTING devices should also communicate information about your product.
- ADVERTISEMENTS for products sold through self-service outlets should contain a picture of the package.
- The MEMORABILITY of a campaign is no guarantee of its persuasiveness.
- INTERNET advertising can be effective without click-throughs.

REFERENCES

1 A discussion of the spreading activation associative network model of memory can be found in most cognitive psychology textbooks. An early formulation of the model can be found in J.R. Anderson, *The Architecture of Cognition* (Cambridge, MA: Harvard University Press, 1983). There have been numerous modifications of the model, but the basic idea behind the model as described here has not changed.

2 What we refer to here as implicit attitudes are also sometimes referred to as automatic evaluations.

3 A better description of this procedure can be found in R.H. Fazio, D.M. Sanbonmatsu, M.C. Powell, and F.R. Kardes, "On the Automatic Activation of Attitudes," *Journal of Personality and Social Psychology* 50, no. 2 (1986): 229–38. There are also other procedures available for measuring implicit attitudes.

4 See R.J. Rydell and A.R. McConnell, "Understanding Implicit and Explicit Attitude Change: A Systems of Reasoning Approach," *Journal of Personality and Social Psychology* 91 (2006): 995–1008.

5 See A.A. Mitchell and J.C. Olson, "Are Product Attribute Beliefs the Only Mediator of Advertising Effects on Brand Attitude?" *Journal of Marketing Research* 18, no. 3 (1981): 318–32.

6 We use the term "information" loosely. It may be in verbal, visual, or auditory form. For instance, the music that is used in an advertisement provides information about the advertised product or service as do the people who may appear in the advertisement.

7 Two models have been proposed based on these two types of processes. These are the Elaboration Likelihood Model from R.E. Petty and J.T. Cacioppo, *Communication and Persuasion: Control and Peripheral Routes to Attitude Change* (New York: Springer-Verlag, 1986); and the Heuristic and Systematic Model from S. Chaiken, "Heuristic and Systematic Information Processing and the Use of Source and Message Cues in Persuasion," *Journal of Personality and Social Psychology* 39, no. 5 (1980): 752, 766. While there are subtle differences in the models, both models propose that two different processes may cause attitude change.

8 See M.A. Dempsey and A.A. Mitchell, "The Influence of Implicit Attitudes on Consumer Choice When Confronted with Conflicting Attribute Information," *Journal of Consumer Research* 37, no. 4 (2010): 614–25.

9 See A. Mitchell and A. Valenzuela, "How Banner Ads Affect Brand Choice Without Click-Through," in C. Haugtvedt, K. Machleit, and R. Yalch, *Online Consumer Psychology* (Hillsdale, NJ: Lawrence Erlbaum Associates, 2005), 125–42.

10 Technically, evaluative priming does not operate in this manner since there would need to be links from the brand to words that have the same valence. With evaluative priming, activating the brand node also creates a positive or negative feeling if the node has an implicit attitude. This positive or negative feeling creates a response bias when responding to the appropriate and inappropriate keys.

11 This procedure is also called sequential priming. By varying the length of time between the prime and the appearance of the string of letters, one can determine if the activation of the related node occurs with or without conscious thought. If the latter occurs it is based on an expectation. See J.H. Nealy, "Semantic Priming and Retrieval of Lexical Memory: Roles of Inhibitionless Spreading Activation and Limited Capacity Attention," *Journal of Experimental Psychology: General* 106, no. 3 (1977): 226–54.

6 Hedonomics: Why People Do Not Buy What They Enjoy the Most

CLAIRE I. TSAI[1]

Virtually all consumers want to maximize the happiness that comes with consumption. In recent decades, the debate has expanded to include behavioural marketing researchers, psychologists, and economists, all of whom have accumulated empirical data and developed testable theories on happiness.

People do not seem to know how to choose a product or service that they will enjoy the most among their available options. This is by and large attributed to two pitfalls in decision-making. First, people are notoriously poor in predicting their happiness (i.e., positive or negative feelings that come with consumption). For example, in chapter 9 of this book, Min Zhao discusses studies showing that people often experience difficulty in simulating the experience of consuming a newly developed product and underpredict the benefits of that product. Even with familiar product categories such as snacks, they may overpredict satiation and want to choose different snacks for future consumption. Second, even when people can accurately predict their happiness, they often base their decision on product attributes that are unrelated to their happiness. This is because people have a strong tendency to undervalue *soft* information ("How much pleasure would I derive from the slick, pretty stereo versus the ugly, bulky stereo?") and overvalue *objective* information ("How much more wattage, a measure of power, does this ugly stereo have over the pretty one?") in making decisions.

Marketers can of course take advantage of the decision biases and try to sell more products to their customers. But we would like to advocate a different approach that benefits both consumers and practitioners. As the virtual social community proliferates, consumers have become more vocal in expressing their opinions about a product or service and such word-of-mouth plays an important role in driving sales and repeat purchases (see David Dunne's chapter 2 for a more thorough discussion concerning word-of-mouth and the empowerment of consumers). So it is imperative for practitioners to gain insight into the psychology of consumer decision-making and use that knowledge to help consumers choose a product or service that they will enjoy most of the available options. Marketers can develop tools and design shopping environments that help to enhance consumer satisfaction in two ways, by enabling people to (a) reduce biases in their predictions about how much happiness a product can bring them, and (b) base decisions on the predictions that are the most accurate. This chapter summarizes major findings about the psychology of happiness and common mistakes in consumer decision-making.

There are at least two general approaches to improving happiness. The first is to enhance the magnitude of desired stimuli (e.g., the amount of income, size of home, or number of shoes) or their quality (e.g., higher-quality home appliances, vehicles, or better view from one's home). The second is to find the optimal relationship between stimuli and happiness. The following analogy illustrates the distinction between these approaches. Suppose a child loves wooden blocks and possesses some. He has played with the ones he owns for a while and is bored with them. How can he increase his happiness? One approach would be to obtain more blocks; the other would entail finding a new and better way to combine the existing pieces and build more enjoyable projects.

The first approach is embraced by most consumers in our society. Many consumers often think that if they got that promotion, owned a vacation home, or had the new iPad their life would be better and they would finally be happy. Indeed, most consumers become increasingly wealthy over their working lives and possess more goods now than ever before. However, it is well established that these increases in or improvement of material goods often lose their appeal quickly as consumers become used to them. The second approach is the focus of this chapter; it seeks to optimize the relationship between external stimuli and happiness without having to increase the magnitude or quality of the external stimuli per se. A better understanding of the second approach can potentially increase consumer happiness without expending more financial resources. We refer to this approach as *hedonomics*.

Hedonomics would not be important if either of the following statements were true. First, happiness depends primarily on the absolute magnitude or quality of desired external stimuli. Second, consumers fully understand the relationships between external stimuli and happiness, and in making consumption decisions they are already maximizing their happiness. As we will show, both of these statements are false.

Hedonomics challenges two commonly held, often tacit assumptions in traditional economics: that maximizing desired external stimuli (including goods and services) approximates maximizing consumer happiness; and that what consumers choose reflects what makes them happy. In marketing textbooks, it is assumed that consumers can store and process as much information as Google's servers, think logically like Spock, and have consistent preferences over time without being affected by their internal states (moods, feelings) and external environments (e.g., relaxing on a beach vs. stressing out during an exam). Intuitively, this depiction deviates significantly from how consumers actually behave and make decisions.[2] For example, many people have problems with long division, not to mention their ability to compare information from tens or hundreds of options when shopping for electronic products or kitchen appliances. Scholarly research has also confirmed that, contrary to the lay belief, consumers often overestimate their ability to use and process large amounts of information effectively.[3] When faced with large amounts of information, consumers tend to use only a few cues to make judgments. While consumers seem to recognize that some cues are better than others, they also let non-diagnostic information affect their judgment (e.g., they feel less confident in their choice if the options are advertised using blurry images).[4] As well, when consumers receive redundant information that confirms their existing opinions but offers little new insight, they often misinterpret this as confirmation of their judgment, which can lead them to be overconfident about their judgments and make decisions based on such unwarranted confidence.

External Stimuli and Happiness

We will first review major findings concerning the psychology of external stimuli and its impact on happiness.

1. Everything Is Relative – Gains and Losses

Consider a consumer, Jack, making investment decisions and predicting his experience with potential outcomes of the investment. A financial advisor, George, recommends two stocks to Jack: stock X and stock

Y, each $10 per share. Jack decides to invest $1,000 in stock X. The fluctuations of the price (per share) for the next four months are summarized below.

	Month			
Stock	1	2	3	4
X	10	12	8	3
Y	10	15	8	2

When evaluating his investment, Jack has (at least) two options. He can either focus on stock X alone or use the performance of stock Y as a benchmark. Depending on the points of comparison, Jack will react positively or negatively towards the price fluctuations of stock X. For example, in month 2, the price of X goes up by $2 per share. This change is perceived as a gain if Jack only focuses on Stock X. However, the same change can be perceived as a loss if stock Y is used as a benchmark, and in this case Jack could be upset with his financial adviser George. By contrast, when both stocks plummet in the last two months because of the financial crisis, Jack might actually feel happier with George if he uses stock Y as a reference point rather than focusing on stock X only, because stock X performs better than stock Y during month 4.

The investment example is captured by Kahneman and Tversky's influential prospect theory,[5] which was originally proposed to describe choice under risk but also has important implications for consumption experience with riskless external stimuli. These implications can be briefly summarized as follows. First, one's experience with an external stimulus depends not on its absolute value, but on the difference between the absolute value and some reference point. A positive difference is a gain and evokes a positive experience, whereas a negative difference is a loss and evokes a negative experience. Second, the negative experience evoked by a loss is more intense than the positive experience evoked by a gain of the same absolute value – a principle termed loss aversion. In the investment example, Jack is likely to experience more intense feelings when the value of his investment drops by $200 than when the value increases by $200. Finally, consumers are less sensitive to incremental changes in gains or losses as overall gains or losses increase. In the stock example, as the value of stock X continues to decline, Jack probably feels less strongly about an increase in loss from

Figure 6.1 Gains/Losses of Investment

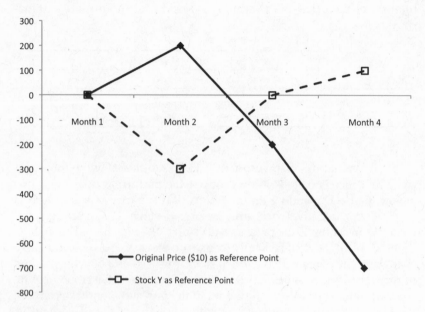

$200 to $500 in comparison to a loss from status quo (no loss/gain) to a loss of $300, despite these losses being the same amount.

Prospective theory has several prescriptive strategies to maximize happiness.[6]

Strategy one: if a consumer has two good events to enjoy (e.g., dining out with a charming friend and watching a favourite video), he/she should enjoy them on separate occasions, because multiple gains will yield greater total happiness if they are experienced separately than if they are experienced as one aggregate gain.[7]

Strategy two: if a consumer has to experience two bad events (e.g., seeing a dentist and spending time with his/her in-laws), it is better to experience them in close proximity, because multiple losses will yield less total pain if they are experienced as one integrated loss than if they are experienced separately.[8]

Strategy three: if a consumer has a big, bad event and a small, good event to experience, he/she should experience them separately so that the negative experience with the bad event does not contaminate the good event.

Strategy four: if a consumer has a small, bad event and a big, good event to experience, he/she should experience them in close proximity so that the positive experience with the good event can eliminate the pain from the small, bad event.

We are aware of only one paper that systematically demonstrates consequences of strategy one in consumer decision-making. Specifically, Tsai and Zhao[7] look at unpacking a virtual social event of chatting with a group of six contacts on the internet into chatting with individual contacts. The study found that the time people expect to spend on chatting increases when the contacts are likeable friends but decreases when they are disliked acquaintances. More importantly, the greater the time estimates, the more people want to acquire software that helps them manage their contacts better.

Loss aversion can cause market inefficiency. For example, people may feel negatively about giving up or selling their possessions (e.g., their homes) or paying money to acquire an item. As a result, there is often a discrepancy between the asking price set by a seller and the offering price set by a buyer.[8] Recent research has identified a number of important moderators for loss aversion. For example, intentions to improve the status quo can reduce loss aversion because people with these intentions focus more on the benefits of the good they intend to acquire (or the money they will gain from selling their possessions) instead of obsessing about the loss (i.e., the good or money they have to give up in the transaction).[9] Reducing emotional attachment can decrease loss aversion; in other words, consumers are more willing to give up utilitarian than hedonic items.[9] Further, ambiguity in the status quo might also reduce loss aversion, given that in this case the reference point is not as rigid and thus consumers are not as attached to a particular status quo.[10] Finally, having consumers recall the benefits of a good starting with the least important benefit (as opposed to the most important one) can reduce loss aversion as the first benefit that comes to mind tends to carry more weight in a consumer's evaluation of that product.[11]

2. A Raise Is Only Better If It Is Greater Than What Your Colleague Got – Quantity and Value

Most economics theories assume that more of a desired stimulus is always better. For example, an airline passenger will always be happier if he/she receives 3,000 bonus miles than if he/she receives 2,000 bonus miles. Is this assumption true? Recent research suggests that a consumer's sensitivity to the magnitude (e.g., amount, quantity, duration, probability, or mileage) associated with a stimulus depends on at least two factors: evaluation mode and the evaluability of the relevant attribute.[12]

What is evaluation mode? The evaluation of any stimuli proceeds in one of two modes, or in some combination of them: joint evaluation (JE) and single evaluation (SE). In JE, two or more stimuli are juxtaposed and evaluated comparatively. For example, if a passenger receives two sets of bonus miles from two different airlines, he/she is in JE of these two sets of bonuses. Under SE, only one stimulus is present and evaluated in isolation, for example, a passenger receives only one·set of bonus miles at a time.

Some attributes are inherently more evaluable than others. For example, without any learning or point of comparison, we can tell which temperatures make us comfortable and happy and which do not.[13] Similarly, consumers are sensitive to changes in their amount of sleep or their social relationships (isolation or connectedness).[13] Time and mileage are examples of attributes of lower evaluability when assessed in JE. (Some people may find these attributes easy to evaluate after some learning but their ability is unlikely to be innate. See Dilip Soman's chapter 12 for extensive discussion on the evaluation of time.)

Now let us return to the mileage example. Do 3,000 bonus miles always make a consumer happier than 2,000 bonus miles? Not necessarily. Passengers receiving 3,000 bonus miles are unlikely to be happier than passengers receiving 2,000 bonus miles if they do not compare the awards in JE. If passengers are in SE and if they are not familiar with the distribution or range of such promotions (i.e., if they lack a reference point for comparison, making mileage an attribute that is difficult to evaluate), they may feel equally happy about receiving 2,000 miles and 3,000 miles – but the differential cost of promotion to airline companies can be substantial.

Life often presents itself in SE. For example, most passengers do not receive multiple sets of bonus miles from different airlines at the same time. Although most passengers know the more miles they receive the happier they will be, they often have difficulty in deciding exactly how happy they would be with a specific amount like 2,000 or 3,000 miles. However, passengers often have to make purchase decisions in JE (i.e., simultaneously compare many airline companies when planning a trip) and their positive reaction towards the airline that sends them bonus miles does not necessarily translate to the purchase decision. Furthermore, consumers do not have much information about the range and distribution of most product attributes. Thus, *more* of a good thing does not necessarily make consumers happier or generate greater sales for marketers.

In summary, consumers differ in how they respond to an increase in external stimuli when the stimuli are presented in JE versus SE. In JE, the relationship between happiness and the value of external stimuli is relatively linear and steep. In SE, we often observe a step-function such that happiness increases around a neutral reference point (e.g., a jump in happiness from no promotional miles to receiving some bonus miles) and flat elsewhere (little change in happiness for additional bonus miles).[14] This tendency is more pronounced the less evaluable the attribute is.

3. Time and Distribution – Remedies for Short-Lived Increases in Happiness

Many things consumers care about change over time. If a stimulus one cares about changes – for example, moving from this small apartment to a larger unit – one will at first experience a positive feeling that will fade away with the passage of time. This process is called hedonic adaptation.

Hedonic adaptation occurs for multiple reasons. One is basic psychophysical adaptation. That is, the longer we are exposed to a stimulus, the less sensitive we are towards it.[15] For example, when a person first immerses his/her hand in water that is 10 degrees Celsius, he/she will feel cold. After a while he/she will adapt to the temperature and no longer find the water cold. Another reason for hedonic adaptation is dilution of attention. For example, after a person moves to a large apartment from a smaller place, he/she will first be overjoyed with the extra size, but before long his/her attention will shift away from the house to many other things, such as his/her crying baby and nagging spouse. The size of his/her new apartment is just one of the myriad of events that causes the ups and downs in his/her life.

A third reason for hedonic adaptation is what has been referred to as "ordinization."[24] Once an affective event happens, consumers have a tendency to rationalize it, make it seem ordinary, and thereby dampen its affective impact. This can happen to both positive and negative events. For example, if a bidder wins an auction for a painting on eBay, he/she might think to him/herself, "It's no surprise. I bid a lot." If he/she is outbid, he/she might quickly recover from the loss by thinking, "It wasn't a very good painting anyway."

Although prior research has focused primarily on documenting the phenomena of hedonic adaptation, recent research has begun investigating the antecedents that systematically influence the speed at which consumers adapt to changes in external stimuli. For example, consumers satiate or habituate less when they can more easily perceive the variety of a hedonic experience,[17] or take a break during consumption.[17] Similarly, researchers found that knowing the exact (vs. approximate) duration of a boring study session made the session more painful to students.[19] In the positive domain, knowing the exact duration of a pleasant music clip versus an unpleasant one rendered the pleasant clip more enjoyable and the unpleasant one more aversive. Duration knowledge can therefore decelerate adaptation. However, the researchers also found that counting down an aversive experience (e.g., counting the experience of listening to construction noise in seconds) can mitigate the unpleasant experience and help people adapt to the noise faster.[19] In a follow-up study, the authors observed that counting down items that are being consumed (such as potato chips or a movie) can increase consumption enjoyment because the act of down-counting increases awareness of the available supply in decline. By contrast, when people focus on the fact that the potato chips are running out or the movie is coming to an end (a less pleasant fact compared with consuming tasty food or viewing a fun movie), then counting down the remaining chips or movie time can prevent people from fully enjoying the experience.

Some events are more resistant to adaptation than others by nature. First, variable, uncertain events are more resistant to adaptation than certain, stable events (e.g., good views, additional space, or upgrades in a new apartment). For example, studies have shown that a gift from a mysterious source (uncertain condition) creates longer-lasting happiness than an equivalent gift from a known source (certain condition). In the negative domain, people who live by an airport or highway do not adapt to the noise from airplanes and traffic[19] because this type of noise comes and goes rather than remaining at a constant level (by contrast, people get used to the noise inside an airplane during a flight because the noise level is stable and constant). In the area of health issues, researchers found that colostomy patients with hope of recovery (uncertain outcome) adapted more slowly to their misery than patients with little chance of recovery.[21]

Second, events associated with inherently evaluable attributes are probably more resistant to adaptation than events associated with inherently inevaluable attributes.[12] For certain attributes, people have an innate, shared, and stable scale to assess which level of the variable is desirable and which is not. These attributes include ambient temperature, amount of sleep, stress, fatigue, and so forth. An attribute is less evaluable when people do not have an innate scale for gauging its desirability and must rely on external reference information, such as what others have or objective value (e.g., income, size of a home, jewellery). For example, raising one's room temperature in the winter from 10 degrees Celsius to 20 degrees Celsius will probably have a longer-lasting effect on happiness than will upgrading one's kitchen countertop from laminate to granite, assuming that the two events have the same initial effect on happiness.

Many events we care about constantly change over time – for example, gas prices, stock prices, and body weight – and adaptation to these changes is less likely. How do people react to such ongoing changes? First, our momentary experience with such ongoing changes depends on the direction of the change; it is positive if the change is in a desirable direction and negative if the change is in an unwanted direction.[22] Second, our momentary experience depends on the rate of change (or velocity), in that we feel happier the faster a positive change and less happy the faster a negative change.[22] Finally, certain snapshots of our momentary experiences heavily influence our retrospective evaluation.[23] For example, our overall evaluation or impression of a movie is largely determined by how much we like or dislike its opening and its ending, as well as the moments of climax that induce extremely positive or negative feelings during the movie. We tend to pay less attention in our evaluation to the middle parts that trigger mild feelings or none at all. In sum, consumers adapt to states but react to changes. They react more the faster the change, and they react not only to the rate of change but also to changes in the rate.

4. Too Many to Enjoy – Choice and Options

Many believe that having a choice is always better than having none, and that having more choices is always better than having fewer. In reality, neither is true. Research shows that if consumers have to experience one of several undesirable options, they will feel happier if someone else makes the choice for them than if they have to make the choice themselves.[24] For example, a consumer who is on diet and can only eat meals that are unappealing to him/her will feel better if someone else chooses the meal for him/her than if he/she has to make a choice herself, because choosing an unappealing meal will make the consumer feel responsible for causing their negative feelings towards it while delegating the choice to others will shift the blame to them.

When people make a choice themselves, they will be less satisfied with that choice if they have many options to choose from than if they have only a few options to choose from. Too many options can be demotivating because they can become too complex and involve too many trade-offs for consumers to manage.[25] For example, shoppers will be less happy with the chocolate they choose if they have thirty truffles to choose from than if they have only six options.

Actually, simply having more than one option can reduce happiness.[26] That is, if consumers are presented with one good option, they will be happy, but if they are presented with two good options, they will notice the disadvantages of each option relative to the other and will be less happy with either option. For example, if a consumer wins a free trip to Paris, he/she will be happy; if the consumer wins a free trip to Hawaii, he/she will also be happy. But if the consumer wins a free trip and has to choose between Paris and Hawaii, he/she may be less happy because each option contains shortcomings compared with the other. Whereas Paris does not have Waikiki Beach, Hawaii does not have the Louvre.

Finally, research shows that consumers will be less happy with their decision if they closely consider the options available to them than if they do not. In most cases a consumer can choose only one of the available options and has to forgo the other options. Close deliberations can prompt consumers to form an emotional attachment to all the options, including those they have to forego. Thus, choosing one feels like "losing" the others to which they already have some emotional attachment.

5. Fear Is Pain Arising from the Anticipation of Evil (Aristotle) – Cognition Utilities

Imagine that a person participated in a sweepstakes a month ago. He/she has just been informed that he/she has won a three-day vacation in Paris. What is the utility of this trip to the consumer? Intuitively, one would say that the utility is the happiness he/she will derive from the vacation. That can be referred to as consumption utility. But he/she experiences three other types of utility besides that: news utility – the feeling he/she experiences upon hearing the news that he/she has won the vacation; anticipation utility – the feeling he/she experiences when anticipating the trip; and memory utility – the feeling he/she experiences when recalling the trip afterwards.

In a recent study, students were prompted to report their momentary experiences five times during a class.[1] The first time was about fifteen minutes into the class (which established the baseline of happiness). The second time was immediately after the instructor announced that he would give each student a Kit Kat chocolate bar to eat later in the class; this measured news utility. The third time was about ten minutes after the announcement of the news; this measured anticipation utility. The fourth time was right after the students had received the chocolate and were eating it; this measured consumption utility. The last time was some ten minutes after the consumption; this measured memory utility.

Compared with the baseline level of happiness, the students reported the greatest happiness when they heard the news, followed by when they ate the chocolate, and lastly when they anticipated and when they recalled the consumption. This study indicates the possibility for news to generate even greater happiness than consumption.

In an ingenious study on anticipation utility, respondents were asked to indicate how much they were willing to pay to receive a kiss from their favourite movie star immediately, in three hours, or in three days.[27] According to traditional discounted utility theory, people should be willing to pay more for the immediate kiss than for the delayed kisses, because experiences in the future are discounted and their appeal is diminished. However, the researchers found that respondents were willing to pay more for receiving the kiss in three days than for receiving it immediately or in three hours. Presumably, waiting for the kiss brought happiness. In one recent study, we observed that people enjoy a snack less when they count down its remaining items because the anticipation that the snack is running out evokes negative feelings. As a result, counting down a hedonic experience induces negative anticipation utility, which contaminates the consumption experience and reduces happiness.

Memory utility is another important cognition utility. Memory of past events can influence happiness in two ways. First, consumers may relive a positive (versus negative) experience from their past and derive positive (versus negative) utility when recalling the past (consumption effect). For example, a person can derive pleasure by recalling the details of his/her last trip to Paris. Second, past experience can serve as a point of comparison and create a contrast effect or spill over to one's current experience and create an assimilation effect. Which effect will dominate depends on the context. For example, if the past event is similar to the current event (e.g., a fancy French dinner versus a mediocre French dinner), the past experience will create a contrast effect (the mediocre dinner becomes even more unbearable). If the past event is dissimilar to the present event (e.g., a fancy French dinner versus a mediocre movie), the past event will create an assimilation effect (watching the mediocre movie becomes less miserable as the happy feeling from the fancy dinner carries over to the movie).

Intuitively, the primary source of happiness that a desirable stimulus (e.g., a chocolate bar or a vacation) brings is the consumption of the stimulus, whereas news, anticipation, and memory are all secondary. In reality, cognition utilities may comprise a large portion of the happiness from the stimulus, and sometimes even a portion that is larger than consumption utility. Consumption utility is like a light source while cognition utility is like its halo; without the light source, there will be no halo – but with the light source, the halo may be brighter than the source itself.

Obstacles to Maximizing Happiness

We will now review consumption biases that serve as obstacles for maximizing happiness. These biases are attributed to either failure to make accurate predictions about happiness derived from consumption (numbers one to four) or failure to follow predictions even when they are accurate (numbers five to eight).

1. Decision in a Vacuum – Impact Bias

When asked to predict the experiential consequence of an event (e.g., moving to a larger apartment), consumers often ignore the power of adaptation and thereby over-predict the duration and the intensity of the experience.[28] This type of misprediction is known as "impact bias."

Impact bias can be attributed to two causes. One is neglect of ordinization. As we reviewed earlier, when an emotion-triggering event happens, people will make sense of it and make the event seem ordinary.[16] Yet most people underestimate this ordinization effect. Another reason for this bias is focalism; that is, consumers pay too much attention to the focal event, overlook the dilution-of-attention effect (as we reviewed earlier), and thereby overestimate the affective impact of the focal event.[28] For example, when a consumer is predicting how much happier he/she will be if he/she moves from a smaller apartment to a larger one, he/she focuses his/her attention on the size dimensions, but once he/she moves into the larger apartment, size will be just one of many things that affect his/her life.

2. Just Do the Math? Distinction Bias

A recent graduate who currently lives in a 500-square-foot studio without indoor parking has found a job and has two options for housing: one is a 1,250-square-foot apartment with indoor parking and the other is a 1,500-square-foot apartment without indoor parking (rent is the same for both options). In comparison, he/she notices the clear difference in size between the two options and predicts that he/she will be happier living in the bigger apartment despite the lack of indoor parking, thus he/she chooses the bigger place. Is this the optimal choice? Probably not. In reality, he/she may well be happier if he/she rents the smaller apartment, because the difference between 1,250 and 1,500 square feet may make less of a difference in his/her day-to-day consumption (living) experience than whether he/she has access to indoor parking or not. As the example illustrates, when making a choice, the person tends to over-predict the difference in experience generated by two apparently distinct values on a particular dimension (in this case, square footage). We refer to this prediction bias as the distinction bias.[29]

The distinction bias arises because consumers are in different evaluation modes during prediction versus consumption. Predictions are often made in joint evaluation (JE) while consumption often takes place in separate evaluation (SE). For instance, prospective house buyers typically compare alternative homes in JE and predict their experiences. When they actually live in a home, they experience that place alone in SE. If consumers do not recognize their distinction bias, they may sacrifice things that are actually important to their consumption experience (e.g., the availability of indoor parking) for things that are not as important (e.g., the difference between 1,250 and 1,500 square feet).

3. Contrary to Popular Beliefs . . . Belief Bias

People often have good intuition, but we also know that many popular beliefs are invalid and that basing decisions on such erroneous beliefs leads to suboptimal decisions. For example, people believe that having more information improves their decision-making, so they tend to feel more confidence in their decisions as they acquire additional information over time. However, in reality, decisions do not improve with more information beyond the first three to five cues.[3] Mispredictions about consumption experience may also result from consumers' inaccurate theories concerning relationships between external stimuli and happiness. Consumers may expect adaptation or satiation when it does not exist. For example, in one study, students believed that their liking for their favourite ice cream would decrease if they had it every day, but in reality their liking did not decrease as much as predicted.[30] Similarly, consumers are notorious for predicting contrast effect. For example, although people believe a negative *past* event (e.g., having a wheatgrass-flavoured jelly bean) would render the current positive experience (e.g., having a pineapple-flavoured jelly bean) more enjoyable, in reality such contrast effect does not occur.[31] On the contrary, people can under-predict contrast effects such that they predict that anticipating a negative *future* event (e.g., listening to construction noise) would contaminate the current experience (e.g., listening to pleasant music) and make it less pleasant, whereas in reality the comparison with construction noise makes the music more enjoyable (contrast effect).[32]

Another common belief is that more options are better.[25] As we reviewed earlier, this is not always true; it depends on the size of the choice set, the mode of evaluation, the level of involvement, and the cost of searching and processing information. A related common belief is that having the right to choose makes people happier than having someone else make the choice for them.[24] Again, as we discussed earlier, this belief is not true when the choice must be made among undesirable alternatives.

According to recent research, people intuit that knowing the exact duration of a hedonic experience (e.g., movie, music, or study session) will weaken the experience and slow down adaptation, rending a positive event less pleasurable and a negative event even more unpleasant. As reviewed earlier, this lay belief is the opposite of the actual effect of duration knowledge.[19] Similarly, we observed in one set of studies that people enjoy a tasty beverage or snack better if they know the exact quantity of the item to be consumed, but the same quantity information worsens their experience if the item is unappetizing. Contrary to the actual effect of quantity information, people want to avoid the quantity information if they expect the item to be tasty and acquire it if they expect it to be unappetizing.

Finally, in one recent study, we observed that people enjoy a product better if they get a discount for it – but, importantly, this positive effect only occurs if consumption takes place immediately after the payment is made. For delayed consumption, price promotions actually decrease the enjoyment derived from the product. This work has important practical implications because many products are typically consumed only after some time has transpired following the sales transaction (e.g., grocery items, books, and prepaid vacation packages).

4. If I Am Hot Now, I Am Also Hot Six Months from Now – Projection Bias

Consumers often find themselves in different visceral (arousal) states. Sometimes they are rested or satiated; other times they are tired and hungry. When consumers in one visceral state predict experiences in another visceral state for themselves or others, they often project their current state into their predictions.[33] For example, if a person is full now, he/she will underestimate how much he/she will enjoy his/her next meal when he/she is hungry again.

Projection bias can result in important behavioural consequences. For example, hungry shoppers at a grocery store may buy more items than they need or planned to buy,[34] unless they are reminded of their grocery list.[35] A currently hungry person may choose a candy bar over an apple for a future consumption occasion on which he/she will be full, only to find that he/she would actually have preferred the apple when that moment comes.[36]

5. As a Rule of Thumb . . . Rule-Based Choice

In decision-making, consumers may base their choices on factors other than predicted experience. One such factor is "decision rules." These rules come into being because they simplify decisions and lead to optimal consequences under certain circumstances. Nevertheless, once these rules are internalized, people over-apply them to circumstances where they do not lead to experientially optimal choices. Examples of decision rules include "seek variety or diversification," "waste not," and "don't pay for delays." For example, consumers may intuitively recognize the importance of anticipation and predict greater happiness from a concert that will take place in a week than a similar concert that will take place tonight, yet they are not willing to pay extra for the concert in a week, presumably because they want to adhere to the "don't pay for delays" rule.

Variety seeking can also lead to an inconsistency between predicted experiences and decisions. For example, diners tend to order different items than what their friends choose even if they would prefer to eat the same thing.[37]

Similarly, the "waste not" rule can lead consumers to forego options that they predict to be more enjoyable and choose a less enjoyable one. For example, researchers asked participants to imagine that they had purchased a $100 ticket for a weekend ski trip to Michigan and a $50 ticket for a weekend ski trip to Wisconsin.[38] They later found out that the two trips were for the same weekend and had to pick one to use. Although the participants were told that the trip to Wisconsin would be more enjoyable, the majority of them chose the more expensive trip to Michigan.

6. Armchair Economist – Lay Rationalism

Consumers have a general tendency to resist immediate affective influence and base their choices on factors they consider rational.[39] This tendency is termed lay rationalism and it manifests itself in different forms. One is lay scientism – a tendency to base decisions on "hard" (objective and quantitative) attributes rather than "soft" (subjective and hard-to-quantify) attributes. In one study, participants were given a choice between two fictitious stereo systems, one having more power and the other having a richer sound.[40] For half of the participants, power was described as an objective wattage rating and sound richness as a subjective experience. For the other half, power was described as a subjective experience and sound richness as an objective quantitative rating. When power was framed as objective, more participants chose the powerful stereo over the richer sounding stereo. The results were reversed when sound richness was framed as objective. However, when people were asked to predict the enjoyment they would get from listening to the stereos, their choice did not vary by the presentation format of the attributes. That is, the objectivity/subjectivity manipulation had a greater influence on choice than on predicted experience.

In addition to affecting purchase decisions prior to consumption, lay scientism also systematically influences the way in which consumers place value on the worth of their purchase after it has been made. For example, when deciding on the compensation for a broken product or a lost concert ticket, consumers largely ignore owner's value (i.e., consumption enjoyment in dollar amount; cash equivalent) and decide on the compensation amount solely based on the price they paid for the product – even when they are aware that the paid price is often irrelevant to the worth/value of the product to consumers.[41] This is because consumers feel it is more legitimate to base their decision on paid price (objective information) than value (subjective, malleable information). These findings corroborate the notion that consumers base their choices not purely on predicted experience, but also on what they consider to be "rational" – or, in this case, objective.

Recent research seeks to further understand lay scientism and demonstrates that the tendency to base choice on seemingly objective information is mainly driven by the instrumentality of hard attributes. In one study, researchers reduced the weight placed on a hard attribute (memory size for two smartphones) by increasing the range of the attribute such that an increase in memory by two megabytes was either very attractive (for a small range) or very trivial (for a wide range).[42] When the increased memory was perceived as trivial, this attribute was less instrumental for choice than the soft attribute (attractiveness of the smart phones) and carried less weight in the consumers' choice.

7. Fever Pitch – Impulsivity

We define an impulsive choice as choosing an option that yields a better short-term (immediate) experience over an option that yields a better long-term (immediate plus future) experience. For example, eating fatty food may produce better short-term enjoyment than eating healthy food, but it may also cause obesity and other health-related problems in the long run. Thus, eating fatty food rather than healthy food can be considered an impulsive choice.

Consumers sometimes behave impulsively because they mispredict their behaviour's consequences. For example, some people eat fatty foods because they under-predict its negative consequences. But more often than not, consumers commit impulsive behaviour even though they are keenly aware of its aversive consequence because they simply cannot resist the temptation.[43] For example, many substance abusers are fully aware that drugs are ruining their lives and may even warn their friends to stay away from drugs, but they simply cannot resist their cravings. In other words, impulsive choosers fail to base their choices on what they predict will bring them the best overall experience. Here, overall experience refers to long-term experience, in other words, the sum of immediate and future experiences.

8. Failure to See the Forest for the Trees – Medium Maximization

When people exert effort to obtain a desired outcome, the immediate reward they receive is usually not the outcome per se, but a "medium" – an instrument that they can trade for the desired outcome. For example, points for consumer loyalty programs and mileage for frequent flyer programs are both media.

In decisions involving a medium, consumers may maximize the medium rather than their predicted experiences with the ultimate outcomes.[44] In an experiment designed to test the effect of media, respondents were given a choice between a shorter task which would award them 60 points or a larger task which would award them 100 points. Respondents were told that with 60 points they could get a serving of vanilla ice cream and with 100 points they could get the same amount of pistachio ice cream. Most respondents chose to work on the long task. However, when asked which type of ice cream they preferred or which type of task they preferred, most favoured the vanilla ice cream and the short task. It seems that the presence of a medium led the respondents to work more and enjoy less.

In Closing

Although it is tempting to profit by taking advantage of the consumer biases reviewed here, this myopic approach will hurt profitability in the long run. Given that consumption experience plays an essential role in influencing customer satisfaction, repeat purchase, word of mouth, and consumer loyalty,[45] it is imperative for practitioners to first understand what product makes people happy (as that will drive repurchase and word of mouth) rather than what people will choose. This approach is even more relevant to marketing that has moved away from transactions to focus on relationships as a result of the proliferation of online social networks. This chapter reviewed academic research offering insight into how to help consumers overcome their judgment biases and make decisions that will maximize their consumption enjoyment.

Several prescriptive strategies can be inferred from these academic findings about consumer decision-making and happiness. First, marketers can help consumers better predict their happiness. In the apartment example involving a trade-off between parking and space, a renter can better appreciate the convenience of indoor parking if he/she is prompted to recall prior experiences of having to carry groceries from his/her car back to the apartment on a cold, rainy (or even snowy!) day. Second, marketers should strive to help consumers base their purchase decision on happiness that comes with consumption rather than attributes that are less relevant to happiness. As mentioned earlier, consumers tend to compare features or attributes jointly when viewing product information of available options, regardless of how meaningful or impactful these differences are in their actual experience. One way to mitigate this decision bias is by educating salespeople to guide consumers to focus on relevant attributes for happiness in decision-making. Alternatively, marketers may consider presenting soft attributes (e.g., sound quality, the pleasure of consumption) in an objective fashion by, for example, developing a quantitative scoring system that complements qualitative descriptions (e.g., the numeric scores in wine magazines). That way, consumers will be more willing to base their decision on soft attributes, which are most relevant to their happiness. Finally, marketers can utilize academic findings to help consumers maximize happiness during consumption. For example, given that duration knowledge or quantity information enhances pleasurable experiences but exacerbates unpleasant experiences, marketers may consider highlighting the duration of a movie at the ticket booth in the box office or highlight the quantity information on a snack's packaging (e.g., number of potato chips) by using visual cues. But for less pleasant products with long-term benefits (e.g., weight-loss program or diet, training workshops for standardized tests), marketers should de-emphasize the duration or quantity information.

In the end, to create a good wooden-block project, a child needs to accurately predict what a project will look like if he/she combines the blocks in a particular way and then combine the blocks based on his/her predictions. Likewise, to pursue happiness, consumers need to accurately predict the affective consequences of their options and make their choices based on these predictions.

A Prescription for Dealing with the Mispredicting Consumer
Hedonomics shows that people frequently fail to buy products they enjoy the most because (a) they mispredict and (b) their choices are often based on product attributes that are not relevant to happiness. Marketers can improve long-term profitability through repeat purchase and positive word of mouth (WOM) by:

- SIMULATING actual consumption experiences at the point of purchase.
- GUIDING consumers to base their choice on attributes that are most relevant to happiness.
- HELPING consumers maximize happiness during the consumption process.

REFERENCES

1 This chapter was written in collaboration with Professor Christopher Hsee (University of Chicago) and is based on the article "Hedonomics in Consumer Behaviour," in Curtis P. Haugtvedt, Paul M. Herr, and Frank R. Kardes, eds., *Handbook of Consumer Psychology* (Mahwah, NJ: Lawrence Erlbaum Associates, 2008), 639–58. Used with permission of Taylor & Francis Group LLC; permission conveyed through Copyright Clearance Centre, Inc.

2 Richard H. Thaler and Cass R. Sunstein, *Nudge: Improving Decisions about Health, Wealth, and Happiness* (New Haven, CT: Yale University Press, 2008).

3 Claire I. Tsai, Joshua Klayman, and Reid Hastie, "Effects of Amount of Information on Judgment Accuracy and Confidence," *Organizational Behavior and Human Decision Processes* 107, no. 2 (2008): 97–105.

4 Claire I. Tsai and Ann L. McGill, "No Pain, No Gain? How Construal Level and Fluency Affect Consumer Confidence," *Journal of Consumer Research* 37, no. 5 (2011): 807–21.

5 Daniel Kahneman and Amos Tversky, "Prospect Theory: An Analysis of Decisions Under Risk," *Econometrica* 47 (1979): 313–27.

6 Richard H. Thaler, "Mental Accounting and Consumer Choice," *Marketing Science* 4 (1985): 199–214.

7 Claire I. Tsai and Min Zhao, "Predicting Consumption Time: The Role of Event Valence and Unpacking," *Journal of Consumer Research* 38, no. 3 (2011): 459–73.

8 Richard H. Thaler, "Toward a Positive Theory of Consumer Choice," *Journal of Economic Behavior and Organization* 1 (1980): 39–60.

9 Z. Carmon and D. Ariely, "Focusing on the Forgone: How Value Can Appear So Different to Buyers and Sellers." *Journal of Consumer Research* 27 (2000): 360–70.

10 Ravi Dhar and Klaus Wertenbroch, "Consumer Choice between Hedonic and Utilitarian Goods," *Journal of Marketing Research* 37 (2000): 60–71.

11 Eric J. Johnson, Gerald Haubl, and Anat Keinan, "Aspects of Endowment: A Query Theory of Value Construction," *Journal of Experimental Psychology: Learning, Memory, and Cognition* 33, no. 3 (2007): 461–74.

12 Christopher K. Hsee and Jiao Zhang, "General Evaluability Theory," *Perspectives on Psychological Science* 5, no. 4 (2010): 343–55.

13 Christopher K. Hsee, Yang Yang, Naihe Li, and Luxi Shen, "Wealth, Warmth and Wellbeing: Whether Happiness Is Relative or Absolute Depends on Whether It Is about Money, Acquisition, or Consumption," *Journal of Marketing Research* 46, no. 3 (2009): 396–409.

14 Christopher K. Hsee and Yuval Rottenstreich, "Music, Pandas and Muggers: On the Affective Psychology of Value," *Journal of Experimental Psychology: General* 133, no. 1 (2004): 23–30.

15 Harry Helson, *Adaptation-Level Theory: An Experimental and Systematic Approach to Behavior* (New York: Harper and Row, 1964).

16 See the discussion of happiness on page 115 above.

17 Barbara E. Kahn and Brian Wansink, "The Influence of Assortment Structure on Perceived Variety and Consumption Quantities," *Journal of Consumer Research* 30, no. 4 (2004): 519–33.

18 Leif Nelson and Tom Meyvis, "Interrupted Consumption: Disrupting Adaptation to Hedonic Experiences," *Journal of Marketing Research* 45, no. 6 (2008): 654–64.

19 Min Zhao and Claire I. Tsai, "The Effects of Duration Knowledge on Forecasted vs. Actual Affective Experience," *Journal of Consumer Research* 38, no. 3 (2011): 525–34.

20 S. Cohen, G. Evans, D. Krantz, D. Stokols, and S. Kelly, "Aircraft Noise and Children: Longitudinal and Cross-Sectional Evidence on Adaptation to Noise and the Effectiveness of Noise Abatement," *Journal of Personality and Social Psychology* 40 (1981): 331–45.

21 Dylan M. Smith, George Loewenstein, Aleksandra Jankovich, and Peter A. Ubel, "Happily Hopeless: Adaptation to a Permanent, but not to a Temporary, Disability," *Health Psychology* 28, no. 6 (2009): 787–91.

22 Christopher K. Hsee and Robert P. Abelson, "Velocity Relation: Satisfaction as a Function of the First Derivative of Outcome Over Time," *Journal of Personality and Social Psychology* 60 (1991): 341–47.

23 B. Fredrickson and D. Kahneman, "Duration Neglect in Retrospective Evaluations of Affective Episodes," *Journal of Personality and Social Psychology* 65, no. 1 (1993): 45–55.

24 Simona Botti and Ann L. McGill, "When Choosing Is Not Deciding: The Effect of Perceived Responsibility on Satisfaction," *Journal of Consumer Research* 33 (2006): 211–19.

25 S.S. Iyengar and M. Lepper, "When Choice is Demotivating: Can One Desire Too Much of a Good Thing?" *Journal of Personality and Social Psychology* 76 (2000): 995–1006.

26 Christopher K. Hsee and France Leclerc, "Will Products Look More Attractive when Evaluated Jointly or when Evaluated Separately?" *Journal of Consumer Research* 25 (1998): 175–86.

27 G. Loewenstein, "Anticipation and the Valuation of Delayed Consumption," *The Economic Journal* 97 (1987): 668–84.

28 T.D. Wilson, T. Wheatley, J. Meyers, D.T. Gilbert, and D. Axsom, "Focalism: A Source of Durability Bias in Affective Forecasting," *Journal of Personality and Social Psychology* 78 (2000): 821–36.

29 Christopher K. Hsee and Jiao Zhang, "Distinction Bias: Misprediction and Mischoice due to Joint Evaluation," *Journal of Personality and Social Psychology* 86 (2004): 680–95.

30 D. Kahneman and J. Snell, "Predicting a Changing Taste: Do People Know What They Will Like?" *Journal of Behavioral Decision Making* 5 (1992): 187–200.

31 Nathan Novemsky and Rebecca K. Ratner, "The Time Course and Impact of Consumers' Erroneous Beliefs about Hedonic Contrast Effects," *Journal of Consumer Research* 29 (2003): 507–16.

32 T. Meyvis and L. Nelson, "Contrast Against the Future: The Unexpected Effect of Expectation," *Advances in Consumer Research* 37 (2009): n.p.

33 G. Loewenstein, T. O'Donoghue, and M. Rabin, "Projection Bias in Predicting Future Utility," *Quarterly Journal of Economics* 118 (2003): 1209–48.

34 R.E. Nisbett and D.E. Kanouse, "Obesity, Hunger, and Supermarket Shopping Behavior," *Journal of Personality and Social Psychology* 12 (1969): 289–94.

35 D.T. Gilbert, M.J. Gill, and T.D. Wilson, "The Future is Now: Temporal Correction in Affective Forecasting," *Organizational Behavior and Human Decision Processes* 88 (2002): 430–44.

36 D. Read and B. van Leeuwen, "Predicting Hunger: The Effects of Appetite and Delay on Choice," *Organizational Behavior and Human Decision Processes* 76 (1998): 189–205.

37 D. Ariely and J. Levav, "Sequential Choice in Group Settings: Taking the Road Less Traveled and Less Enjoyed," *Journal of Consumer Research* 27 (2000): 279–90.

38 H.R. Arkes and C. Blumer, "The Psychology of Sunk Cost," *Organizational Behavior and Human Decision Processes*, 35 (1985): 124–40.

39 Claire I. Tsai and Manoj Thomas, "When Does Feeling of Fluency Matter? How Abstract and Concrete Thinking Influence Fluency Effects," *Psychological Science* 22, no. 3 (2011): 348–54.

40 Christopher K. Hsee, J. Zhang, F. Yu, and Y. Xi, "Lay Rationalism and Inconsistency between Predicted Experience and Decision," *Journal of Behavioral Decision Making* 16 (2003): 257–72.

41 Claire I. Tsai and Christopher K. Hsee, "A Behavioral Account of Compensation Awarding Decisions," *Journal of Behavioral Decision Making* 22, no. 2 (2009): 138–52.

42 Jaewoo Joo and Claire I. Tsai, "Asking About and Predicting Consumer Preference: Implications for New Product Development," working paper, University of Toronto, 2012.

43 R. Kivetz and I. Simonson, "Self-Control for the Righteous: Towards a Theory of Pre-commitment to Indulgence," *Journal of Consumer Research* 29 (2002): 199–217.

44 C.K. Hsee, F. Yu, J. Zhang, and Y. Zhang, "Medium Maximization," *Journal of Consumer Research* 30 (2003): 1–14.

45 Arjun Chadhuri and Morris B. Holbrook, "The Chain of Effects from Brand Trust and Brand Affect to Brand Performance: The Role of Brand Loyalty," *Journal of Marketing* 65, no. 2 (2001): 81–93.

7 Marketing Management When Facing Forward-Looking Consumers

ANDREW T. CHING

Introduction

As information technology improves rapidly and becomes more accessible, it becomes much easier for consumers to gather product information and spend more time thinking about how to get the most out of their budget constraints. This means that consumers are getting "smarter" and more forward-looking, as well as acting more strategically. Recent academic research has substantially improved our understanding of how forward-looking consumers make decisions. In this chapter, I will discuss some of the research in this area and the challenges a manager faces when customers are forward-looking and strategic. What exactly do I mean by "forward-looking"? Let me use some examples to illustrate this. Whenever Mrs Prescott goes grocery shopping, she needs to decide what to buy. When she sees that her favourite brand of toilet paper is on sale, she may decide to stock up and buy several packs, even though she knows her family cannot use all of them within one or two weeks. She buys more than her current needs because she anticipates that such a good price will not be available until at least a few weeks later. By stockpiling while the price is "good," she can save quite a bit.[1] Here is another example. A diligent college student needs to buy a textbook for a marketing management course he has just registered for. His professor assigns a textbook that costs $200! This student wonders whether it is worth spending his parents' money on this brand new textbook or if he should get a used copy to save $50. While making this decision, he goes to the bookstore, finds a copy, opens the cover, and checks for the current edition's release date. Why does he do this? He is trying to figure out how likely it is for him to sell the textbook after the semester is over. He knows that textbooks typically have a new edition every three to four years. Once a new edition is released, the previous edition is worth almost nothing on the resale market. If the current edition was released less than two years ago, it is fairly safe to assume that he can sell it and get at least $80 back. This means the new book will likely cost him a net price of $120. But if the current edition was released more than three years ago, his chance of selling it will be much lower. Well, it turns out that the textbook is a new edition released just last year. Given that he prefers to use a brand new book, he decides to purchase the new copy. This scenario suggests that a forward-looking student takes the future resale opportunity into account when determining his willingness to pay for a brand new item. These two examples illustrate that grocery stores may need to think about how to run price promotions carefully and durable goods producers may need to reconsider how often they should release a new edition when facing consumers who are forward-looking. In this chapter, I will discuss several examples and use them to show the importance of measuring the degree to which consumers are strategic, as well as what quantitative marketing and economics research can offer to help managers make marketing decisions.

The Smart Grocery Shopper Example

Let me elaborate on the smart grocery shopper example. If all shoppers behave like Mrs Prescott, it may not be wise for grocery stores or supermarkets to run temporary price promotions – they will not be able to sell items at regular prices! Apparently, not all shoppers are so strategic. Some of them are impatient and some of them may simply follow some rules of thumb. Therefore, temporary and random price cuts can serve as a useful way to carry out price customization or price discrimination. Consumers who are impatient or have high opportunity costs of doing mental calculations (and hence behave as if they are myopic when buying small-budget items) may not even pay attention to whether prices are at the regular level or not. These are consumers who will buy products whenever based on need. They may not have much incentive to stockpile and may find it troublesome to keep track of their inventory. This type of consumer is likely to buy products at the regular price level. But consumers who are forward-looking appear to be more price-sensitive. Economic theory tells us that if a firm can practice perfect price discrimination (or first-degree price discrimination), it can extract all possible consumer surplus from consumers. But the truth is that this is usually very difficult to do because it requires the firm to know not only the distribution of consumer demand, but also which demand curve is associated with a particular consumer. When a firm has only some ideas about the distribution of consumer demand and cannot tell the identity of consumers, the best it can do is use second-degree price discrimination. This practice is usually done by offering products in different package sizes and charging different prices per unit. The main idea is that we want consumers to self-select and sort themselves according to their preferences. For instance, we would like to have price-insensitive consumers (perhaps a family with two incomes and no children) to buy a small package at a higher per-unit price, and price-sensitive consumers (perhaps a family with one income and four children) to buy the large package at a lower per-unit price. A lesser known fact is that random temporary price promotions can also be used as a way of implementing the second-degree price discrimination.[2] Price-sensitive consumers usually behave more strategically and choose to wait for price promotions in order to stockpile. But price-insensitive consumers are more likely to pay the regular price. Using this strategy, a firm could sort consumers according to their preferences and charge price-sensitive consumers a lower price.

It is important to note that the second-degree price discrimination is often welfare-enhancing for both firms and consumers (yes, a win-win outcome!). If a firm can only set one price for all consumers, the price may be so high that some of the price-sensitive consumers will decide not to buy the product and hence will not be able to enjoy the potential consumer surplus associated with consumption. The tricky issue is how often managers should run a promotion and how deep the discount should be. This would depend on the distribution of consumers in terms of how forward-looking they are. This is where quantitative marketing research can help. I will return to this point later.

New and Used Goods Example

The presence of the used-goods market often has important implications for a consumer's willingness to pay for new goods. The housing market is a good example. When the condo market is booming, we see that the demand for pre-construction condos rises significantly. Many buyers have already owned a house. They jump into the pre-construction condo market because they expect to make profits by selling their condos once the whole building is finished. For them, this is an investment opportunity because they believe that the net price they are paying is negative!

The housing market example clearly illustrates that expectations regarding resale value help to boost demand for the new product market. But another factor we need to pay attention to is the competition between new and used goods. In many situations, they are highly substitutable. This is particularly true of products with information content, such as textbooks, video games, music CDs, and so on. If you look at a new and used video game with the same title, they are identical in every observable attribute. As long as the disc is not damaged, the only major difference may be the psychological benefit of having a brand new copy.

In these markets, manufacturers of new goods are often afraid that competition from the used-goods market will force them to set a lower price in order to compete. This is why we observe that original manufacturers attempt to "kill off" the used-goods market. Examples include introducing new editions of a textbook with a content update of less than 5 per cent, video game manufacturers filing lawsuits against the used-goods retailers,[3] and so forth. Such a belief seems to rely on the assumption that consumers are myopic and do not take the resale value into account when they decide if they should buy a new product.

However, a recent study by Chevalier and Goolsbee has challenged this traditional view.[4] Their study investigated the textbook market and found strong evidence that most college students do take the resale value of textbooks into account. They also found that the average length of the revision cycle varies across disciplines. Right before a new edition is released, the resale value of the textbook drops dramatically. This variation of the data allowed them to test if consumers are forward-looking by checking the following testable implication: *If consumers are forward-looking, their elasticity of demand for the new book should increase when the current edition has been out for a few years; moreover, their elasticity of demand for the new book should be the lowest when a new edition is just out.* Using a large data set from a college bookstore and a data set from Amazon Marketplace, they indeed found strong evidence that consumers' behaviour is consistent with this hypothesis. This suggests that the conventional wisdom of attempting to "kill off" the used-goods market may be questionable.

The "textbook" example is particularly simple. Note that consumers (i.e., students) do not need to worry about when to buy the durable-goods item and when to sell it. This is because instructors typically decide which textbook to use, and students seldom choose a course based on the price of the assigned textbook. Moreover, students usually sell their textbooks the following year. But in general, the timing of buying and selling a durable-goods item is a choice made by consumers. So the general problem is actually much harder than what Chevalier and Goolsbee analysed. Because of the difficulty of the problem, there are only a few studies that focus on the interaction between the new and used-goods markets. Another reason why previous research has hardly studied this problem is because for traditional durable goods (e.g., cars), used goods suffer from physical depreciation and asymmetric information problems (the so-called market for lemons).[5] These two problems have limited the impact of used goods on the demand for new goods. But I believe that we will not be able to avoid studying the role of the secondary market anymore. The advance of digital technology has made physical depreciation of many products (e.g., books, video games, music CDs, DVD movies, etc.) irrelevant; this will likely increase the role of the secondary/used-goods market because these goods look almost identical to new goods. This is recognized by Ishihara,[6] who argues that in order to analyse the demand for these types of products, it is important to take three fundamental characteristics into account. First, although these types of products seldom depreciate physically, their *consumption values to owners* could decline quickly due to satiation. As a result, it is not uncommon for cheaper used products to become available shortly after a new product's release date. Second, *the expected consumption value to potential buyers* may also decline over time because they may have a preference for how "fresh" a new product is. Third, even if a used-goods item is physically the same as its new counterpart, *the availability of used goods* could be another important factor that affects the choice between new and used goods. Ishihara argues that these three characteristics play crucial roles in determining the substitutability between new and used goods, which in turn has important implications for the marketing strategies of the players for these types of products – for example, how manufacturers of new goods should price their products over time, whether they should attempt to kill off the used-goods market, how the used-goods retailers should set their prices for selling and buying used goods, and so on.

To address this problem, Ishihara developed a new empirical demand model wherein consumers are forward-looking and form expectations about the future. More precisely, when a potential buyer is deciding whether to buy a new or used video game in the current period or to wait instead, he/she needs to consider (1) how quickly his/her expected consumption value decreases over time; (2) the availability of used games today and in the future; (3) the evolution of the prices of new and used goods; and (4) how much he/she can realize if he/she sells the item to the used market in the future. The final point actually requires the potential buyer to consider the owner's problem: once a consumer owns the game, he/she needs to consider the optimal time for selling it. This would require the owner to consider how quickly he/she will become satiated with the video game and the evolution of its resale value (i.e., how much an owner will get when he/she sells the product to used-goods retailers). This model highlights why mangers should care about consumers' forward-looking behaviour. Moreover, it sheds new light on how we should design marketing strategies for durable products that do not exhibit physical depreciation.

Consumer Learning and Uncertainty about the New Product

When a new goods item is introduced, it often takes a while before it can penetrate the market. One obvious reason is that consumers are uncertain about the quality of these products. Due to their risk-averse behaviour, they may be reluctant to try a new product. Giving away free samples is one way that manufacturers get consumers to experiment with their new products. But how many free samples should we give away and who should we give them to? The answer to this question again depends on the extent to which consumers think about the value of experimentation. If consumers are sufficiently forward-looking, they actually have incentives to experiment with a new product themselves. The idea is that if the product turns out to be of a high quality, they will keep buying it in the future and enjoy higher utility. Even if the product is not so great, they will only suffer once as they can choose not to buy it again. Given that consumers have incentives to experiment themselves, is it still necessary for retailers or manufacturers to run special promotions to encourage consumers to try their new products? This depends on how many consumers have strong incentives to self-experiment. In other words, it depends on how consumers value the future pay-offs of their current choices.

This has several important implications for the marketing mix. If most consumers are reluctant to experiment, we may want to design our advertising in a way that is more informative about the features of products. On the other hand, if we know most consumers are going to experiment regardless, we can focus on designing our ads so that they mainly build brand image. This has further implications for the true costs of introducing a new product. If consumers do not have incentives to self-experiment, it means that in addition to the fixed costs of developing a product, we also need to factor samples into the size of the marketing budget in order to have consumers adopt this product quickly.

Adoption Costs of New Technology in the Consumer Life Cycle

Even when uncertainty about the benefits of a new product or technology is not an issue, sometimes we still observe that certain segments of consumers are reluctant to adopt new products. This is particularly true of the elderly. It is important for both public policymakers and managers to understand what causes this stylized fact. Getting this segment of consumers to adopt a new product could significantly change the implications on total consumer welfare and firms' profits. This is because the elderly population is increasing in both relative and absolute terms – the number of Americans aged 65 and over is expected to increase from 35 million in 2000 to over 70 million by 2030.[7] Moreover, many elderly are also financially well off because of their lifetime-accumulated savings.

According to explanations proposed by most existing researchers, elderly individuals are slow learners due to their deteriorating cognitive abilities. In economics, this explanation can essentially be generalized to adoption costs or switching costs. Yang and I have proposed an alternative explanation that is orthogonal to this traditional explanation.[8] We argued that one can explain elderly behaviour based on a story about adoption benefits. The key idea is that elderly individuals have a shorter lifespan. Therefore, even if we assume that the per-period benefits of a new technology are the same across age groups, the elderly would have a lower total of expected discounted benefits. As a result, the incentive to adopt a new technology is smaller for the elderly.

To our knowledge, we have made the first attempt to incorporate the total discounted lifetime benefits of adopting a new technology in an empirical behavioural model. Our empirical framework can be applied to any new technology's adoption environments, such as smartphones, tablet PCs, and so forth. Yang and I applied our model to the adoption of ATM cards using a panel survey data set collected by the Bank of

Italy during the 1990s. The advantage of this data set is that it is publicly available and hence other researchers can try to replicate our results. At first, it may seem difficult to disentangle the relative importance of adoption benefits versus costs. Our hypothesis implies that the total expected discounted benefits of adopting new technology decreases with age. Traditional hypotheses imply that adoption costs increase with age. Both approaches can explain why consumers become reluctant to adopt as they become older. Indeed, if all we observe are consumer adoption decisions at different ages, it would not be possible to separately measure the relationship between costs and age versus that between benefits and age. To uncover the relationship between adoption costs and age in addition to adoption decisions, we need to observe the variation in adoption benefits independent of adoption costs. The Bank of Italy's data give us this type of variation. Note that one benefit of adopting ATM cards is that consumers can put more savings into their bank accounts to earn interest, depending on interest rates and the amount of cash required for financing consumption.

Our results can be summarized as follows: unlike previous literature, which found that adoption costs are higher for the elderly, we found that average adoption costs remained fairly stable across age groups in this particular application. Our parameter estimates implied that the adoption cost for ATM cards ranged from U.S.$137 to U.S.$202 (2002 base); however, previous parameter estimates implied that the upper bound of the adoption cost was only U.S.$28 (2002 base),[9] which would appear to be too low if one wanted to use it to explain the slow adoption behaviour of the elderly. Why was our estimated adoption cost much higher? This was because we explicitly took the total expected lifetime benefits of adopting ATM cards into account. Previous work simply incorporated the benefits of adopting in the current period. Getting a more precise estimate of adoption costs is important for marketing management. For instance, this would allow us to forecast the impact of a sign-up bonus on adoption rates. Our findings suggested that explicitly incorporating consumers' forward-looking behaviour into marketing research can bring a very substantial return.

Rewards Program Example

A rewards program is a frequently used marketing tool in today's world. The effectiveness of rewards programs also depends on how forward-looking consumers are. Let's consider a simple example. A consumer collects a stamp each time he/she visits a chain coffee shop. Once he/she fills up the stamp card, he/she gets a free gift and then starts with a new, blank stamp card. For the sake of argument, let's assume that this free gift is a lottery ticket. Consumers do not know exactly what they will get, but they have a good idea about the list of gifts available and the odds of getting any one of them. This problem is inherently dynamic. If a consumer is forward-looking and values the lottery ticket, he/she cares about the number of stamps he/she has collected. The closer he/she is to completing the stamp card, the more eager he/she is to visit the coffee shop. But if he/she is entirely myopic, the number of stamps should not affect his/her decision about which coffee shop to visit. In fact, in this set-up, it can be shown that consumer behaviour with respect to which coffee shop to visit varies systematically with consumer time preference.[10] This implies that if we observe consumer choice data, which is the database that retailers maintain, it is possible to learn how individual consumers make inter-temporal trade-offs. This is important because when retailers want to change the structure of the rewards program, they need to forecast revenue under the new program. Similar to the applications discussed above, quantifying the way individual consumers evaluate future pay-offs is the key to making accurate forecasts.

For more discussion about rewards programs, readers can refer to chapter 11 by Mengze Shi. This example is also related to the "virtual progress" theory discussed in chapter 12 by Dilip Soman.

How Can Quantitative Research Help Marketing Management?

By now, I hope that the examples presented above have demonstrated the importance of understanding consumers' forward-looking behaviour. But for managers, simply understanding theory is not enough. In order to optimally set the marketing mix, we need to know the distribution of time preferences in the population. How do we measure this distribution? Or, more generally, can we measure the way consumers think about the expected future pay-offs associated with the choices they make today? Quantitative research in economics and marketing has made two headways in attacking this problem. The first approach that I would like to discuss is by Geweke and Keane.[11] They proposed using a flexible functional form to approximate the expected future pay-offs associated with each alternative that consumers choose. In order to apply this approach, the dynamic problems faced by consumers need to have some factors that affect their expected future pay-offs, but not their current pay-offs.[12] This condition is called "exclusion restriction" in the literature. In the new and used goods example, "the number of years that the current edition of a textbook has been out" satisfies this condition because it does not affect the student's utility of using the book in the current semester, and yet it affects the expected return of selling the book in the future. In the rewards program example, "the number of stamps that a consumer currently has" also satisfies this condition because it does not affect a consumer's current utility of visiting a coffee shop, but it affects his expected return in the future. Here is the logic for why the exclusion restriction helps estimate the extent to which consumers are forward-looking. Suppose consumers are totally myopic. In this case, all they care about are current pay-offs. Even if we observe a lot of variation in the factors that satisfy the exclusion restriction, consumers' choice behaviour should not correlate with them. So the estimated coefficients in expected future pay-offs should all be zeros. On the other hand, if consumers are forward-looking, then consumer choice should vary systematically with the values of the factors that affect future pay-offs. So in principle, we should be able to infer how consumers form expectations about future pay-offs. This approach is simple to use, but it comes with a cost. The number of parameters required to form a flexible function increases exponentially with the complexity of the problem (roughly speaking, complexity can be measured by the number of factors a dynamic problem has). This implies that the number of observations required to get "precise" inferences also increases with the complexity of the problem. With this limitation in mind, it is important to point out that there is still much we can learn from this method.

For instance, one can apply this method to investigate what decision rules consumers use to solve a dynamic problem that requires them to consider future pay-offs. I should mention that it is quite common for academic economists and marketing scientists to assume that consumers solve dynamic choice problems using dynamic programming. One of the reasons is that dynamic programming is a well-understood mathematical technique with many useful tools available for obtaining solutions (including numerical solutions). Academic researchers hope that consumers with real-life experiences will behave in a way that is relatively close to the solution of dynamic programming. It does not mean that we truly believe that consumers can solve a difficult dynamic programming problem. However, as Manski and Keane have forcefully argued, with only choice data available, we cannot infer consumer preferences if we do not make more assumptions about the functional form of the utility function, and about the way consumers think about their objectives and form expectations about future outcomes conditional on their choices.[13,14]

Therefore, an important research question is whether the solution to dynamic programming serves as a good proxy for actual decision rules adopted by consumers.[15] Using Geweke and Keane's approach, Houser, Keane, and McCabe conducted their investigation in an experimental setting, which allowed them to control for consumers' objectives, constraints, and the exact structure of the dynamic problem they were facing. As a result, they were able to learn how consumers formed expectations about future pay-offs. Their methodology allowed them to draw inferences about the number of consumer types and the nature of the decision rules used by each type of consumer when they needed to solve a decision problem that involved future pay-offs. The game they set up was challenging – the optimal solution could only be obtained by using dynamic programming. They found that there were three types of consumers, and that about one-third of the subjects actually used a decision rule close to the one generated by dynamic programming. The other two types did substantially worse than the optimal solution. But their decision rules still showed that they understand the importance of "investment" – in other words, they are willing to choose an option that gives them low current pay-offs, but can raise expected future pay-offs. Remember that I keep emphasizing the importance of measuring consumer preferences for expected future pay-offs in the examples above. The research method proposed by Geweke and Keane serves as a fruitful way to address this issue.

This approach can also be applied to choice data generated from non-experimental/real-life settings. In another recent study, Erdem, Keane, and I extended this idea to test whether consumers have incentives to experiment when they face uncertainty about the brands they need to choose.[16] We applied our framework to scanner panel data in the diaper category collected by a marketing research company called AC Nielsen. We selected households where there were likely to be new parents who could hence be uncertain about the quality of diapers across different brands. Our results suggested that consumers do have incentives to experiment with new products. According to the commonly used statistical model selection criteria, we found that the data are in favour of the hypothesis that consumers are forward-looking instead of myopic.

The second approach that I would like to discuss was proposed by Manski, who argued that in addition to observed choice data, one can add self-reported preference data by conducting a survey and using carefully phrased questions to solicit consumers' expectations about the future. This is a new research agenda and the literature that adopts this approach has been growing rapidly. In the context of studying forward-looking behaviour, the survey can be designed to solicit consumer expectations about future events, such as expected future prices,[17] expected amounts of future advertising,[18] and so on. This approach has been shown to be very useful in relaxing strong assumptions made in studies that only used observed consumer choice data.

Let me point out that the quantitative marketing and economics literature usually assumes that consumers are either forward-looking or myopic. When researchers assume consumers are forward-looking, they typically assume that consumers are "rational" and hence will discount future pay-offs according to interest rates. Suppose the annual interest rate is 5 per cent. Receiving $100 a year later is roughly equivalent to receiving about $95 today, because if I put $95 in a savings account, it will become roughly $100 with interest one year later. But does every consumer necessarily think this way? Maybe not. In general, choice data alone do not allow us to estimate the discount factor. Consumer survey data can also help here. One can also design survey questions to directly elicit consumer time preferences. For instance, the "Survey of Income and Wealth" conducted by the Bank of Italy used the following question to solicit the discount factor for each respondent:

Imagine you won the equivalent of your household's net annual income. The sum will be paid to you in a year's time. However, if you give up part of the sum, you can have the rest immediately. To get the money right away, would you give up…?

(a) I'd wait a year to collect the whole amount

(b) 2 per cent of this sum

(c) 3 per cent of this sum

(d) 5 per cent of this sum

(e) 10 per cent of this sum

(f) 20 per cent of this sum[20]

Consumers' answers to this question show that they are quite heterogeneous in discounting the future. For instance, 25 per cent of the respondents chose option a and 32 per cent chose option d. Yang and I incorporated this information when estimating our dynamic model.[8] The information garnered from this survey has certainly helped us measure adoption benefits (and hence adoption costs) more precisely in our study.

Conclusion

I would like to conclude by saying that frontier quantitative marketing and economics research has the potential to make a real difference in marketing management. Academic research has already developed models to capture the examples that I discussed in this chapter, and there are other applications that I did not cover here. Although estimating these types of dynamic models with forward-looking consumers is still computationally demanding, with the improvement of computer technology and new estimation methods, the adoption hurdle is not as high as one might perceive. Nowadays, one can purchase a very powerful workstation by spending less than $3,000. It is also possible to link several workstations together to build a cluster that will work like a supercomputer. Moreover, companies have collected very rich consumer-level databases from their own loyalty programs and social networks. The advanced research techniques described here can be applied to these data, allowing us to better understand consumers' forward-looking behaviour and hence improve marketing management. Qualitative research in marketing will continue to give new insights into marketing management. But if companies also adopt advanced quantitative research as one of their marketing management tools, I believe that they can capitalize on these insights much further.

This chapter focused on discussing recent research that improves our understanding of consumers' forward-looking behaviour. I also briefly discussed how managers could take advantage of this information, for example, by practising price customization (or price discrimination). But I have not discussed how managers should set the marketing mix in a forward-looking manner. In two studies, I developed a dynamic model to explain how forward-looking managers should determine price levels over time when they introduce a new product. The model takes into account both consumer uncertainty about product quality as well as the competitive environment.[19] Readers who are interested in learning more about forward-looking marketing management can also refer to chapter 8 by Ron Borkovsky. In that chapter, Borkovsky uses examples of version release, new product development, advertising, and repositioning to explain how managers should anticipate reactions from rivals and take their future possible actions into account when practising marketing management.

A Prescription for Dealing with the Forward-Looking Customer

With better access to information and decision-making aids, many customers are getting smarter and look forward before they make decisions. To better and more profitably serve these customers, marketers should:

- IDENTIFY the differences in behaviour of myopic and forward-looking customers in response to marketing actions.
- ESTIMATE the composition of the marketplace using recently developed, advanced research techniques.
- COLLECT rich customer-level data from loyalty programs or social networks to feed these advanced research techniques.

REFERENCES

1 Tülin Erdem, Susumu Imai, and Michael P. Keane, "Brand and Quantity Choice Dynamics under Price Uncertainty," *Quantitative Marketing and Economics* 1, no. 1 (2003): 5–64.
2 Martin Pesendorfer, "Retail Sales: A Study of Pricing Behavior in Supermarkets," *Journal of Business* 75, no. 1 (2002): 33–66.
3 Taro Hirayama, "A Sequel to the Used Game Lawsuit," *Research Center for the Legal System of Intellectual Property*, accessed 13 May 2012 from http://www.21coe-win-cls.org/rclip/activity/e_index29.html.
4 Judith Chevalier and Austan Goolsbee, "Are Durable Goods Consumers Forward-Looking? Evidence from College Textbooks," *Quarterly Journal of Economics* 124, no. 4 (2009): 1853–84.
5 George A. Akerlof, "The Market for 'Lemons': Quality Uncertainty and the Market Mechanism," *Quarterly Journal of Economics* 84, no. 3 (1970): 488–500.
6 Masakazu Ishihara, "Dynamic Demand for New and Used Durable Goods Without Physical Depreciation" (PhD diss., Rotman School of Management, University of Toronto, 2011).
7 Department of Health and Human Services, "A Profile of Older Americans: 2010," accessed 13 May 2012 from http://www.mowaa.org/document.doc?id=410.

8 Botao Yang and Andrew T. Ching, "Dynamics of Consumer Adoption of Financial Innovation: The Case of ATM Cards," working paper, Rotman School of Management, University of Toronto, 2010. Available at http://ssrn.com/abstract=1434722.

9 Orazio R. Attanasio, Luigi Guiso, and Tullio Jappelli, "The Demand for Money, Financial Innovation, and the Welfare Cost of Inflation: An Analysis with Households' Data," *Journal of Political Economy* 110, no. 2 (2002): n.p.

10 Andrew T. Ching and Masakazu Ishihara, "Identification of a Dynamic Model of Rewards Program," working paper, Rotman School of Management, University of Toronto, 2012.

11 John F. Geweke and Michael P. Keane, "Bayesian Inference for Dynamic Discrete Choice Models without the Need for Dynamic Programming," in Robert Mariano, Til Schuermann, and Melvyn Weeks, eds., *Simulation-Based Inference and Econometrics: Methods and Applications* (Cambridge: Cambridge University Press, 2000), 100–31.

12 An alternative condition is that researchers observe the actual pay-offs received by consumers. But in most choice problems other than those in labour economics, we usually do not observe this type of data.

13 Charles Manski, "Measuring Expectations," *Econometrica* 72, no. 5 (2004): 1329–76.

14 Michael P. Keane, "Structural vs. Atheoretic Approaches to Econometrics," *Journal of Econometrics* 156, no. 1 (2010): 3–20.

15 Daniel Houser, Michael P. Keane, and Kevin McCabe, "Behavior in a Dynamic Decision Problem: An Analysis of Experimental Evidence Using a Bayesian Type Classification Algorithm," *Econometrica* 72, no. 3 (2004): 781–822.

16 Andrew T. Ching, Tülin Erdem, and Michael P. Keane, "Learning Models: An Assessment of Progress, Challenges and New Developments," working paper, Rotman School of Management, University of Toronto, 2011.

17 Tülin Erdem, Michael P. Keane, T. Sabri Öncü, and Judi Strebel, "Learning About Computers: An Analysis of Information Search and Technology Choice," *Quantitative Marketing and Economics* 3, no. 3 (2005): 207–46.

18 Tat Y. Chan, Barton H. Hamilton, and Christopher Makler, "Using Expectations Data to Infer Managerial Objectives and Choices," working paper, Washington University, St. Louis, 2010.

19 Andrew T. Ching, "A Dynamic Oligopoly Structural Model for the Prescription Drug Market after Patent Expiration," *International Economic Review* 51, no. 4 (2010): 1175–207; Andrew T. Ching, "Consumer Learning and Heterogeneity: Dynamics of Demand for Prescription Drugs after Patent

Expiration," *International Journal of Industrial Organization* 28, no. 6 (2010): 619–38.

20 "Survey of Italian Households' Income and Wealth 2004," *Bank of Italy*, 2004, accessed 13 May 2012 from http://www.bancaditalia.it/statistiche/indcamp/bilfait/docum/ind04/Quest_ing2004.pdf.

8 Strategic Forward-Looking Marketing Management

RON N. BORKOVSKY

The marketing management landscape has changed dramatically in recent years. There has been a drastic increase in the availability of data on consumers *and* competitors, and a reduction in the costs of storing such data. Moreover, increased computing power and enhanced marketing analytics software systems are making it possible for marketers to truly exploit the wealth of data that is available. Ultimately, this makes it possible for marketers to develop much more sophisticated data-intensive marketing management programs and to execute them more effectively. One area that stands to benefit greatly from this trend is *strategic forward-looking marketing management*.

Today, many of the industries that are of the greatest importance to marketing managers are characterized by oligopolistic competition – that is, competition amongst relatively few firms that collectively dominate a market. This is true of many segments of consumer packaged goods, electronics, pharmaceutical, automotive, and retail industries, among others. In such industries, marketing managers behave *strategically* – taking rival firms' anticipated responses into consideration when devising marketing strategy. For example, a marketing manager considering an increase in advertising spending will take into consideration how its rivals would respond to such a change in order to forecast the effectiveness of the increased spending. Game theory provides us with tools that are ideal for studying such interdependence and marketing scholars have used these tools to great effect over recent decades in studying product positioning, pricing, retailing, channel management, advertising, entry, and product introductions, among other topics.[1] Furthermore, in recent years, the marketing literature has also begun to account for the fact that marketing managers must often make decisions in a *forward-looking* manner – that is, taking into consideration the implications of those decisions not only for the present but also for the future. Below, I discuss several circumstances under which it is important to model marketing managers as being forward-looking as opposed to myopic.

The importance of these two facets of marketing management has recently spawned a literature on strategic forward-looking marketing management. In this chapter, I discuss strategic forward-looking marketing management and its managerial implications. I present some illustrative examples and discuss several useful managerial insights that this literature has yielded. Finally, I explain how the insights and the methodological toolbox provided by this literature can help marketing managers improve the ways in which they make strategic forward-looking marketing management decisions. First, they can help marketing managers understand the circumstances under which it is particularly important to be forward-looking. Second, even if a manager is fully aware of the extent to which he/she must be forward-looking, making forward-looking marketing management decisions optimally – especially in the face of oligopolistic competition – is extremely difficult. For example, even if a marketing manager deciding on a schedule of advertising has determined that a pulsing strategy is optimal, one critical question still remains: exactly how often and with what intensity should the firm pulse? The insights and tools described in this chapter can help managers make exactly these types of decisions. (The particular problem of devising an optimal advertising pulsing strategy is discussed further below.) Finally, at the end of this chapter, I provide suggestions as to how marketing scholars should strive to make the insights and tools that this literature has yielded more accessible to marketing managers.

Why Model Marketing Managers as Forward-Looking?

There are two general reasons as to why one might want to model marketing managers as being forward-looking. First, as explained in chapter 7, there is a vast marketing literature that has explored forward-looking consumer behaviour. Consider the following examples (discussed in detail in chapter 7). First, consumers take their expectations about future prices into consideration when making their buying decisions today and therefore may stockpile when prices are low.[2] Second, consumers take their expectations about future resale value into consideration when deciding whether to purchase a durable good.[3] Finally, consumers take the future benefits they expect to receive from reward programs into consideration when making consumption decisions today.[4] If consumers are forward-looking and marketing management decisions can influence consumer behaviour, it follows that the marketing manager must also be forward-looking.

Second, even when it is sensible to model consumers as being myopic, one should model marketing managers as being forward-looking if the marketing decisions that a firm makes today affect its strategic positioning in the future. There are various reasons why this would be the case. A marketing manager may learn from promotional activities undertaken today and thus be better positioned to make decisions about future promotional activities. A firm investing in research and development (R&D) in order to enhance product quality must take into consideration that these investment decisions have the potential to impact both current and future product quality.[5] A firm that is repositioning its product, brand, or pricing format must take into consideration that this will have long-term effects because the costs that must be incurred and the effects of such repositioning on reputation are often only partially reversible.[6] The same is true of a decision to release a new version of a product[7] or enter a new market. A firm in a market characterized by network effects or indirect network effects must take into consideration that marketing activities undertaken today will enhance demand directly in the present and indirectly in the future. For example, a reduction in the price of a video game console will directly enhance demand today, which will spur software developers to produce more games for the console, thus indirectly enhancing future demand.[8] Several examples of this are discussed in detail below.

Chapter 7 discusses forward-looking consumer behaviour and its implications for marketing management decision-making. This chapter builds upon chapter 7 in two ways. First, this chapter explains why and how firms need to think about the long-term effects of marketing management decisions even when consumers themselves are myopic in their decision-making. Second, this chapter explores the implications of the forward-looking nature of *both* consumer behaviour and firm behaviour for marketing management *in oligopolistic industries*.

Product Development

In this section, I explain why product development that entails repeatedly improving a particular product's quality is an inherently dynamic process. I discuss a research study that explores such product development within the context of a duopolistic industry. Finally, I discuss this study's managerial implications.

In many industries in which R&D is undertaken to enhance product quality, a firm accumulates the successes of R&D and strategically decides when to incorporate these improvements into a new version of its product. Prominent amongst the reasons for accumulating R&D successes is that incorporating these successes into a product by releasing a new version is costly. A version release (or *product upgrade*) typically entails costly marketing activities such as advertising, branding, and package design. Moreover, a version release may require changes to production facilities, recontracting with suppliers, and retraining of personnel. Thus, a firm has an incentive to defer releasing a new version of its product until the new version offers a sufficiently large improvement over the current version. Such product development occurs in many R&D-intensive consumer packaged goods categories. For example, since the 1970s, Procter & Gamble (Pampers, Luvs) and Kimberly-Clark (Huggies) have waged an intense "diaper war" by investing heavily in R&D to develop improvements in their diapers' comfort, absorbency, and containment, then bringing these improvements to market via product upgrades.[9] Both Procter & Gamble and Kimberly-Clark have developed and incorporated reusable tabs, elastic leg bands, gel technology, and breathable material, among other improvements. Other R&D-intensive consumer packaged goods categories – such as toothpaste and laundry detergent – have exhibited similar competitive dynamics. More generally, R&D-intensive consumer packaged goods categories tend to be characterized by competition of this nature in the introduction and growth stages of their product life cycles, and perhaps later. For example, even today – with the diaper category arguably being in its maturity – Procter & Gamble and Kimberly-Clark are still investing heavily in R&D to improve their diapers' fit, absorbency, durability, and odour protection.[10]

Borkovsky[7] explores such industries in an oligopolistic model that includes forward-looking firms and myopic consumers. It is essential to model firms as forward-looking because in making both R&D-investment and version release decisions, a firm must take into consideration the benefits that such decisions will yield in both the present and the future. The primary research question Borkovsky poses is: How does the intensity of price competition affect firms' product development strategies? He finds that when firms engage in aggressive price competition – for example, because the degree of horizontal differentiation between their products is relatively low – this induces the firms to also employ very aggressive product-development strategies. In particular, firms engage in pre-emption races characterized by heavy investment in R&D and very frequent version releases. However, when firms engage in less aggressive price competition, the intensity of such pre-emption races decreases significantly and firms sometimes enter *phases of accommodation*. In a phase of accommodation, the market leader releases new versions less frequently and its rival reduces its R&D-spending significantly, thus *both* firms are able to save on the high costs of product development.

Borkovsky[7] also explores the effect of an increase in the cost of releasing a new version. There are several reasons why this cost might uniformly increase or decrease in an industry. First, as explained above, to release a new version a firm must undertake costly marketing activities. Over time, the costs of these marketing activities and/or the industry norms governing the extensiveness of these activities may change. This is discussed further below. Second, as explained above, in order to create, produce, and support a new version, a firm may have to undertake a wide variety of changes relating to its production facilities, supply chain, and personnel. The costs of such changes and the extensiveness of such activities could change over time as well.

An increase in the cost of releasing a new version has two countervailing effects. First, intuitively, an increase in the cost of releasing a new version would induce a firm to release new versions less frequently simply to save on the higher cost of doing so. Second, perhaps counter-intuitively, this increase induces firms to release new versions *more* frequently for the following reason. As the cost of releasing a new version increases, a product quality lead achieved by one firm becomes more secure because it is more costly for its rival to catch up and therefore its rival is less likely to do so. As such, when neither firm has too large a lead, firms compete more intensely for the lead by engaging in more aggressive pre-emption races – investing *more* heavily in R&D and releasing new versions *more* often. As long as the cost of releasing a new version is not too high, the second effect overwhelms the first and when neither firm has too large a lead, firms do indeed release new versions more frequently despite the higher cost.

This model yields several useful managerial insights. First, suppose a potential entrant is contemplating entering a monopoly market by releasing the initial version of its product into that market. In doing so, it would transform that market from a monopoly into a duopoly. From observing the monopolistic behaviour of the incumbent firm, the potential entrant cannot infer how this incumbent firm would behave if the potential entrant did indeed enter. That is, how would the move from monopolistic to duopolistic market structure cause the incumbent firm to change its R&D investment and version-release strategies? It would be unwise of the potential entrant to assume that the incumbent firm's behaviour would not change. The insights of the model in Borkovsky[7] can allow the potential entrant to make predictions about the changes that may occur. In particular, if the degree of horizontal differentiation between the product it is considering launching and the incumbent firm's product is very low, then it can anticipate that upon entry, the firms will engage in intense pre-emption races that will ultimately yield an asymmetric industry structure. In this case, in making an entry decision, the potential entrant should take into consideration that such pre-emption races are *very* expensive. Moreover, the potential entrant should launch its product only if it is confident that it will ultimately prevail in this pre-emption race; this is quite likely to occur if its product is of higher quality than the incumbent firm's product and rather unlikely if it is not. Alternatively, if the firm is considering launching a product that is sufficiently differentiated from the incumbent firm's product, then it could predict that if it enters, the firms would engage in less aggressive pre-emption races and may enter into phases of accommodation. This would make the prospect of entry more attractive. Finally, the firm may have some control over the extent to which its product is differentiated from the incumbent firm's product. In this case, it is of course trivial to assert that greater differentiation is preferable because it weakens price competition. However, the model in Borkovsky[7] would allow a firm to predict the particular implications that this weakening of price competition would have for firms' respective R&D investment and version-release strategies.

Second, marketing managers may be able to exert some influence on the cost of releasing a new version. As explained above, many of the costs that must be incurred in order to release a new product are related to marketing activities. A marketing manager can decide how much to spend on such activities. In doing so, he/she may be able to influence the industry norm and therefore affect the cost of future releases in the industry. For example, if one firm undertakes a product launch that is much more extensive than product launches conducted in the industry in the past, then its rivals may feel that they too must undertake more extensive product launches when releasing future versions. The counterfactual exercise in Borkovsky[7] that is discussed above allows marketing managers to predict the impact of such a change and can therefore be useful in making such decisions. For example, as explained above, if neither firm has too large a lead, then such a change could induce firms to invest *more* heavily in R&D and release new versions *more* frequently. This would be costly for all firms in the industry and a firm may therefore want to avoid taking such action. If, however, a firm has a lead over its rivals, then increasing the cost of releasing a new version for all firms in the industry by affecting the industry norm would serve to secure the firm's lead. As explained above, since this would make it more costly for rival firms to catch up to the leader, they would be less likely to do so. Under such circumstances a leader may indeed want to increase the cost of releasing a new version.

Finally, consider that Borkovsky[7] devises and solves a theoretical model. While the insights that the model yields can be useful to managers, as explained above, the model also provides a framework for studying this problem empirically. Using data on prices, sales, and product qualities and characteristics for a particular market, one could estimate a demand system. One could then use the model in Borkovsky[7] to compute the optimal R&D investment and version release strategies for that market. In this respect, such a model can help marketing managers solve the very complicated problem of deciding *exactly* how much to spend on R&D and *exactly* when to release new versions. In the next section of this chapter, I discuss a research study that takes this very approach in solving an advertising scheduling problem. In the final section of this chapter, I discuss the challenges that scholars must overcome in order to make these tools accessible to marketing managers.

Advertising

This section of the chapter explains why firms must be forward-looking in making advertising decisions. Furthermore, it presents an example that illustrates exactly how the tools found in the literature on strategic forward-looking marketing management can help a marketing manager devise an optimal advertising schedule.

Several studies have established that advertising has carry-over effects – in other words, that advertising today affects a consumer's propensity to buy a product not only in the present but also in the future.[11]

It follows that firms must be forward-looking in making advertising decisions. Taking this into consideration, Dubé, Hitsch, and Manchanda[12] studied the problem of optimally scheduling advertising over time. In particular, they explored whether it is optimal to employ the commonly observed strategy of "pulsing," which entails concentrating advertising in some periods while not advertising at all in others.[13] They explained that firms have the incentive to pulse if there is a threshold below which advertising has no impact on consumers *and* if the extent of carry-over is sufficiently high. Using data from the "frozen entrée" product category, they estimated a demand system that allowed them to test whether such a threshold exists and whether advertising has carry-over effects. They found strong evidence for both. To explore the implications of this, they devised and solved a dynamic model of advertising competition in which firms faced the estimated demand system. They found that it is indeed optimal to pulse and that optimally scheduling advertising would entail advertising for one to two weeks and then ceasing to advertise for one to three weeks. Comparing the equilibrium advertising schedules that they compute to the advertising schedules observed in the data, they concluded that firms should advertise more frequently and would moderately increase their profits by doing so.

Repositioning

Marketing managers face a wide variety of repositioning decisions regarding particular products, brands, distribution strategies, and pricing strategies, among other elements of the marketing mix. When making such decisions, marketing managers must take into consideration that these strategies have long-term effects because the associated costs and the effects on reputation are often only partially reversible.[14] Consider the following examples.

I first present an example in which it appears that a firm was not sufficiently forward-looking in making a critical repositioning decision and irreparably damaged its reputation as a result. While Krispy Kreme Doughnuts had always engaged in some off-premises sales, it had built its reputation and strong brand on the back of the hot, freshly baked doughnuts that are sold in its factory stores. However, in 2000, Krispy Kreme famously repositioned its distribution strategy by initiating a significant increase in its off-premises sales.[15] At this time, Krispy Kreme increased its sales to supermarkets and grocery stores and ultimately began to sell its products to a wide variety of third-party retailers such as gas stations and to mass merchants such as Target and Walmart.[16] The goal was to utilize the excess production capacity of existing stores in order to increase sales, market penetration, brand awareness, and customer convenience.[17] It was estimated that by 2005, off-premises sales constituted roughly half of Krispy Kreme's total sales.[18] However, this repositioning spurred several problems. First, it hurt Krispy Kreme's reputation for serving fresh, high-quality products. Second, the extensive off-premises sales made Krispy Kreme seem ubiquitous, which caused its mystique to dissipate.[19] Third, the wide availability of Krispy Kreme reduced store traffic; this was particularly unfortunate given the higher margins associated with on-premises sales.[20] In retrospect, Krispy Kreme may not have been sufficiently forward-looking in deciding to change its distribution strategy. While this change did allow it to utilize excess production capacity and increase sales in the short run, it ultimately had a detrimental impact on Krispy Kreme's brand equity and its in-store sales. This is regarded as having played a key role in Krispy Kreme's subsequent decline.

In the above example, Krispy Kreme unintentionally damaged its reputation in repositioning its distribution strategy. Next, I discuss an example in which a firm in the video game console market, Nintendo, made a repositioning decision that *intentionally* damaged its reputation amongst consumers in its previous target market (serious gamers) and enhanced its reputation amongst consumers in a new target market (casual gamers). Moreover, this is the first of several examples that I discuss in which a firm decides to reposition in order to differentiate itself from rivals and therefore escape intense competition.

In 2006, Nintendo repositioned its brand by launching the Nintendo Wii video game console. The Wii console differed drastically from previous consoles – including its predecessor, the Nintendo GameCube – in terms of both its technology and its target market.[21] Its motion-sensing wireless controller encouraged interactive play and physical activity. Furthermore, its simplicity and ease-of-use encouraged casual gamers and non-gamers to adopt the Wii in great numbers. Nintendo successfully repositioned its brand as one that offers a family-oriented, interactive, and social experience. This repositioning is responsible for having propelled Nintendo to market leadership in the seventh generation of video game consoles after having been only third in terms of unit sales during the sixth generation, lagging far behind the market leader, Sony's PlayStation 2.[22] This repositioning decision has had long-term implications for Nintendo. Prior to the release of the Wii, Nintendo's reputation among serious gamers had already faltered because of its poor performance relative to the Sony PlayStation and Sony PlayStation 2 in the fifth[23] and sixth video game console generations, respectively. The repositioning brought about by the launch of the Wii only further hurt Nintendo's reputation among serious gamers. In embarking on the development of the Wii, Nintendo surely took into consideration the long-term implications that their repositioning would have. That is, if the Wii failed, it would have been extremely difficult for Nintendo to reverse its repositioning decision and rebuild a brand that would appeal to serious gamers. Today, it is clear that Nintendo's repositioning has been hugely successful. However, as Nintendo prepares to launch its eighth-generation console, the Wii U – which is supposed to appeal to both casual *and* serious gamers – it remains to be seen whether Nintendo will succeed in again catering to serious gamers despite the repositioning of its brand.

I now discuss a research study that developed a model allowing one to formally study the types of repositioning decisions discussed in the above anecdotes. Ellickson, Misra, and Nair[6] studied the repositioning of supermarkets' pricing formats – in particular, their decisions of whether to use Every Day Low Price (EDLP) or Promotional (PROMO) pricing formats. EDLP entails charging consistently low prices. PROMO entails charging higher regular prices but frequently offering steep price discounts or *sales*, thus involving greater variability in prices. Each of these pricing strategies has its benefits. PROMO allows a firm to inter-temporally price-discriminate by selling goods at lower prices to more price-sensitive consumers who make an effort to take advantage of sales, and selling at higher prices to others. Moreover, both the frequency of sales and the unpredictability of their timing may induce consumers to visit the store more often. As EDLP entails less variability in prices over time, it accordingly induces less variability in demand; this allows a firm to reduce inventory costs, better coordinate its supply chain, and reduce the risk of stockouts. Changing pricing formats is costly in the sense that a store must advertise the change and must alter its inventory and supply-chain management systems in order to accommodate such a change. Moreover, a store's consumers may be averse to a change in pricing format and – if the advertising of the change is not successful – consumers may continue to regard the store as having the old pricing format. It follows that it would be very difficult and costly for a firm to switch back after changing its pricing format. Therefore, such repositioning has long-term implications.

Ellickson, Misra, and Nair[6] estimated the cost of such pricing format repositioning. To do so, they exploited the introduction of Walmart Supercenters, which always employ EDLP. The entry of a Walmart Supercenter into a market is a shock that induces each local competitor to consider whether it should exit and, if not, whether it should reposition its pricing format. The authors thus devised a model in which supermarkets make both entry/exit and pricing format decisions. They estimated this model using data on pricing format decisions of all supermarkets in the United States during the 1994–8 period, in which there was extensive entry of Walmart Supercenters. They found that the cost of switching from PROMO to EDLP was four times higher than the cost of switching from EDLP to PROMO, consistent with the fact that there were many more switches from EDLP to PROMO in their period of observation. They also found that PROMO generates higher revenues in the following sense: if all stores were to choose PROMO, then the median store's revenue would be U.S.$6.4 million higher than if all stores were to choose EDLP. Finally, they estimated that the median gross margin was significantly higher under PROMO (16.5 per cent) than under EDLP (12.2 per cent). These results help explain why EDLP adoption has been somewhat limited despite earlier predictions that this format would become more prominent.[24]

Finally, I present two additional examples in which iconic Canadian retailers – Canadian Tire and The Bay – have made repositioning decisions in order to differentiate themselves from rivals and escape competition. While both of these firms' repositioning efforts are still ongoing, it is already extremely clear that both have been forward-looking and strategic in devising their repositioning strategies.

In recent years, Canadian Tire – the iconic Canadian retailer of automotive parts and service, tools, hardware, sporting goods, housewares, and seasonal goods, among others – has faced increasing competition from U.S. retailers that have expanded operations north of the border. Walmart – the discount department store behemoth – and Home Depot – America's largest home improvement retailer – both entered the Canadian market in 1994 and have since continued to expand their Canadian operations.[25] Lowe's – another American home improvement chain – launched its Canadian operations in 2007 by opening stores in Ontario and has since expanded into Western Canada.[26] More recently, Target – another dominant U.S. discount retailer – purchased the leases for 220 Zellers stores from the Hudson's Bay Company and plans to enter the Canadian market as early as 2013 by converting some of these locations into Target stores. After years of flat sales and an unsuccessful attempt to establish itself as a general goods retailers – for example, by trying to appeal more to female shoppers and entering the home decor market – Canadian Tire is responding to the competitive pressure by repositioning to focus on the categories in which it had traditionally been strong: tools, home supplies, sporting goods, and especially automotive parts and service.[27] To this end, it is opening automotive concept stores that provide express automobile servicing and detailing. It is also streamlining its auto parts supply chain, training employees to be tire experts, and testing a new automotive-centric store format.[28] It has also relaunched its online store – after abandoning a previous attempt in 2009 – and is currently selling an extremely wide variety of tires and wheels online, but nothing more. It remains to be seen how successful this repositioning will be as the Canadian retail landscape continues to change. However, Canadian Tire is surely being both strategic and forward-looking in making this repositioning decision. The categories on which it is focusing are not only those in which it has traditionally been strong, but also those that overlap the least with the product mixes of the major competitors mentioned above, among others. Therefore, it anticipates that they are extremely unlikely to respond to Canadian Tire's repositioning by focusing on these categories themselves.

The final example I present shows that when a firm repositions in order to escape intense competition from rivals in one market, it may be forced to enter into more intense competition with rivals in another market. This other market presumably has the potential to be more lucrative, thus justifying the repositioning effort. Of course, the firm must be strategic in the sense that it must anticipate the ways in which rivals in this other market will respond to its decision to compete more intensely with them. These very dynamics play prominently in the recent repositioning effort of yet another iconic Canadian retailer, The Bay.

Since 2008, The Bay – the Hudson's Bay Company's full-line department store – has been striving to reposition itself as a major *fashion* department store.[29] The Bay's repositioning is motivated by increased competition for the middle-class and upper-middle-class shoppers that constitute its target demographic. In recent decades, The Bay's sales have been eroded as these shoppers were lured first by specialty stores and later by the low prices of discount retailers such as Walmart and Winners.[30] The fashionable clothing category is attractive because it is both lucrative and less competitive. Presently, Holt Renfrew is the only high-end Canadian department store, and with its current repositioning efforts, The Bay is entering into direct competition with it.

As part of its repositioning effort, The Bay has thoroughly redesigned its flagship downtown Toronto store. The store's crown jewel is "The Room," an upscale store within a store that carries only high-end designer clothing. The Room includes a posh private lounge accessible only to VIPs – typically, affluent upper-class Toronto socialites – and hosts exclusive events at which such customers fraternize with designers and fashion celebrities. The store has also introduced valet parking.[31] While these are clear attempts to lure Holt Renfrew's most affluent customers, The Bay's primary objective is to appeal to shoppers who are in search of designer clothing at more reasonable prices.[32] This *low end of luxury* category is even more lucrative than the high end simply because there is a much bigger market for it. To achieve this, The Bay has drastically changed its product assortment, dropping 850 fashion brands and carefully adding 250 others. In its flagship store, it has completely redesigned the department that stocks second-tier designer labels. It has also installed in-store boutiques for several designer brands. It hopes to be able to replicate these efforts at other stores.[33] Further intensifying the competition between the two retail chains, Holt Renfrew has recently stretched its range of prices downward and has relaunched its more reasonably priced private label.[34] While this decision has surely been influenced by the economic downturn, it is perhaps also a response to The Bay's repositioning.

Opportunities and Challenges

Marketing scholars who study strategic forward-looking marketing management have both made use of and contributed to a set of very useful methodological tools. These tools allow us to devise rich models that incorporate forward-looking consumer and firm behaviour as well as the strategic interaction that characterizes decision-making in oligopolistic industries. Furthermore, they allow us to both estimate models using appropriate data sets and explore how firms would behave in counterfactual scenarios of interest. These achievements represent an opportunity for marketing managers and accordingly a challenge for scholars.

The challenge to scholars is twofold. First, we must convey the insights from this literature both in general and with respect to particular industries. In short, for many important marketing management decisions such as those discussed above, straightforward cross-sectional and longitudinal analysis is not sufficient. Marketing managers can benefit greatly from accounting for both the long-term impact of their marketing management decisions *and* the strategic interaction that characterizes such decision-making in concentrated industries. Ignoring either of these when analysing a marketing management decision could lead to a mistaken conclusion. For example, the result from Borkovsky[7] that an increase in the cost of releasing new versions could induce firms to begin releasing new versions *more* frequently comes only because he accounts for both forward-looking behaviour *and* strategic interaction.

Second, scholars must strive to develop tools that will make these methods more accessible to managers in terms of both education and application. Regarding education, in a very recent Harvard Business Publishing online marketing simulation,[35] students play the role of CEO of a manufacturer of medical motors. They are tasked with making a wide array of marketing management decisions – including pricing, distribution, promotion, targeting, positioning, and sales force management. As the simulation includes twelve consecutive fiscal quarters, students learn about the implications of their marketing management decisions not only for the present but also for the future. And as each student CEO competes against fictitious competitors, he/she must take the competitive response of rivals into consideration. Furthermore, the instructor can modulate the aggressiveness of competitor response, therefore giving students an opportunity to learn about the implications of more and less aggressive competition for marketing management. As students can play the simulation repeatedly, they have the opportunity to learn and become more sophisticated in their decision-making. This is an excellent tool for teaching practitioners how to make marketing management decisions in a strategic forward-looking manner. Similar tools could be developed for the marketing management decisions and industries discussed above. A simulation that allows the instructor to modulate the extent to which the CEO is forward-looking (by varying the interest rate that the firm faces and accordingly the rate at which it discounts future income) could help practitioners learn about the implications of being more or less forward-looking. Furthermore, a simulation that allows students to compete against one another – instead of fictitious competitors – could provide for richer competitive interaction.

Regarding application, it is important for scholars to develop analytical tools that allow marketing managers to benefit from the progress that has been made in the literature on strategic forward-looking marketing management. This is no small challenge. At present, both the estimation of such models and the exploration of counterfactual scenarios are theoretically and technically challenging and computationally burdensome exercises. Therefore, the challenge lies in devising tools that allow practitioners to approach these problems in a sound, albeit perhaps less rigorous manner than scholars, and that will produce results in a timely fashion. These tools would certainly have to be tailored to specific marketing management decisions and particular industries. Moreover, these tools should be designed taking into consideration that marketing managers often have a wealth of historical data on their firm's marketing management – typically, much more than is available to scholars. While firms do not have as much data on competitors' marketing management, they can often purchase rich data sets from market research companies such as the Nielsen Company and the SymphonyIRI group. This is crucial because in order to estimate a model that incorporates strategic interaction, one naturally requires data on competitors.

If marketing scholars can make these tools more accessible, marketing managers could benefit in two ways. First, marketing managers could use these tools to assess whether the forward-looking marketing strategies they employ are optimal by conducting an exercise similar to that of Dubé, Hitsch, and Manchanda.[12] Having estimated a demand system that a product faces, one could compute the optimal marketing strategies that all firms in the industry should employ when facing such demand. One could also conduct a similar exercise with the assumption that rivals will continue to behave as suboptimally as they did in the past. By comparing the optimal strategies that have been computed to the strategies actually employed, the marketing manager could assess the extent to which his/her firm and rival firms are successful in accounting for the complexities introduced by the long-term impacts of marketing management decisions and strategic interaction with rival firms. Accordingly, this could help marketing managers improve their marketing management decision-making.

Second, these tools can be used to explore counterfactual scenarios of interest. That is, a marketing manager could explore how it should react and infer how its rivals would react to some change in the fundamentals of the industry. Turning again to the example of Walmart Supercenters, suppose that a supermarket in a market that Walmart has *not* entered anticipated that Walmart *might* enter in the future. That supermarket might be interested in predicting the effect of Walmart

Supercenter entry on its local market. If Walmart enters, should the supermarket change its pricing format? Would rival supermarkets change their pricing formats? Would Walmart's entry induce rival supermarkets to exit? Would Walmart's entry forestall future entry by rival supermarkets that might otherwise occur? Exploring this counterfactual scenario using a model of strategic forward-looking firm behaviour would help answer such questions. The answers to such questions could help the supermarket firm prepare for the possible eventuality of Walmart's entry into the market. Furthermore, exploring a similar scenario in which Walmart is a *potential* entrant could help the firm decide how to forestall Walmart's entry.

A Prescription for Engaging in Strategic Forward-Looking Marketing Management

In many industries, the importance of being forward-looking and strategic in making marketing decisions has increased. To maximize the effectiveness of marketing actions, managers need to be:

- CONSISTENT with consumers – because the more forward-looking their customers, the more forward-looking their strategies should be.
- Forward-looking on PRODUCT development – because investment in R&D to develop or improve products today affects strategic positioning in the future.
- Forward-looking on ADVERTISING decisions – because advertising affects a consumer's propensity to purchase not only in the present but also in the future.
- Forward-looking on REPOSITIONING decisions – because the associated costs and the effects on reputation are often only partially reversible.

REFERENCES

1 See S. Moorthy, "Using Game Theory to Model Competition," *Journal of Marketing Research* 22 (1985): 262–82; P. Kotler, G. Lilien, and S. Moorthy, *Marketing Models* (Englewood Cliffs, NJ: Prentice Hall, 1992); S. Moorthy, "Competitive Marketing Strategies: Game-Theoretic Models," in J. Eliashberg and G. Lilien, eds., *Handbooks in Operations Research and Management Science: Marketing* (Amsterdam: NorthHolland, 1993), 143–90.
2 See I. Hendel and A. Nevo, "Sales and Consumer Inventory," *The RAND Journal of Economics* 37, no. 3 (2006): 543–61; I. Hendel and A. Nevo, "Intertemporal Price Discrimination in Storable Goods Markets," working paper, Northwestern University, Evanston, IL, 2011.

3 M. Ishihara, "Dynamic Demand for New and Used Durable Goods without Physical Depreciation" (PhD diss., Rotman School of Management, University of Toronto, 2011).

4 A. Ching and F. Hayashi, "Payment Card Rewards Programs and Consumer Payment Choice," *Journal of Banking and Finance* 34, no. 8 (2010): 1773–87.

5 R. Borkovsky, U. Doraszelski, and Y. Kryukov, "A Dynamic Quality Ladder Duopoly with Entry and Exit: Exploring the Equilibrium Correspondence Using the Homotopy Method," *Quantitative Marketing & Economics* 10, no. 2 (2012): 197–229; R. Goettler and B. Gordon, "Does AMD Spur Intel to Innovate More?" *Journal of Political Economy* 119, no. 6 (2012): 1141–200.

6 P. Ellickson, S. Misra, and H. Nair, "Repositioning Dynamics and Pricing Strategy," *Journal of Marketing Research* (forthcoming 2012).

7 R. Borkovsky, "The Timing of Version Releases in R&D-intensive Industries: A Dynamic Duopoly Model," working paper, University of Toronto, 2012.

8 J. Dubé, G. Hitsch, and P. Chintagunta, "Tipping and Concentration in Markets with Indirect Network Effects," *Marketing Science* 29, no. 2 (2010): 216–49.

9 See K. Elzinga and D. Mills, "Innovation and Entry in the US Disposable Diaper Industry," *Industrial and Corporate Change* 5, no. 3 (1996): 791–812; M. Parry and M. Jones, "Pampers: The Disposable Diaper Wars (A)," working paper, Darden Business Publishing, Charlottesville, VA, 2001; D. Dyer, F. Dalzell, and R. Olegario, *Rising Tide: Lessons from 165 Years of Brand Building at Procter & Gamble* (Cambridge, MA: Harvard Business School Press, 2004).

10 S. Alfonsi, U. Fahy, and K. Brown, "Battle for Baby's Bottom: Diaper Wars Heat Up," *ABC News*, 2010; "The Bottom Line Diaper Wars," *ABC News: Nightline*, 2010.

11 D. Clarke, "Econometric Measurement of the Duration of Advertising Effect on Sales," *Journal of Marketing Research* 13 (1976): 345–57; G. Assmus, J. Farley, and D. Lehmann, "How Advertising Affects Sales: Meta-Analysis of Econometric Results," *Journal of Marketing Research* 21 (1984): 65–74; L. Lodish, M. Abraham, J. Livelsberger, B. Lubetkin, B. Richardson, and M. Stevens, "A Summary of Fifty-Five In-Market Experimental Estimates of the Long-Term Effect of TV Advertising," *Marketing Science* 14, no. 3 (1995): G133–40.

12 J. Dubé, G. Hitsch, and P. Manchanda, "An Empirical Model of Advertising Dynamics," *Quantitative Marketing and Economics* 3 (2005): 107–44.

13 See M. Vijay and E. Muller, "Advertising Pulsing Policies for Generating Awareness for New Products," *Marketing Science* 5, no. 2 (1986): 89–106; S.

Park and M. Hahn, "Pulsing in a Discrete Model of Advertising Competition," *Journal of Marketing Research* 28, no. 4 (1991): 397–405; M. Villas-Boas, "Predicting Advertising Pulsing Policies in an Oligopoly: A Model and Empirical Test," *Marketing Science* 12 (1993): 88–102.

14 P. Ellickson, S. Misra, and H. Nair, "Repositioning Dynamics and Pricing Strategy," *Journal of Marketing Research* (forthcoming 2012).

15 Krispy Kreme Doughnuts Inc., *Annual Report for the Period Ending 1/28/2001* (Winston Salem: Krispy Kreme Doughnuts Inc., 2001).

16 See Krispy Kreme Doughnuts Inc., *Annual Report for the Period Ending 1/30/2005* (Winston Salem: Krispy Kreme Doughnuts Inc., 2005); K. O'Sullivan, "Kremed!" *CFO Magazine*, 2005; B. Cohen, "Krispy Kreme: The Franchisor That Went Stale," working paper, Kellogg School of Management, Evanston, IL, 2009.

17 Krispy Kreme Doughnuts Inc., *Annual Report for the Period Ending 1/30/2005* (Winston Salem: Krispy Kreme Doughnuts Inc., 2005).

18 K. O'Sullivan, "Kremed!" *CFO Magazine*, 2005.

19 Ibid.

20 Krispy Kreme Doughnuts Inc., *Annual Report for the Period Ending 1/28/2001* (Winston Salem: Krispy Kreme Doughnuts Inc., 2001).

21 M. Dahlén, F. Lange, and T. Smith, *Marketing Communications: A Brand Narrative Approach* (West Sussex, UK: John Wiley, 2010).

22 See "Playstation 2 Sales Reach 150 Million Units Worldwide," Sony Computer Entertainment Inc., Press Release, 14 February 2001; "2010: The Biggest Year in Xbox History," Microsoft Xbox, Press Release, 11 January 2011; "Consolidated Sales Transition by Region," *Nintendo*, 31 March 2011, accessed 28 July 2011 from http://www.nintendo.co.jp/ir/en/library/historical_data/index.html.

23 See "Cumulative Production Shipments of Hardware (Until March 2007)," *Sony Computer Entertainment Inc.*, accessed 28 July 2011 from http://www.scei.co.jp/corporate/data/bizdataps_e.html.

24 R. Bolton, V. Shankar, and D. Montoya, "Recent Trends and Emerging Practices in Retailer Pricing," in M. Krafft and M. Mantrala, eds., *Retailing in the 21st Century: Current and Future Trends* (Berlin: Springer-Verlag, 2010), 245–59.

25 S. Ho and J. Tilak, "Factbox: U.S. Retailers Eye Canada for Expansion," *Reuters*, 13 January 2011.

26 Ibid.

27 C. Sorensen, "Canadian Tire's Baffling Strategy to Sell You Everything," *Maclean's*, 11 October 2011, accessed 24 May 2012 from http://www2.macleans.ca/2011/10/11/so-wrong-that-its-right/.

28 S. Freeman, "Canadian Tire Launches New Auto-centric Store Format," *Canadian Press*, 19 October 2011.

29 L. McLaren, "The Bay vs. Holts: The Bay's Scheme to Steal the Fashion Crown from Holts," *Toronto Life*, 1 November 2010, accessed 24 May 2012 from http://www.torontolife.com/daily/style/from-the-print-edition/2010/11/01/the-bay-vs-holts-the-bay%E2%80%99s-scheme-to-steal-the-fashion-crown-from-holts/.

30 Ibid.; R. Giese, "Retail: HBC's Cinderella Moment," *Canadian Business*, 23 November 2009, accessed 24 May 2012 from http://www.canadianbusiness.com/article/16838--retail-hbc-s-cinderella-moment.

31 Ibid.

32 See M. Mattos, "Designing a Bulletproof Retail Experience," *Strategy*, 1 March 2011; L. McLaren, "The Bay vs. Holts: The Bay's Scheme to Steal the Fashion Crown from Holts," *Toronto Life*, 1 November 2010.

33 L. McLaren, "The Bay vs. Holts: The Bay's Scheme to Steal the Fashion Crown from Holts," *Toronto Life*, 1 November 2010.

34 D. Flavelle, "Holts Boosts Sales with Expanded Prices and Sizes," *Toronto Star*, 1 September 2010, accessed 24 May 2012 from http://www.thestar.com/business/article/855491 --holts-boosts-sales-with-expanded-prices-and-sizes.

35 D. Narayandas, *Marketing Simulation: Managing Segments and Customers,* 3341-HTM-ENG Series (Boston: Harvard Business Publishing, 2010).

9 Just Imagine: The Role of Visualization in New Product Evaluation

MIN ZHAO

With new product failure rates as high as 80 per cent, marketing managers always have their eyes and ears open for ways to reduce their risk of failure. Consider the Segway Human Transporter, a hydrogen-powered personal transportation device, designed for eco-transportation over short distances, that mimics the human body's ability to maintain its balance. The Segway offers greater mobility in an environmentally friendly way, and yet consumers have been slow to adopt it. When the Segway was introduced in 2002, the predictions were that it would make its first billion dollars faster than any company in history, but by the summer of 2004, fewer than 10,000 units had been sold.[1] It turns out that consumers often feel enthusiastic about adopting a new product before it is launched, but are much more lukewarm about it when it comes time to make an actual purchase decision.[2] This reluctance to accept the Segway (and other new products) can be attributed to the learning cost associated with new product adoption and consumers' underestimation of the value of new benefits.[3] A similar phenomenon exists after purchase: consumers may purchase a new product intending to make the full use of its benefits, but they may never take the time to learn how to make each feature work. As a result, they may end up regretting their purchase decision over time.

How can marketers increase consumers' adoption of – and satisfaction with – new products? Research has proposed that providing relational analogies using existing products may help enhance consumers' comprehension and acceptance of new products.[4] However, the lack of commonality between new products and existing ones often makes it challenging to find ways to draw analogies.

Another method that has been employed to help consumers learn about the benefits of new products is visualization, or mental simulation. In this chapter, I will discuss different types of mental simulation as effective cognitive tools for increasing consumers' adoption of new products. Mental simulation is the imitative mental representation of events. Essentially, it is using one's imagination. For example, without actually using the product, consumers can mentally simulate driving a new car or using the latest tablet PC. Indeed, advertisers often ask consumers to imagine themselves completing some type of activity with a new product, hoping thereby to improve the product's evaluation. For instance, a recent ad for a new washing machine asks consumers to "imagine clothes looking new, longer." The California lottery encourages consumers to "dream a little dream" of how they would spend their millions were they to win.[14]

Not all types of visualization are equally effective, however. In this chapter, I review recent research on visualization in the new product domain, identify key ways in which marketing managers can improve consumers' evaluations of new products, and show how visualization contributes to the evolving role of the marketing manager. I summarize the effect of different types of visualization in new product evaluation in four sections, and in closing I discuss how these strategies can be implemented in marketing practice.

1. The Role of Process and Outcome Simulation in Preference Consistency over Time

One of the big challenges faced by marketers is consumers' inconsistency over time when it comes to expressing preferences for new products. In chapter 6, Claire Tsai discussed consumers' misforecasting of their future preferences in general. In the new product domain, this preference inconsistency can manifest in several ways. During a concept test, consumers may state their warm intention to purchase the new product, and yet not follow through when it comes time to make the actual purchase. Or, when asked to make a purchase decision in advance, they may choose a new product (rather than a more familiar one) and then feel unhappy with that decision when the time comes to use the product. This is also consistent with the notion that Dilip Soman discusses in chapter 12 regarding how people's behaviour can change after waiting. Applying that thinking to the new product adoption process, we can say that consumers' attitudes towards new products changes during the waiting period between committing to a product and actually purchasing it or using it.

The psychological mechanism underlying this inconsistency can be explained by a theory called Construal Level Theory, or CLT.[5] According to this theory, temporal distance between the present and the time at which people make a product decision changes the way they think of the product. For example, when a typical consumer, Mark, thinks of adopting the Segway in the future, he tends to focus on the novel benefits of the Segway, such as its great mobility. He ignores how using the Segway will mean changing his everyday routine. In other words, Mark has a positive attitude towards the Segway when he's forecasting how he'll use it in the future. The same thing happens when a different consumer, Joe, purchases a product for future consumption – let's say a new digital camera that he intends to use on his vacation in two months. He focuses primarily on the product's benefits when ordering it. However, when the time comes for Mark to decide whether to actually buy the Segway in the store, or when Joe is on his vacation and actually needs to use the digital camera he bought earlier, they will switch their primary focus from the product benefits to the usage process, which highlights the learning cost of the Segway and difficulties of using the fancy features on the digital camera. As a result, they lower their evaluation of the new products: Mark decides not to buy the Segway while Joe feels frustrated with the camera he purchased and doesn't use it. They both started with warm intentions, but ended up failing to carry through.

My work on mental simulation has shown how different types of simulation can overcome this time-related preference discrepancy. Prior research distinguishes between process simulation, which encourages people to imagine the step-by-step process of reaching a certain goal, and outcome simulation, which encourages people to think about the desirable outcome of fulfilling the goal.[6] Multiple studies have shown that process-focused simulation makes people more likely to follow through on adoption intentions for everyday products such as shampoo or vitamins.[7]

I and my colleagues propose that both process-focused and outcome-focused mental simulation are effective in helping people be consistent in their preferences over time when these simulations are used to encourage people to focus on whatever element in a situation they would otherwise ignore.[8] Specifically, when people are considering events in the distant future and are therefore more likely to be focused on overall benefits while neglecting process-related drawbacks, asking them to practice process simulation can get them to consider how they will use the product (product usage), which will lead them to consider process-related drawbacks and thereby bring their product evaluation closer to what it would likely be at the time of actual use (or consumption). Outcome simulation, which highlights the naturally salient product benefits, on the other hand, would be redundant – it would encourage these people to do what they already are doing.

However, when people are considering events in the immediate future, they focus on practical usage considerations rather than more general or abstract benefits. In this situation, outcome simulation offers the right corrective, as it stimulates them to focus on the naturally ignored product benefits, which brings their attitude towards the product more in line with what it was when they considered the product in the more distant past. Process simulation, on the other hand, would be redundant in this situation.

For example, in one of our experiments, 225 participants were asked to evaluate two software packages that they would use to create a photo essay. Software Package A had better features but was more difficult to use; Software Package B had fewer features but was easier to use. Participants were told that the decision was either for now or for later, and then were asked either to engage in process simulation, outcome simulation, or no simulation (as the control condition). Participants in the process simulation groups were asked to imagine the process of using each software package and to focus on the procedure of using it to create their project. Participants in the outcome simulation groups were asked to imagine the final outcome of using each software package and to focus on the quality of the project created with this software. Participants in the control group did not do any simulation and simply answered questions regarding their preferences for the two software packages.

The results confirmed that people's preferences change over time and that when they did not engage in either simulation, participants in the "now" condition liked the easier software package more than participants in the "later" condition. How did the different types of mental simulation affect their preferences? When the decision was for now, process simulation had no effect on participants' preferences, but outcome simulation significantly increased their preference for the software package with more features, despite its usage difficulty. In fact, when participants in the "now" condition engaged in process simulation, their preferences fell in line with those of participants in the control segment of the "later" condition.

When the decision was for later, outcome simulation had no effect on participants' preferences, but process simulation significantly increased their preferences for the easier software package. As a result, their preferences matched those of participants in the control segment of the "now" condition.

These results show that asking consumers to practice process simulation before making a decision for the distant future, or asking them to practice outcome simulation for a near future decision, can change how they consider the product and promote preference consistency over time. This preference can be consistently low over time, in which case consumers' over-enthusiasm about the new product during preference forecasting is reduced; or it can be consistently high over time, in which case people are less likely to experience disappointment or regret when they actually purchase or use the product. In other words, preference consistency is beneficial regardless which direction it leads to; when making a decision for the far future, consumers who are guided by process simulation are more likely to develop a preference that is closer to what their attitude will be at the time of actual consumption. Conversely, consumers who practice outcome simulation at the time of product use or consumption are more likely to recall the features and benefits that led to their forecasted preference back when they made their decision, and therefore they are better equipped to cope with any difficulties involved in using or consuming the product.

Extending these visualization strategies beyond preference inconsistency in the new product domain, these findings also have important implications in other aspects of consumer life. For example, when it comes to self-control – for example, in situations where there is a discrepancy between consumers' ambitious plan of saving or healthy diet and their actual overspending and overeating behaviours – thinking about the naturally ignored aspect of how to save or how to eat healthy will help consumers set up realistic goals for the long run. On the other hand, at each moment of actually implementing their goals, thinking about the benefit of achieving those goals will enhance their self-control and help them to resist the temptation of buying an unnecessary pair of shoes or eating a rich chocolate cake.

2. The Role of Process and Outcome Simulation in Improving New Product Evaluation

While preference consistency can help marketers obtain a more accurate prediction of consumer preference for a new product as well as higher levels of customer satisfaction, it does not fully address another key problem that marketers face when a new product has already been introduced to the market: low adoption rates. In this section, I review findings in relevant visualization literature that describe how to use process and outcome simulation to improve new product evaluations.

As mentioned earlier, process simulation is more effective than outcome simulation in increasing achievement of goals and improving people's evaluation of familiar products such as shampoo or vitamins. Because really new products have a salient high learning cost and people are uncertain of how to use them,[9] asking people to think about how they might use such a product could focus their attention on the high learning cost and weaken the advantage of process simulation over outcome simulation. Indeed, one of my studies has shown that, although process simulation encouraged more favourable evaluations for an existing product (the IBM ThinkPad), asking people to think about the process of using a new product (an audio PC) did not stimulate any higher evaluation than asking them to think about the benefit of using it, because people felt uncertain about how to use an audio PC. Clearly, the best way to use process and outcome simulation to improve new product evaluation is an interesting question.

In my recent work, I have pointed out that the classic mental simulation literature has combined cognitive and affective components to different degrees, which may have masked some of their unique effects. Drawing on the dichotomy of affect and cognition, I argue that process and outcome simulation can each have unique and predictable effects on new product evaluation in both affective and cognitive modes.[10] My predictions are based on a well-known distinction in behavioural research: whereas cognitive information processing is based on "cold," deliberate, and analytic thinking, affective information processing is based on "hot," rapid, and emotional feelings.

A large body of research has examined the role of affective and cognitive processing modes and has demonstrated that focusing on one or the other leads to very different attitudes, evaluations, and decisions. This question of cognitive versus affective processing modes is particularly critical for new products; consumers have both cognitive and

emotional uncertainty with new products, either of which might negatively impact the other. As such, having both the affective and cognitive
components within each type of simulation could lead to interference
between the two mental processes, which can adversely affect evaluations.

People tend to give more weight to negative information than to
positive information. Therefore, when a new product both provides
novel benefits and has a high learning cost, they naturally focus more
on the product usage process (i.e., the negative learning cost) than on
the positive product benefits, and therefore they evaluate the product
less favourably. Prior work with a cognitive focus has indicated that for
these types of products, switching consumers' cognitive focus from the
usage process to the product benefits improves product evaluations.
In conjunction with the finding that each type of mental simulation is
effective when it augments the aspect of the product that would otherwise tend to be ignored, my colleagues and I predict that when people
are operating in a cognitive mode, outcome simulation (i.e., thinking
about the product benefit) will be more effective at enhancing evaluation than process simulation (i.e., thinking about the usage process),
because outcome simulation will shift attention away from the learning
cost and towards the otherwise underweighted product benefits.

From the affective perspective, research has demonstrated that when
people relate a product to themselves, an affective orientation (rather
than a cognitive orientation) results in less critical analysis, fewer negative thoughts, and more positive affective responses, which in turn improves their attitude towards the product. For new products, because
the mental representation of the usage process is more salient than the
representation of the product's benefits, thinking about the emotions
that go along with using the product is more likely to switch attention
away from the difficult aspects of the product and evoke a positive affective response than is thinking about the product's benefits. Thus,
in an affective mode, process simulation is predicted to result in more
positive product evaluation than outcome simulation.

Those predictions are supported by empirical evidence. In one of our
experiments, participants received a product ad for the Sony e-Reader.
Depending on the group to which the participants were assigned, the
ad either encouraged them to imagine how they would incorporate this
product into their daily routine (process/cognitive conditions), how
they would feel while incorporating this product into their daily routine (process/affective conditions), how they would benefit from using

this product in their daily routine (outcome/cognitive conditions), or how they would feel about the benefit they would receive from using this product in their daily routine (outcome/affective conditions). The ad included a picture of the product, a brief product description, and the mental simulation instructions. Participants were asked to write down what they imagined and to answer evaluative questions relating to the product. The results showed that in a cognitive processing mode, outcome simulation improved product evaluations much more than process simulation. However, in an affective mode, process simulation was more effective than outcome simulation in improving product evaluation.

Because the predictions for this effect were made based on the assumption that consumers naturally focus more on the usage process for new products than the product benefits, I also argue for an exception: if the new product is a hedonic product rather than a utilitarian one – that is, if it is a product that offers experiential benefits rather than merely functional benefits, and consumers choose this product mainly because of the feelings that they can obtain from using it (i.e., fun, pleasure, and excitement) – then in that case, because consumers are primarily seeking enjoyment, they will focus on these experiential benefits when evaluating the product rather than on the usage process. In this case, the best corrective, under a cognitive focus, is process simulation because it activates usage process thoughts, which otherwise do not arise much. Under an affective focus, on the other hand, outcome simulation should be more effective because it is more salient and more likely to facilitate affective immersion. Indeed, in the experiment described above, when participants received an ad for the Apple iPad (a hedonic product) instead of the Sony e-Reader (a functional product), the results showed that in a cognitive processing mode, focusing on the usage process enhanced product evaluations significantly more than focusing on the product benefits, whereas in an affective mode, the opposite was true.

These results demonstrate the unique effects of process and outcome simulation in improving new product evaluation, both when consumers rely on their feelings and when they rely on thinking. While feelings and thinking are often interrelated and feelings often occur automatically, I suggest that encouraging consumers to shift their relative focus between feelings and thinking can impact their evaluation of new products. The basic takeaway is that for a new product that is functional (e.g., audio PC, e-reader, GPS), under a cognitive focus where cognitive thinking is recommended and relatively little emphasis is given to feelings, encouraging consumers to think about the product's benefits leads to higher evaluations than encouraging them to think about the usage process. On the other hand, under an affective focus where reliance on feelings is more emphasized, encouraging consumers to imagine the feelings associated with using the product leads to higher evaluations than encouraging them to imagine the feelings associated with the product's benefits. For a new product that is hedonic, the reverse is true. Marketers can easily implement the appropriate mental simulation instructions by incorporating them in their product ads, promotion messages, or personal interactions with consumers.

3. The Effect of Past- and Future-Oriented Visualization on New Product Evaluation

How does past- or future-oriented visualization impact new product evaluation? When marketers launch a new product such as the iPad, they could ask consumers to visualize having the iPad on their last business trip, or they might ask them to imagine having it on their next business trip. In my work, I have compared the effect of memory-focused visualization with that of imagination-focused visualization and found an advantage for the imagination-based approach.[11] Because people's creativity in general is enhanced when they move away from a default routine and employ divergent thinking, I proposed that encouraging consumers to engage in imaginative visualization that is future oriented, rather than past oriented, would better illuminate the value of a product's benefits and lead to more favourable evaluations.

In one of my studies, participants were asked to evaluate either a new product (audio PC) or a control product (ThinkPad) and were instructed either to simply free their mind to visualize activities with the computer (which is naturally memory-focused) or to free their imagination to visualize new activities that they had never been able to do with computers before. The results showed that while there was no difference between the two types of visualization when the participants were evaluating the ThinkPad, imagination-focused visualization improved participants' evaluations of the audio PC more than memory-focused visualization did. Further analyses showed that this effect was due to participants' increased perception of the value of the new product benefit arising from the imagination-focused visualization.

Those findings suggest that when marketing new products, marketing managers should encourage customers to use their imagination to focus on new uses they have never experienced before. Having consumers imagine new uses and the benefits of those new uses helps them to recognize the value of those benefits, leading to higher product evaluations. Managers could use different promotion methods to stimulate consumers to use their imagination regarding the new product. In their print ads, advertising on TV, and on the web, managers could encourage consumers to look forward and imagine new uses for the product rather than simply visualizing how they would use the product in their current daily activities.

Another way marketing managers commonly help consumers visualize and evaluate new products is by giving them usage examples or visualization aids. But what kinds of examples work best and how many should marketers give? Drawing on literature on retrospection, anticipation, and the congruency of mindsets, I have suggested that if marketers can match the usage examples to consumers' temporal perspectives, new product evaluations will improve.[12] In particular, because people tend to think of past events in a more detailed and concrete way and future events in a more general and abstract way, I argue that providing detailed product usage examples for a past-oriented visualization while providing abstract product usage examples for future-oriented visualization should create a match between visualization aids (product examples) and time, and thereby enhance new product evaluation. These predictions are supported by empirical evidence. In one scenario, I asked participants to evaluate a new computer (tablet PC). When the participants were asked to relate the product to past usage scenarios, concrete product usage examples led to higher purchase intentions than abstract examples. However, when participants were asked to relate the product to future usage scenarios, contrary to conventional wisdom, concrete examples and greater numbers of examples did not increase product evaluation – it was fewer and more abstract product usage examples that led to increased purchase intentions.

4. The Effect of Metacognitive Experience on New Product Evaluation

Thus far, I have reviewed research on how the content of visualization impacts product evaluation. In this section, I will discuss how the ease or difficulty of the task of imagining can influence new product evaluation. Prior research has shown that ease of retrieving the experience (or images) can often be more diagnostic than the content. For example, researchers have demonstrated that people who were asked to give ten reasons for choosing a BMW gave the BMW a lower evaluation than people who were asked to give only one reason. The theory is that the difficulty of calling ten reasons to mind was what caused the lower evaluation.[13]

This stream of research has typically had participants take a retrospective view by asking them to look back and recall things from their memory. In the new product domain, a common approach using mental imagery is to ask people to look forward using their imagination. It is unclear how the findings from the previous paragraph will apply in the new-product-learning domain. One might suggest that for radically new products, people might take difficulty of information processing as an indication of greater product innovativeness and might therefore give it a better evaluation. In my work, however, I have found that higher levels of difficulty lowers the perceived usefulness of the product and ultimately results in lower product evaluations. For example, in one of our studies, we asked participants to evaluate a new product (an audio PC). Participants were simply asked to envision either one or eight new activities they had never been able to do with computers but would be able to do with the audio PC. The results showed that even if participants were able to envision more new activities with the target product in the eight-activity condition, they gave the product a lower evaluation than did participants in the one-activity condition, and we theorize this is because visualizing eight new activities was more difficult than visualizing one new activity, and the increased difficulty stimulated a lower product evaluation.[15] A study with another new product (a wearable optical language translator) replicated the effect: difficulty imagining new uses resulted in lowered product evaluation when participants had high involvement in the task. When the involvement was low, the effect of imagination difficulty was attenuated.

The results suggest that managers should encourage customers to focus on the new benefits or the new uses for a new product, but encouraging consumers to imagine *multiple* uses may lead to lower evaluations because of the difficulty of imagination in this instance.

Conclusion

In this chapter, I have reviewed the latest research findings in visualization and new product evaluation in four different domains: (1) the role of process and outcome simulation in preference consistency over time; (2) the role of process and outcome simulation in improving new product evaluation; (3) the effect of past- and future-oriented visualization on new product evaluation; and (4) the effect of metacognitive experience on new product evaluation. There are three key takeaways:

1. To help consumers accurately predict their preference for new products when there is a large temporal distance between when they choose a product and when they actually use it, marketers should develop promotion strategies that encourage consumers to visualize how/when/where they will use the product (i.e., process simulation) because such visualization yields a preference that is similar to the preference they will have at the time of actual use. This way, their prediction will be more accurate or they will make a more realistic advance purchase. Alternatively, at the time of consumers' actual use of a product, marketers can encourage consumers to visualize the benefits the product will give them (i.e., outcome simulation), despite the challenges that usage poses. Doing so will help consumers switch their focus from learning cost to product benefit and will help them make the most of the novel benefits the new product provides. This further increases consumers' welfare and will also promote repeat purchases from the same company. Beyond the new product domain, the same rationales can be applied to any other domain where consumers demonstrate inconsistent preferences over time, such as helping them with their self-control.

2. To improve consumers' evaluations of new products, because it is not always easy to understand how to use the new products, marketers should try to switch consumers' focus away from thinking too much about how to technically use the product. They could do this by encouraging consumers to imagine how they will feel when they use the product, which will switch consumers' focus away from a cognitive interpretation of the usage process and will improve new product evaluation. However, if the product is primarily hedonic such that consumers care more about the affective experience they get than the way that the technology works (e.g., the iPad or iPhone), encouraging consumers to imagine their feelings about the overall benefits of the product is more effective in enhancing evaluation because benefit considerations are more vivid and lead more easily to affective immersion. It is very important to note that because consumers are lazy information processers, marketers should encourage consumers to go beyond simple visualization based on their current consumption routine and imagine new uses for and benefits of the product.

3. When, for product evaluation purposes, marketers want to encourage consumers to look back at their past experiences, the marketers should provide concrete, detailed product usage examples to aid consumers' visualization. However, when marketers want to encourage consumers to imagine future experience, they should avoid giving too many details and should instead provide general and abstract examples. Furthermore, when encouraging consumers to imagine using a new product, marketers should make it easy. Encouraging consumers to imagine multiple uses of a new product without providing specific examples may lead to lower evaluations because of the difficulty of imagination in this instance.

In the case of something like the Segway Human Transporter, marketers should encourage consumers to visualize how/where/when they will use this product so that consumers don't just focus on the novel benefits but also consider the usage process. At the time of consumption, when people are feeling intimidated by the challenges of using the product and no longer are as interested in its novel benefits, marketers should emphasize those positive benefits. In particular, to improve evaluations of products like the Segway, marketers should ask people to focus on its benefits and ignore all the emotional uncertainty, or focus on the way they will feel while they are travelling on the scooter. It is very important that marketers push consumers to use their imagination rather than letting consumers simply rely on their memories of past routines in similar scenarios. If asking consumers to think about a scenario in the past in which they might have used the Segway, marketers should provide abundant usage examples to aid their visualization, whereas if asking them to think about a future scenario in which they might use the Segway, examples should be brief. Finally, it is important that marketers keep the visualization process easy, because imagination difficulty leads to lower evaluations for new products.

How can different types of visualization be employed in the marketing practice? How can marketers direct consumers to perform a certain type of visualization? All these visualization strategies can be implemented through interaction with salespeople, in TV commercials or printed advertisements, or even through product descriptions on the product's packaging. In our studies, we simply gave participants an ad for the new product with appropriate visualization instructions and observed the effect that we expected. Recall the ad for a new washing machine that we mentioned in the beginning of this chapter, asking consumers to "imagine clothes looking new, longer." Depending on what the marketers would like the consumers to visualize, this message on the ad could easily be changed into, "Imagine how you feel about your clothes looking new, longer," and so on.

Lastly, while my research has focused on technologically new products such as the audio PC, other products that consumers have not used before or have not experienced before (e.g., baby stroller for first-time parents; first trip to China; first 3D movie) also share the characteristics of technologically new products: they provide consumers with new benefits, but bring along learning costs at the same time. As such, the visualization strategies reviewed above can also be applied to those new products and specific consumer groups. Such strategies can also be effectively employed in the tactics of brand management discussed by Sridhar Moorthy in chapter 3.

A Prescription for Harnessing the Psychology of Visualization to Increase New Product Adoption

Increasing new product adoption is vital to the ultimate success of marketing managers. The psychology of visualization implies that managers need to:

- ENCOURAGE consumers to visualize
  - how to use new products when forecasting their preference
  - the novel benefits at the time of usage.
- PROVIDE a limited number of general examples if consumers associate the product with future consumption.
- PROVIDE a significant number of detailed usage examples if consumers associate the product with past consumption.
- Make the visualization EASY, because difficulty of visualization decreases new product evaluation.

REFERENCES

1 Steve Kemper, *Code Name Ginger: The Story Behind Segway and Dean Kamen's Quest to Invent a New World* (Boston: Harvard Business School Press, 2003).
2 David Alexander, John G. Lynch, Jr., and Qing Wang, "As Time Goes By: Do Cold Feet Follow Warm Intentions for Really-New vs. Incrementally-New Products?" *Journal of Marketing Research* 65 (2008): 307–19.
3 John Gourville, "Eager Sellers and Stony Buyers: Understanding the Psychology of New Product Adoption," *Harvard Business Review* 84 (2006): 98–106.

4 Jennifer Gregan-Paxton and Deborah Roedder John, "Consumer Learning by Analogy: A Model of Internal Knowledge Transfer," *Journal of Consumer Research* 24 (1997): 266–84.

5 Yaacov Trope and Nira Liberman, "Temporal Construal," *Psychological Review* 110 (2003): 403–21.

6 Shelley E. Taylor, Lien B. Pham, Inna D. Rivkin, and David A. Armor, "Harnessing the Imagination: Mental Simulation, Self-Regulation and Coping," *American Psychologist* 53 (1998): 429–39.

7 Jennifer Edson Escalas and Mary Frances Luce, "Understanding the Effects of Process-Focused Versus Outcome-Focused Thought in Response to Advertising," *Journal of Consumer Research* 31 (2004): 274–85.

8 Min Zhao, Steve Hoeffler, and Gal Zauberman, "Mental Simulation and Preference Consistency Over Time: The Role of Process- versus Outcome-Focused Thoughts," *Journal of Marketing Research* 44 (2007): 379–88.

9 Steve Hoeffler, "Measuring Preferences for Really New Products," *Journal of Marketing Research* 40 (2003): 406–20.

10 Min Zhao, Steve Hoeffler, and Gal Zauberman, "Mental Simulation and Product Evaluation: The Affective and Cognitive Dimensions of Process- versus Outcome-Focused Thoughts," *Journal of Marketing Research* 48, no. 5 (2011): 827–39.

11 Min Zhao, Steve Hoeffler, and Darren Dahl, "The Role of Imagination-Focused Visualization on New Product Evaluation," *Journal of Marketing Research* 46 (2009): 46–55.

12 Min Zhao, Darren Dahl, and Steve Hoeffler, "Matching Temporal Perspective and Visualization Aids to Enhance New Product Evaluation: The Role of Retrospective and Anticipatory Views," working paper, University of Toronto, 2011.

13 Michaela Wanke, Gerd Bohner, and Andreas Jurkowitsch, "There Are Many Reasons to Drive a BMW: Does Imagined Ease of Argument Generation Influence Attitudes?" *Journal of Consumer Research* 24 (1997): 170–7.

14 Jennifer Edson Escalas, "Imagine Yourself in the Product: Mental Simulation, Narrative Transportation, and Persuasion," *Journal of Advertising* 33, no. 2 (2004): 37–48.

15 Min Zhao, Steve Hoeffler, and Darren Dahl, "Imagination Difficulty and New Product Evaluation," *Journal of Product Innovation Management* (forthcoming).

10 The Role of Morality in Consumer Decisions

NINA MAZAR

As Avi Goldfarb outlines in chapter 4, the commercialization of the internet has revolutionized the way consumers communicate with companies as well as with each other; it has led to a fall in search costs and an increase in the availability of products in the long tail. The internet has become a giant candy store in which consumers can find virtually everything at their fingertips. But the new possibilities come with new challenges for managers. While over the last decade the market for digital content such as music, movies, and books has seen incredible growth (today, already half of Amazon's book sales are digital),[1] it has also seen record levels of illegal downloading through peer-to-peer software (P2P), cyberlockers, MP3 search engines, overseas pay sites, emails, and instant messaging that undermine growth, erode values for talent as well as investors, and discourage innovation. Perhaps even more disturbing, statistics suggest that people of all ages, across the board, are engaging in some form of unauthorized downloading. In other words, these transgressions are not just committed by a few bad apples.

The truth is, even though most of us consider ourselves to be moral human beings, most of us engage in less-than-virtuous behaviours from time to time. This is why immoral acts are all too prevalent in day-to-day life. This is why "wardrobing" – the purchase, use, and then return of the used clothing – costs the U.S. retail industry an estimated $16 billion annually,[2] and why the overall magnitude of fraud in the U.S. property and casualty insurance industry is estimated to be 10 per cent of total claims payments, or $24 billion annually.[3] And this is what makes it a challenge for managers: How should one fight and deter illegal, immoral, or asocial actions when a large share of one's customer base engages in such actions?

To make it even more challenging, what if, for example, people who illegally download music from the internet spend more money on legal music than anyone else? What? Unlikely to be true? Think twice! A study in the UK[4] found that those who admitted to illegally downloading music on average 75 per cent more a year on legal music than those who claimed that they never downloaded music illegally, and another study in Canada[5] concluded that P2P file sharing had increased music sales: for every twelve P2P downloads (one album), music purchasing had been estimated to increase by 0.44 CDs per year. In light of such statistics, how can a manager fight the serious threats that illegal downloading brings about without alienating its core customers?

Let's look at a second type of conundrum. Why do consumers with energy-efficient washing machines end up washing more clothes,[6] or why do purchasers of eco-cars end up driving their cars more often?[7] In fact, it has been estimated that one-third of consumers who make energy-efficiency efforts at home do not see a decrease in their energy bills at all.[8] Why? It turns out that even if we consider ourselves to be responsible members of the society and make, for example, environment-friendly purchases or investment decisions, we sometimes unconsciously and quickly adjust our consumption patterns to the new circumstances – and these adjustments can neutralize or even reverse our initial efforts. Aside from directly diminishing societal marketing efforts, the danger of such paradoxical behaviour is that it can lead to customer dissatisfaction with a purchased product and negative changes in attitudes towards a brand because of consumers' lack of awareness of their change in consumption patterns. That is, similar to what my colleague Claire Tsai discussed in chapter 6 of this book when she talked about why people do not buy what they enjoy the most, there is a lack of consumer insight into their own motivations when it comes to moral and prosocial actions.

Thus, while the mixed signals that a manager receives from consumers may seem confusing, what they clearly show is that when it comes to the role of morality, a distinction between black-and-white, immoral individuals – who only engage in calculative cost-benefit analyses and display immoral behaviour whenever beneficial to them – and those individuals that are 100 per cent moral is too simplified and displaced. Instead, most people consider themselves to be honest human beings and engage in naïve, irrational judgments and decisions. This type of behaviour requires a different way of thinking for companies and societies alike. Thus, the challenge for today's managers is twofold:

1 From a company welfare perspective: How to decrease consumer immorality – and thus the costs or losses that companies directly incur because of it – without punishing their core customers?
2 From a societal marketing perspective: How to help consumers to stay on track and continue acting in line with their standards rather than licensing themselves to transgress after a good deed? That is, how to avoid any backfiring for the sake of consumers' happiness and societal welfare?

To tackle those challenges, the evolving role of the marketing manager encompasses the ability to understand the psychological mechanisms that underlie moral judgment and decision-making and the ability to creatively combine that knowledge with economic principles as well as the latest design and technology trends, such as those found in the gaming and social networking domain. The aim of this chapter is to facilitate this endeavour: it introduces a theoretical framework to help managers think about their customers in terms of morality and offers guidelines on how to nudge consumers to behave more in line with their standards.[9,10]

Immorality

Rational Immorality

Rooted in the standard economic model of the "homo economicus" – a rational and selfish human being – is the belief that people carry out immoral acts consciously and deliberately by trading off the expected external benefits and costs of the act.[11] According to this perspective, consumers would consider three aspects as they debate whether to engage in illegal downloading: the expected benefit they stand to gain from illegal downloading (free content), the probability of being caught doing it, and the magnitude of punishment if caught. On the basis of these inputs, people are moral or immoral only to the extent that the trade-off favours a particular action. In addition to being central to economic theory, this view plays an important role in the theory of crime and punishment, which forms the basis for most measures aimed at preventing immoral behaviour and guides punishments against those who exhibit it.

Such a rational view suggests that there are three ways to curb the frequency and magnitude of immoral actions: lowering the magnitude of external rewards, increasing the probability of being caught, and increasing the magnitude of the expected punishment. These measures seem simple and straightforward, yet reality has proven that there are limits to their success. For example, although the music industry has increased its anti-piracy measures – for example, by investing in technologies for better copy-protection of CDs and DVDs and blocking of unauthorized downloads (decreasing external rewards), improving consumer identifiability (increasing the probability of being caught), and increasing fines (increasing the punishment) – P2P music-swapping is still very popular. A recently conducted poll in the UK,[4] which surveyed 1,000 sixteen- to fifty-year-olds with internet access, found that at least three out of four consumers understood that P2P music download was illegal, yet 46 per cent of the people in the survey admitted using one or more of the sites most associated with illegal downloading. That means not only that these large and expensive efforts for increased compliance seem to be (to some extent) a waste of time and money but also that they are likely to hit the core customers the most – in effect alienating valuable customers and decreasing their loyalty. And this observation is not just specific to the music industry; it seems to replicate in other domains. One of the hypotheses put forward to explain the limited effectiveness and even potentially harmful effects of the standard economic interventions has been that rational immoral behaviour is most likely committed only by a few "bad apples." By contrast, this hypothesis suggests that the major damage is being committed by a different type of immorality altogether, one that most people engage in and that needs a different intervention approach: naïve, irrational immorality.[12]

Naïve, Irrational Immorality

From a psychological perspective, and in addition to financial considerations, another set of important inputs to the decision of whether to be, for example, honest (or not) is based on internal rewards. Research has shown that, as part of socialization, people internalize the norms and values of their society,[13] and these serve as an internal benchmark against which a person compares and judges his/her behaviour. Compliance with one's internal value system provides positive rewards, whereas noncompliance leads to negative rewards.

Applied to the context of morality, one major way in which the internal reward system exerts control over behaviour is by influencing the way people view and perceive themselves (i.e., their self-concept).[14] Indeed, it has been shown that people typically value honesty – that is, honesty is part of their internal reward system; that they have very strong beliefs in their own morality; and they want to maintain this aspect of their self-concept.[15,16] This means that if a person fails to comply with his/her internal standards for morality, he/she will have to negatively update his/her self-concept, which is aversive. On the other hand, if a person complies with his/her internal standards, he/she avoids such negative updating and maintains his/ her positive self-view in terms of being a moral person. Interestingly, this perspective suggests that in order to maintain their positive self-concepts, individuals will comply with their internal standards even when doing so involves investments of effort or sacrifices of financial gains.[17] In our illegal downloading example, this perspective suggests that people who contemplate doing it will be influenced not only by the expected external benefits, the probability of being caught, and the magnitude of punishment if caught, but also by the manner in which illegal downloading might make them perceive themselves. In other words, most people are often torn between two competing motivations when there is a temptation to be dishonest: gaining from cheating versus maintaining their positive self-concept as honest individuals. If they cheat, they could, for example, gain financially, but at the expense of an honest self-concept. In contrast, if they take the high road, they might forgo financial benefits but maintain their honest self-concept. This seems to be a win-lose situation; choosing one path involves sacrificing the other.

My co-authors, On Amir and Dan Ariely, and I[18] have found evidence that people typically solve this motivational dilemma adaptively by finding a balance between the two motivating forces such that they can reap some of the benefits from behaving dishonestly but still maintain their positive self-concept in terms of being moral individuals.[19] That is, there seems to be a magnitude range of dishonesty within which people find ways to "trick" themselves; in this way, they can cheat at least a little bit, yet their behaviours – which they would usually consider dishonest – do not bear negatively on their self-concept.

One of the major implications of this process is that attempts to curb this "long-tail" type of limited dishonesty should be directed at shrinking the "fudge factor," and thus making it psychologically harder for individuals to "trick" themselves.

Shrinking and Expanding the "Fudge Factor"

Two of the tricks that individuals employ to morally disengage from their detrimental conduct are categorization and inattention.

For example, for certain types of behaviours and smaller magnitudes of dishonesty, people can categorize their actions in more compatible terms and find rationalizations for them.[20] Behaviours with malleable categorization are ones that allow people to reinterpret them in a self-serving manner, and the degree of malleability is likely to be determined by their context. For example, intuition suggests that it is easier to steal a 10¢ pencil from a friend than to steal 10¢ out of this friend's wallet to buy a pencil, because the former scenario offers more possibilities to categorize the action in terms that are compatible with friendship (e.g., I'll give it back to my friend later; this is what friends do).

This thought experiment suggests that a higher degree of categorization malleability facilitates dishonesty (stealing), but also that some actions are inherently less malleable and therefore cannot be categorized successfully in compatible terms.[21,22] In related work, On Amir, Dan Ariely, and I[18] showed that when the reward from being dishonest was presented as tokens (rather than cash) that participants knew would be exchanged for cash right after the experiment, they cheated more than those for whom the reward was presented as cash. Based on these findings we argued that as society moves away from cash and electronic exchanges become more prevalent in the economy, their impact on increasing naïve, irrational dishonesty should not be underestimated; they provide more opportunities for people to re-categorize their actions. In other words, as the categorization malleability increases, so does the magnitude of dishonesty a person can commit without feeling bad.

In addition to categorization, another "trick" that people employ is to decrease their attention to their moral standards. When people are mindful of their moral standards, any dishonest action is more likely to influence their self-concept, which in turn will cause people to adhere to a stricter delineation of honest and dishonest behaviour.[23,24] However, when individuals are inattentive to their own moral standards, their actions are not evaluated relative to their standards, their self-concept is less likely to be updated, and therefore their behaviour is more likely to diverge from their standards. Thus, in cases in which one's moral standards are more accessible, people will have to confront the meaning of their actions more readily and therefore be more honest about them. For example, Diener and Wallbom[25] showed that confronting people with a reflection of themselves in a mirror increased their self-awareness and turned their attention inwards to their moral standards such that people ended up cheating less. Similarly, in one of our papers, On Amir, Dan Ariely, and I[18] demonstrated that asking people to recall the Ten Commandments eliminated cheating. In this sense, greater attention to standards may be modelled as a stricter range for the magnitude of dishonest actions that does not trigger updating of the self-concept, or a lower threshold up to which people can be dishonest without influencing how they feel about themselves in terms of being a moral person.

Moral Licensing

Moral licensing is another aspect that contributes to the paradoxical findings of consumers with high social and ethical standards engaging in detrimental conduct.

The basic idea behind moral licensing is that, because individuals desire a positive moral self-image but moral or prosocial behaviour typically comes at a cost, people keep a running tab or mental account of their moral actions that they strive to maintain at an equilibrium.[26] For example, when individuals have done something good, their good deed increases their moral self-image, making them feel as though they have earned moral credits or credentials. This in turn evokes the feeling of a "licence" to engage in more self-interested immoral or asocial behaviours that otherwise would have discredited their self-image. Thus, people are more likely to engage in transgressions when their moral self-image positively deviates from the equilibrium. The opposite, however, is true as well: if they have behaved in a way that lowers their self-image, they will engage in compensatory behaviour to re-establish a positive view of themselves as being moral and prosocial individuals.[27]

Day-to-day observations that fit into this framework are all too prevalent. For example, a recent report in *USA Today* claimed that "... even though hybrid owners may be able to save gas, they eat up the savings by driving more on pleasure trips. Their commute habits are about the same as non-hybrid drivers, but they logged up to 25% more on trips not related to their jobs."[28] This observation seems to suggest that the purchasing, owning, and driving of a hybrid car established moral credentials that people used to fulfill their more selfish desires of comfort (avoiding walking small distances) and fun (taking more leisure trips). That is, a constant patting on the back and feeling good about oneself can provide a lasting licence to indulge without the fear of discrediting oneself – a powerful mechanism that has the potential to debilitate progress. On the flipside and a more positive note, the moral balancing act might also contribute to customers who end up purchasing a gas guzzler to compensate any feelings of guilt by driving less.

It is very counterproductive from a welfare perspective and (for example) a cause marketing campaign if consumers who care about the environment and engage in corresponding behaviour subsequently feel licensed to behave more selfishly and less prosocially or morally. In addition, consumers might be unaware of their behavioural changes. Thus, any dissatisfaction that might stem from not observing any of the anticipated changes after having purchased energy-efficient light bulbs or a hybrid car may be passed on to the product, brand, or company, and thus could reflect negatively on consumer attitudes towards them.

While the existing research has shown convincing evidence for the existence of naïve, irrational immorality as well as moral licensing, little is known about how to answer the questions that are most relevant to a manager, such as:

- What can be done to curb naïve, irrational immorality in day-to-day activities?
- How can we help consumers not fall into the licensing trap and its counteractive consequences subsequent to committing a good deed?

One of the key tenets of behavioural economics[9,10] is to not only understand the psychological processes underlying behavioural biases but also to develop psychological/behavioural interventions to counter those biases and their negative consequences to welfare. In line with this approach, the subsequent section discusses some ideas, tools, and techniques that have the potential to successfully nudge consumers into behaving more in line with their moral standards and to help managers curb consumer dishonesty without alienating the majority of their customer base. This in turn will help managers to maintain positive consumer attitudes while increasing the success of cause-related marketing campaigns and societal marketing at large.

Interventions

Naturally, some of the prescriptions for managers are more straightforward than others. When it comes to the question of how to curb naïve, irrational immorality in day-to-day activities, the general takeaway is that one must design measures that increase people's attention to their moral standards or that decrease their possibility of reinterpreting or justifying their actions, thus making it harder for individuals to "trick" themselves into immoral or asocial actions.

For example, the policy review forms sent out by automobile insurance companies ask customers to indicate, among other things, the current odometer mileage of each of their cars, and this serves as an input to calculate the insurance premium. The higher the number of kilometres driven since the last policy review form, the higher the insurance premium for the car. The challenge that companies face when relying on honest customer self-reports is how to enforce honesty when it is in the customers' interest to misreport facts, and when customers know that the likelihood of being caught cheating is small. The approach currently employed by many companies is to ask clients to sign a statement of honour at the end of a self-report form. In my work with Lisa Shu, Francesca Gino, Dan Ariely, and Max Bazerman, we proposed that the location of the statement of honour matters.[29] In particular, we argued that simply moving the statement of honour from the end to the beginning of a form would bring one's moral standards into focus right before it is most needed, and when an individual still has a clean moral conscience: before facing the temptation to be dishonest. Thus, the increased saliency of moral standards could have a positive effect on the truthfulness of the subsequent self-report. In contrast, when signing after the "damage" has been done, individuals have already found ways to "trick" themselves and managed to consider themselves to be good people despite their transgressions. Thus, signing a statement of honour at the end would come too late. To test the hypothesis, together with an insurance company we sent out two types of review forms to car owners: one group received the traditional form with an honour statement to be signed at the end while another group of customers received a variant form that had an honour statement to be signed at the beginning. When the forms came back, we compared the reported odometer mileage to the last report to calculate the kilometres driven. In line with our theory, an intervention as simple as moving the signature field to the beginning of the form increased the average reported kilometres driven per car by roughly 4,000 kilometres – a result we estimated would increase a customer's insurance premium (i.e., the insurance's income) by almost $100 per car. Similar effects might be achieved by putting up mirrors in front of product shelves or designing pop-up windows on a computer screen with random questions such as "how important is honesty in your family?" or "how much do you care about your community?" The key is to raise attention to one's standards *at the point of temptation*, and even subtle cues such as a picture or a schematic representation of a pair of watching eyes[30] has been shown to be successful in increasing compliance.

In addition to increasing attention to one's moral standards, the other option to decrease naïve, irrational immorality is to decrease the consumers' ability to reinterpret or justify their immoral actions as well as the consequences of their actions. Previous findings have shown that the more ambiguous an action and the less direct or certain its consequences,[22,31] the easier for individuals to disregard, minimize, or reinterpret them. For example, On Amir, Dan Ariely, and I[18] showed in one of our experiments that students cheated more for tokens than for cash. In addition, the easier it is to displace or diffuse responsibility for one's actions, and the more dehumanized and blame-worthy the victim of one's transgression, the easier it is to transgress. For instance, individuals appear to be less reluctant to engage in immoral actions if they feel interdependent and part of a larger group,[32,33] and they are much more likely to deceive large organizations and rich counterparts than private individuals.[31,34]

Together, these examples suggest that (a) decreasing hierarchy in a group decision or organizational context, (b) increasing personal responsibility and accountability, (c) humanizing the victims of transgressions, and (d) making the consequences of people's actions much more salient are all important and valuable design features for more effective interventions. Some of these features are already being increasingly exercised. For instance, over the past few years, the music, film, and software industries have featured public messages that illustrated how illegal downloads hurt the rank-and-file workers (and not just the big corporations) by reducing their job security or pay (see, e.g., television advertisements and movie trailers launched by the Motion Picture Association of America in 2003 and 2004). While doing so, however, managers need to be careful not to make their customers feel prejudged as immoral beings or criminals. Such a message would alienate customers and could potentially generate reactance, leading to a backfiring intervention.

The more challenging question revolves around how to counteract the licensing effect. The fact that a good deed produces a warm glow and has the potential to create moral credit that can be subsequently used to one's selfish advantage is a key aspect to focus on when designing interventions. For example, together with my collaborator Chen-Bo Zhong, I[35] showed that the act of purchasing green products (i.e., buying organic and environment-friendly products) can create the licensing effect. If environmentally conscious behaviour is something that a society values and strives for, then it might be useful to use the power of peer effects in running ad campaigns that show how being green is nothing special but simply the norm – something that everyone is doing and that is the right thing to do. In other words, instead of giving people reason to feel too much of a warm glow when engaging in green behaviour, the key might be to create a norm such that not engaging in green behaviour would create feelings of wrongdoing.

The other possibility lies in trying to keep customers interested and involved in doing the "right" thing. Humans have proven to be creatively adaptive in their ideas and strategies for "tricking" themselves into giving in to selfish immoral or asocial temptations without feeling bad about themselves. Yet recent trends in connectivity, mobility, and social media offer promising tools to tackle that challenge and help individuals keep being interested in doing good. In particular, it might be useful to apply some of the design principles of successful Alternate Reality Games (ARGs), such as Kevan Davis' *Chore Wars* or the *Nike + iPod Sport Kit*, which have been designed to improve people's quality of life and effect real-world change. For example, *Chore Wars* is an online role-playing game that aims to make chores fun by rewarding their completion with experience points that help individuals' characters to "level up." In addition, it measures how much work each individual in a household is doing and lets people share that information. The interesting observation to make is that *Chore Wars* encourages participation by setting compelling goals, interesting obstacles, and well-designed feedback systems that tap into our natural desires to master challenges, be creative, and push the limits of our abilities – elements that also could prove useful when thinking about how to help people to not fall into a moral licensing or balancing trap.

According to Jane McGonigal, the author of *Reality Is Broken*, "The best ARGs are the ones that, like the best traditional computer and video games, help us create more satisfying work for ourselves, cultivate better hopes of success, strengthen our social bonds and activate our social networks, and give us the chance to contribute to something bigger than ourselves"[36] (p. 127). Based on these design principles, similar to *Chore Wars* and other ARGs, a company could add a website feature that allows individuals to set clear and attainable goals, log in their good deeds, keep track of them, receive instant feedback about their performance, collect rewards, and be part of a community with which they can share their performance, compete, or collaborate to achieve even bigger goals. In addition, in order to keep individuals interested, it would be important to increase the difficulty level over time by offering more attractive but harder-to-get rewards. Together, such a game might encourage and help individuals – at least, those who sign up voluntarily to play such a game – to continue doing "good" rather than falling into the licensing trap.

A Prescription for Decreasing Consumer Immorality

Consumer dishonesty and immorality is a problem of increased concern for managers. To design programs that encourage ethical actions and curb immorality, managers need to:

- INCREASE customers' attention to moral standards (e.g., through questions, mirrors, eyes-pictures, signatures, honour codes that guide introspection).
- DECREASE the possibility for customers to re-interpret or justify their actions (e.g., decrease the perception of hierarchy in a group decision, increase the perception of personal responsibility and accountability, humanize the "victims" of transgressions, make the consequences of customers' actions more salient and decrease ambiguity).
- SET the right norms and expectations to minimize customers' feelings of warm glow.
- KEEP customers interested and involved in doing the "right" thing (e.g., through challenges or Alternate Reality Games).

REFERENCES

1 Adam Hartung, "Amazon's 4 Keys to Spectacular Revenue Growth," *Forbes*, 28 July 2011, accessed 1 November 2011 from http://www.forbes.com/sites/adamhartung/2011/07/28/amazons-4-secrets-to-spectacular-revenue-growth/.

2 David Speights and Mark Hilinski, "Return Fraud and Abuse: How to Protect Profits," *Retailing Issues Letter* 17, no. 1 (2005): 1–6.

3 "One-Fourth of Americans Say It's Acceptable to Defraud Insurance Companies, Accenture Survey Finds," Accenture Inc. Press Release, 12 February 2003, accessed 8 May 2012 from http://newsroom.accenture.com/article_display.cfm?article_id=3970.

4 Rachel Shields, "Illegal Downloaders 'Spend the Most on Music,' Says Poll," *The Independent*, 1 November 2009, accessed 1 November 2011 from http://www.independent.co.uk/news/uk/crime/illegal-downloaders-spend-the-most-on-music-says-poll-1812776.html.

5 Dave Parrack, "Government Study Proves Illegal File Sharing Increases Music Sales," *Tech.Blorge Technology News*, 3 November 2007, accessed 1 November 2011 from http://tech.blorge.com/Structure:%20/2007/11/03/government-study-proves-illegal-file-sharing-increases-music-sales/.

6 Lucas W. Davis, "Durable Goods and Residential Demand for Energy and Water: Evidence from a Field Trial," *RAND Journal of Economics* 39, no. 2 (2008): 530–46.

7 Satoshi Fujii and Hiroyuki Ohta, "Does a Technology to Reduce Defector's Negative Impacts 'Worsen' Social Dilemmas? – Backfire Effect of Purchasing an Eco-Car," 13th International Conference on Social Dilemmas, Kyoto, Japan, 20–24 August 2009.

8 Traci Watson, "Consumers Sabotage Energy-Saving Efforts," *USA Today*, 22 March 2009, accessed 1 November 2011 from http://www.usatoday.com/money/industries/energy/2009-03-22-energysavings_N.htm.

9 On Amir, Dan Ariely, Alan Cooke, David Dunning, Nicholas Epley, Botond Koszegi, Donald Lichtenstein, Nina Mazar, Sendhil Mullainathan, Drazen Prelec, Eldar Shafir, and Jose Silva, "Behavioral Economics, Psychology, and Public Policy," *Marketing Letters* 16, nos. 3–4 (2005): 443–54.

10 Richard H. Thaler and Cass R. Sunstein, *Nudge: Improving Decisions about Health, Wealth, and Happiness* (New Haven, CT: Yale University Press, 2008).

11 Gary S. Becker, "Crime and Punishment: An Economic Approach," *Journal of Political Economy* 76, no. 2 (1968): 169–217.

12 Nina Mazar and Dan Ariely, "Dishonesty in Everyday Life and its Policy Implications," *Journal of Public Policy and Marketing* 25, no. 1 (2006): 117–26.

13 Joseph Henrich, Robert Boyd, Samuel Bowles, Colin Camerer, Ernst Fehr, Herbert Gintis, and Richard McElreath, "In Search of Homo Economicus: Behavioral Experiments in 15 Small-Scale Societies," *American Economic Review* 91, no. 2 (2001): 73–8.

14 Daryl J. Bem, "Self-Perception Theory," in Leonard Berkowitz, ed., *Advances in Experimental Social Psychology*, vol. 6 (New York: Academic Press, 1972), 1–62.

15 Karl Aquino and Americus Reed, "The Self-Importance of Moral Identity," *Journal of Personality and Social Psychology* 83, no. 6 (2002): 1423–40.

16 Josephson Institute of Ethics, "2010 Report Card on the Ethics of American Youth," 2011, accessed 8 May 2012 from http://charactercounts.org/pdf/reportcard/2010/ReportCard2010_data-tables.pdf.

17 Elliot Aronson and J. Merrill Carlsmith, "Performance Expectancy as a Determinant of Actual Performance," *Journal of Abnormal and Social Psychology* 65, no. 3 (1962): 178–82.

18 Nina Mazar, On Amir, and Dan Ariely, "The Dishonesty of Honest People: A Theory of Self-Concept Maintenance," *Journal of Marketing Research* 45, no. 6 (2008): 633–44.

19 Dan Ariely, *Predictably Irrational* (New York: HarperCollins, 2008).

20 Albert Bandura, "Social Cognitive Theory of Moral Thought and Action," in W.M. Kurtines and J.L. Gewirtz, eds., *Handbook of Moral Behavior and Development*, vol. 1 (Hillsdale, NJ: Erlbaum, 1991), 45–103.

21 Jason Dana, Roberto A. Weber, and Jason Xi Kuang, "Exploiting Moral Wiggle Room: Experiments Demonstrating an Illusory Preference for Fairness," *Economic Theory* 33 (2005): 67–80.

22 Maurice E. Schweitzer and Christopher K. Hsee, "Stretching the Truth: Elastic Justification and Motivated Communication of Uncertain Information," *Journal of Risk and Uncertainty* 25, no. 2 (2002): 185–201.

23 Thomas S. Duval and Robert A. Wicklund, *A Theory of Objective Self Awareness* (New York: Academic Press, 1972).

24 Ellen J. Langer, "Minding Matters: The Consequences of Mindlessness-Mindfulness," in Leonard Berkowitz, ed., *Advances in Experimental Social Psychology* (San Diego, CA: Academic Press, 1989), 137–73.

25 Edward Diener and Marc Wallbom, "Effects of Self-Awareness on Antinormative Behavior," *Journal of Research in Personality* 10, no. 1 (1976): 107–11.

26 Dale T. Miller and Daniel A. Effron, "Psychological License: When it is Needed and How it Functions," in M. P. Zanna and J. M. Olson, eds., *Advances in Experimental Social Psychology*, vol. 43 (San Diego, CA: Academic Press, 2010), 115–55.

27 Chen-Bo Zhong, Katie A. Liljenquist, and D.M. Cain, "Moral Self-Regulation: Licensing and Compensation," in D. De Cremer, ed., *Psychological Perspectives on Ethical Behavior and Decision Making* (Charlotte, NC: Information Age, 2009), 75–89.

28 Chris Woodyard, "Hybrid Car Owners Drive More and Get More Traffic Tickets, Study Finds," *USA Today*, 17 July 2009, accessed 1 November 2011 from http://content.usatoday.com/communities/driveon/post/2009/07-/68494710/1.

29 Lisa L. Shu, Nina Mazar, Francesca Gino, Dan Ariely, and Max H. Bazerman, "Signing at the Beginning Makes Ethics Salient and Decreases Self-Reports in Comparison to Signing at the End," *Proceedings of the National Academy of Sciences of the United States of America* (2012): In press.

30 Mary Rigdon, Keiko Ishii, Motoki Watabe, and Shinobu Kitayama, "Minimal Social Cues in the Dictator Game," *Journal of Economic Psychology* 30 (2009): 358–67.

31 Uri Gneezy, "Deception: The Role of Consequences," *American Economic Review* 95, no. 1 (2005): 384–94.

32 Philip G. Zimbardo, "The Human Choice: Individuation, Reason, and Order versus Deindividuation, Impulse, and Chaos," *Nebraska Symposium on Motivation* 17, no. 17 (1969): 237–307.

33 Nina Mazar and Pankaj Aggarwal, "Greasing the Palm: Can Collectivism Promote Bribery?" *Psychological Science* 22, no. 7 (2011): 843–8.

34 Insurance Research Council, "Public Attitude Monitor" (Malvern, PA: Insurance Research Council, 1991).

35 Nina Mazar and Chen-Bo Zhong, "Do Green Products Make Us Better People?" *Psychological Science* 21, no. 4 (2010): 494–8.

36 Jane McGonigal, *Reality Is Broken: Why Games Make Us Better and How They Can Change the World* (London: Penguin Press, 2010).

PART THREE

Marketing Management to Engage

11 Manage Customer Value through Incentives

MENGZE SHI

Every year billions of dollars are spent on consumer incentives in the form of price discounts, prizes, and rewards. Companies need to incorporate into their strategy the effective use of incentive programs in managing their customer relationships; otherwise, they will fall behind and lose competitive advantage. This imperative mandates a substantially improved understanding of these incentive programs. As today's world is changing faster and faster, only managers equipped with such knowledge can readily adapt the design of their incentive programs to the new marketing landscape. Currently, an array of the emerging market trends has brought new challenges to the effective use and design of incentive programs:

- Consumers are increasingly relying on the internet to search for product information. The emergence of social media has developed numerous online communities. Like their counterparts in offline world, opinion leaders in these online communities have established their status and exhibited strong influences on community members. How should firms manage their relationships with these opinion leaders? Should firms offer incentives to encourage them to spread positive word-of-mouth? Would monetary incentives increase the opinion leaders' propensity to make referrals? Can it backfire?
- Consumers are increasingly connected through telecommunication services and in the virtual world. An incentive offered to one consumer may have a ripple effect through the consumer's social network. A wireless phone service provider tracks the communication network of each individual caller. If the company gives a

customer an incentive, say, a discount for the customer's outgoing calls, should the company evaluate the return of this promotion based on only the changes to the customer's future calling behaviour and loyalty to the company? Should they also consider the changes that occurred to the people within this customer's personal calling network? For example, these callers may have to pay for the incoming calls from this customer, and they may increase the number of calls to this customer next month. Clearly, a proper assessment of promotional effectiveness has to go beyond the boundary of individual consumers. Knowing the social network structure has useful implications on the design of network-based pricing plans like Friends and Family plans. Connected consumers are also the targets of group-based incentives, like the group-buying deals offered through Groupon.com and Livingsocial.com. Online consumers need to coordinate in signing up for these deals in order to achieve the required mass. The design of incentive programs should facilitate such coordination between consumers to improve success rate.

- Incentive programs are expanding beyond industry boundaries. Frequent flyer programs offered by the airlines have formed alliances with other airlines, hotels, gas stations, and even department stores. As the loyalty programs continue to expand in scale and scope, one might ask: Which companies are the right partners? Where should we draw the boundaries? Is a larger program always better? Now that consumers are facing networks of loyalty programs, one may wonder if each consumer would consolidate purchases around a focal program. Does each network plan have an anchoring company? What is a typical entry point to the network, and how does a consumer's relationship with the network and its member companies evolve?

The above scenarios point to the evolving roles played by consumer incentives and promotions: how the popularity of the internet, the prominence of social media, and increasing cross-industry collaborations affect the use of consumer incentives in the broad context of customer relationship management. This chapter will discuss each of these topics. The objective of this chapter is to provide a set of design principles for consumer incentive programs in consideration of these new market features. The chapter will cover a variety of commonly used consumer incentives, including coupons, rebates, prizes, sweepstakes, and customer loyalty programs. This chapter is organized around a set of design principles instead of type of incentive programs. The four principles, (1) align with objectives, (2) create and leverage size advantages, (3) harness the embedding of social relations, and (4) manage psychological perceptions, are outlined below.

1 Designing an effective promotion program should start with clear objectives. In the context of managing customer relationships, are the incentives offered to acquire new customers or to retain existing customers? If the purpose is to acquire new customers, are incentives provided to generate product awareness or overcome the barrier of switching from competing products? Having clear objectives not only dictates the optimal design of incentives, but also entails accurate measures of campaign effectiveness.

2 Size means scale and/or scope. An airline manages the scale of its frequent flyer program (FFP) by selecting flights, routes, and seat classes eligible for earning air miles. The airline expands the scope of its FFP by forming alliances with a large network of other retailers and service providers. Should a loyalty program pursue maximum scale and scope? If not, where should a loyalty program draw the boundary? Now consider a sweepstakes promotion. The size of a sweepstakes promotion is the total number of winning numbers, which increases with the duration of the promotion and the coverage of geographic areas and product categories. Similarly, is larger always better?

3 There are at least two types of social relations that affect incentive designs. One type of social relation is embedded in existing social networks. Consumer incentives can change the nature and strength of ties as well as the structure of networks. A discount on cellular phone prices or a referral reward can encourage people to talk to their friends more often. The dynamics of the social relationship may manifest itself through reciprocal behaviour. Naturally, knowledge of network structure is critical to the proper assessment of the ripple effect of consumer incentives in social networks. Another type of social relation is artificially created by incentives. Many loyalty programs including FFPs create ladders of social status. How should a company manage the supply of such status to balance the benefit of scarcity with accessibility?

4 The design of incentive programs can affect both perceived value of incentives and perceived acquisition cost. Consumer involvement in

such incentive programs like sweepstakes can create an illusion of control. Incentive programs such as loyalty programs require continued effort from consumers. For these programs, setting proper goals and creating the sense of progress is critical to maintain consumer engagement.

Next I elaborate and substantiate each of these four design principles. My discussion will be centred on the research I have conducted over the years. To provide a more comprehensive and stronger support for these principles, I will also draw key results from research conducted by other researchers in the area.

Principle 1: Align with Objectives

Designing an incentive program should start with clearly stated objectives. Research has shown that promotional objectives should dictate the optimal format of consumer incentives. Further elaboration of this connection requires detailed discussions on specific types of promotions including sweepstakes, phone rebates, and customer loyalty programs. All promotional objectives are stated in the context of managing customer relationships.

Promotion Objectives and Sweepstakes Prize Structure

Sweepstakes promotion is a popular consumer incentive. One of the major design questions concerns prize structure. For instance, given a budget of $1 million allocated to prizes, should a sweepstakes offer Winner-Take-All (one single grand prize of $1 million), Multiple Prizes (four large prizes each worth $250,000), or Large & Small Prizes (one large prize worth $250,000 and 100,000 small prizes each worth $5)? Among many factors, such as the risk attitude of target consumers and product categories, research shows that promotion objective should be an important consideration.[1] To illustrate, let us consider two diverse promotion objectives: to acquire new customers by enticing them away from competitors, or to retain existing customers by enhancing their relationship with the brand. Research reveals a stark contrast in the optimal sweepstakes prize structure between these two objectives: a sweepstakes for customer retention should offer Winner-Take-All or Multiple Prizes; in contrast, a sweepstakes intended for customer acquisition should provide Large & Small Prizes. This result is surprising because it seems natural that large prizes are necessary to draw new customers.

Before explaining the reasons behind the above results, it is first useful to explain briefly two important behavioural properties: over-weighing the chances of winning and loss aversion. First, most people do not use actual probabilities in evaluating the sweepstakes. Because the total number of eligible winning numbers often exceeds millions, the chance of winning is too small for most people to engage in objective calculations. Instead, people tend to use heuristics that typically magnify odds of winning. These heuristics are strongly influenced by exposures to "Someone has to win, why not you?" types of advertising on lotteries and sweepstakes that always feature only the winners. Such a decision bias is a major reason why lotteries attract millions of people even though the total payout is only a portion of the entire pool of money. Second, people tend to avoid anticipated loss because loss looms larger than gain of the same amount. When evaluating purchases associated with sweepstakes, consumers can anticipate both gains from winning prizes and losses associated with unfavourable outcomes. Loss aversion suggests that an anticipated loss has a stronger influence on consumer decisions than an anticipated gain of the same amount.

Promotions intended for customer retention should offer Multiple Prizes or even Winner-Take-All sweepstakes because of the tendency to over-weigh winning probabilities. Smaller probabilities (e.g., 1 out of 10 million) are over-weighed more than slightly higher probabilities (e.g., 1 out of 1 million). Therefore, larger prizes will be perceived as more valuable to current customers. In contrast, sweepstakes promotions intended for customer acquisition should offer a large number of small prizes because of loss aversion. When contemplating a switch to a new brand, a consumer anticipates gains if he/she wins prizes but losses if not. People can be attracted by the chance to win large prizes, but also want to avoid the disappointment of making wrong decisions – a switch induced by sweepstakes that does not result in winning any prizes. A good chance of winning a small prize can be employed to compensate such losses. Trivial prizes given by shopping malls and free coffees given by coffee shops are common examples of small prizes to avert the anticipated loss.

While the tendency to over-weigh the odds of winning leads to Winner-Take-All or Multiple Prizes, loss aversion suggests offering many small prizes. The resulting conflict in prize structure has to be resolved by clearly defined promotion objectives. When a sweepstakes promotion is used for customer acquisition, averting the anticipated loss is an important consideration. Therefore, Large & Small Prizes should be offered. When the promotion targets existing customers, loss aversion is less relevant and therefore a company should offer Winner-Take-All or Multiple Prizes.

Promotion Objectives and Phone Rebates

The wireless communication service industry is very competitive due to the commodified nature of services being offered by the competing providers. The competition has become particularly intense as the industry matures with few new customers for revenue growth. A common practice in this industry is to acquire new customers through an upfront phone subsidy, in the form of a large discount towards a new phone or even a free phone. In return, consumers are asked to commit to multi-year service contracts. Customer retention becomes automatic during the contract period because of the penalty clause in the contract. Unless there is a huge price decrease down the road, customers will stay with the service provider to avoid paying the penalty. Clearly, the phone subsidy is used for customer acquisition. Firms can assess the effectiveness of the promotion by comparing the estimated cost of the subsidy with the expected return from the multi-year contract. The incentive design decisions mainly concern the choice of phones and the size of subsidies. In principle, firms should look for phones that offer higher values to consumers with lower costs to the firms. It is also important to design service contracts properly to minimize the anxiety associated with committing to long-term contracts. Options to switch between the service contracts within the service providers can reduce consumer anxiety and make customer acquisition easier.

   Phone subsidy strategies do not have to be for customer acquisition only. In some markets, phone subsidies are used for customer retention, too. Developed economies have well-established legal and credit systems to enforce binding contracts. Once a multi-year service contract is signed, customers have to pay the monthly fees or a one-time penalty for premature ending of contract. However, such an enforcement system is immature or absent in many markets. Due to the high risk of the consumers reneging on the contracts, companies would not hand out a large upfront phone subsidy for fear of low guaranteed return. As a result, many companies offer dynamic phone subsidies. To illustrate, consider a consumer interested in a new phone with a regular retail price of $300. Instead of offering a $240 phone subsidy and charging only $60 for the phone in return for a commitment to a two-year service contract with a monthly fee of $40, the company can spread the $240 subsidy over twenty-four months. Effectively, during the two-year period, consumers would receive the same service package, but pay a reduced monthly fee of $30 instead. The total amount of the phone subsidy still adds up to $240. However, anytime the consumer stops subscribing to the company's wireless services, the phone subsidy stops automatically.

A dynamic phone subsidy contributes to both customer acquisition and retention. Every month the recurring monthly rebate rewards customer loyalty. The remaining balance of the phone subsidy provides forward-looking consumers with an incentive to stay. A dynamic phone subsidy also contributes to customer acquisition. Consumers naturally calculate the total amount of benefits from the entire subsidy plan and choose a firm that provides better values of services. The challenge arises as these two objectives may ask for different types of dynamic phone subsidy plans. For retention purposes, a plan should have a small monthly subsidy spreading over a long time horizon. Since service prices between competing providers are usually quite close, a small subsidy will be sufficient to retain the customers and prevent them from switching to other firms. However, for acquisition purposes, a plan should have a large monthly subsidy spreading over a short time horizon because customers always prefer a large amount of incentives captured over a shorter time horizon. Again, the balance between the monthly amount and duration should be designed according to the promotional objectives.

The idea of spreading consumer incentives out over time is applicable to any situations in which consumers need recurring services or products. In the markets where it is costly to implement long-term commitment contracts, companies may want to spread the incentives to reward recurring loyalties. Companies also need to monitor changes in the market environment constantly. In the wireless communication service industry, when Wireless Number Portability (WNP) was implemented, consumers could switch operators without changing their phone numbers. This policy substantially reduced consumer switching costs, making customer retention more challenging. In the meantime, as switching is more likely and a long-term relationship is more difficult to sustain, customer lifetime value decreases. As a result, companies no longer want to invest heavily in acquiring new customers. This could prompt a reduction in the provision of consumer incentives. In the event of such policy changes, a clear understanding of the underlying objectives for consumer incentives is even more important.

Promotional Objectives and Consumer Reward Programs

Consumer reward programs, also called customer loyalty programs, have become a major marketing tool for many companies. The primary objective of a consumer reward program is to help acquire and retain heavy-user customers. Examples of heavy users are frequent business travellers for airlines or large families for supermarkets. The importance of heavy users is highlighted by the famous "80/20" rule: 20 per cent of customers – those heavy users – account for 80 per cent of the sales. Reward programs can be an effective tool to acquire heavy users because these consumers can accumulate enough points from purchases to qualify for the rewards. Reward programs can also effectively retain customers because, once a customer has accumulated some points, he or she will prefer to stay with the same company to earn rewards. Reward programs can increase customer loyalty by creating additional switching costs.

Companies should be aware that reward programs, which are designed to target heavy users, have an effect on light users too. Light users are not directly affected by reward programs because they do not purchase enough to qualify for the rewards, but they are still indirectly affected. Since it is costly for the companies to offer rewards, they would raise the market prices for their products or services. In the industries in which companies charge all consumers the same prices, the heavy users are effectively subsidized by light users through the reward programs. Is the higher price caused by reward programs a serious concern to the company? It may not be a concern if the light users are not price sensitive or if they are a very small market segment. However, in the industries that are fairly competitive, if the light-user segment is substantial and they are price sensitive, then the company has to take the impact on light users into consideration when making decisions on its reward programs.[2] To gain further insights into this issue, next we discuss one specific reward decision – type of rewards.

When offering a reward program, companies can choose from two types of rewards: own goods or services versus other prizes. For example, a hotel can offer free room stays or cash back, a supermarket can offer free groceries or a set of plates, and a private club can offer free dinners served in its own banquet room or free tickets to a concert. Usually it is more cost-efficient for a company to offer its own goods or services than other prizes that have equivalent value to the consumers, because the company has to procure these prizes from external suppliers. Consequently, one may conjecture that companies should always offer their own goods or services to reward their loyal customers. However, this may not be true. First, as companies use rewards to compete for heavy users, they may hand out an excessive amount of rewards because each unit of reward costs them very little. In practice, it is not uncommon to observe companies engaging in a "mileage war" in competing for heavy users. When heavy users are price sensitive (for example, large families are more price sensitive than light users in grocery purchases), the total cost of rewards could be even higher if competing firms all offer more efficient rewards. Second, by increasing a company's cost in serving heavy users, these rewards will increase the company's market prices. As a result, the company could lose market share in the light-user segment. Consequently, in the markets in which heavy users are relatively small, it can be optimal for the companies to offer less efficient rewards.

Using own products or services as rewards has additional implications in service industries like airlines and hotels that have capacity constraints and seasonal demand fluctuations. In recent years in North America, the airline load factor was about 80 per cent and the hotel occupancy rate was about 55 per cent. Adjusting capacities can be very costly in these industries; for instance, a hotel cannot easily add or cut rooms. The presence of excess capacities typically leads to price wars when demand is low. Interestingly, offering own products or services as rewards in these industries can reduce price competition. With reward programs, companies allocate a portion of their capacities to be given out as rewards, typically a much higher percentage when demand is low. Such a commitment effectively reduces available capacities and sends a credible signal to the competitors about the reduced available capacities. As a result, the price competition during low-demand periods is mitigated without making costly capacity changes.[3]

Another objective of a consumer reward program is to collect information on consumer preferences. Such information allows companies to provide added value to their existing customers (e.g., by offering customized benefits) with minimal additional costs. Examples of such customized benefits include special pillows offered to frequent hotel guests and preferred seats offered to regular restaurant patrons. Such information-based value-creating capabilities are critical to the profitability of consumer reward programs in competitive markets. In fact, when competing firms have the same level of such capabilities, having both firms offering customer reward programs can be a curse rather than a blessing to the firms. This is because such capabilities allow the companies to retain and capitalize on existing customers successfully. As a result, the value of new acquisition increases with a company's ability to create value based on customer information. But the increased value of acquisition can exacerbate competition in initial customer acquisition, so much so that all the future benefits can be competed away through incentives offered to attract customers. However, when competing firms have different levels of information-based value-creating capability, customer loyalty strategies create another dimension of differentiation between these competitors. The company equipped with more advanced information capability will gain customers and earn more profits through unique value-added benefits. In the meantime, its competitors may resort to low-price strategies.[4]

Principle 2: Create and Leverage Size Advantages

Size of Customer Loyalty Programs

Size matters for earning points faster. If a gasoline retailer owns more stations, if an airline operates more routes and flights, or if a hotel chain owns more locations, then consumers are more likely to find one that matches their preferences. This makes it easier to earn points faster. Similarly, size matters for redeeming points for rewards. After accumulating enough points, a consumer is more likely to find a route and flight matching his or her preference in a larger airline. One can consider the size effect as an artificial externality. Without frequent flyer points, airline choice decisions associated with different flight trips are independent. However, with loyalty programs, all flight trips are compatible towards the same goal of accumulating enough points to earn rewards. This externality does not arise naturally: it is created by the loyalty programs designed by the companies.

Should a firm maximize the scale and scope of its loyalty program by including all product categories and locations? For instance, when an airline offers a frequent flyer program, the airline can include all flights and routes, include only a subset of them, or assign different points to different flights and routes. The size advantage underscores the tendency for many companies to join alliance or network programs. Virtually all the airlines join alliance programs. Although many people exhibit "polygamous loyalty" – that is, they are members of multiple airline frequent flyer programs – most consumers tend to have one focal alliance program. When consumers earn points from retail shopping, they accumulate all the points in a focal alliance program to maximize the return. Airlines offering more scale (more service routes) and scope (more destinations) were more likely to be chosen as the focal program. The size, both scale and scope, of the local airport is most relevant to consumers.

But a larger scale is not always better. To illustrate the logic behind this, consider a retail gasoline station chain with some station locations directly competing against rival brands, and other locations far from any of its competitors. These competing locations need loyalty programs for customer acquisition and retention. But the non-competing locations are local monopolies and thus see little benefit from loyalty programs. Whether a firm should include non-competing stations in the program depends on a number of factors. One factor is how frequently people travel between locations. When consumers travel between stations, including unique and non-competing stations, this can substantially enhance the benefit of a larger scale. Taxi drivers are such consumers because they travel to various destinations according to the needs of their clients. Having these locations as participating stations creates a competitive advantage for the loyalty program among these consumers. However, there are other consumers who typically only drive to work and shop, travelling between their home, workplace, and supermarkets. Including these non-competing service locations to the loyalty program adds little value to these consumers. Overall, a larger program scale is more beneficial when a market has more "travelling" consumers.

Another factor is profit loss due to promotional costs. The non-competing locations give out rewards and incur reward costs unnecessarily because they are local monopolies. Such costs are higher the more local non-travelling customers are served by them. The promotional cost also depends on the extent to which the non-competing location can recoup the costs by increasing prices. This location could increase prices to cover the promotional costs; however, depending on demand elasticity, a higher price could drive down the sales.

The same logic applies to loyalty programs in other industries. Consider a company with multiple brands competing in different product categories. The company can create a loyalty program for a subset of brands in a subset of product categories or maximize the scale by creating an umbrella loyalty program covering all of its brands and product categories. For example, eBay excludes a number of product categories such as motors and real estate from its eBay Bucks program. Naturally, as argued earlier, the company should carefully consider cross-category purchase decisions of its target customers, the competitive position of each brand, and the extent of competitiveness in each category. This logic also applies to network programs like Air Miles with participating companies from different industries. In determining the boundaries for these network programs, decision-makers should again weigh the benefits and costs of adding new members. Maximizing the size of the program is not always the optimal decision. Moreover, networks programs should pay careful attention to the marginal contribution of new member companies to the existing members already in the program.

Size of Sweepstakes Promotion

Size matters not just for customer loyalty programs, but also for other types of consumer incentives such as sweepstakes. The size of a sweepstakes promotion refers to the winning base, the total number of winning numbers. In practice, size can be the number of coffee cups, number of chocolate bags, or number of meal packs with potential winning numbers. In many cases, the size of the promotion also increases with the length of duration. Again, is larger better?

One has to consider at least two contrasting forces concerning the size of a sweepstakes promotion. On one hand, a larger number of participants means a smaller winning probability. Given the budget and reward structure, this would imply lower values of participating in such sweepstakes. Consequently, this would lead to smaller promotional impact in the form of reduced new customer acquisition or retention. One the other hand, consumers tend to over-weigh the small odds of winning prizes when they evaluate sweepstakes and lotteries. Stories about the extremely popular multi-state super lotteries attest to such a phenomenon. Despite much smaller winning probabilities with these super lotteries, casual observations seem to indicate incredibly high enthusiasm among the participants.

The sweet spot that optimizes the scale of a sweepstakes promotion would need to balance these two forces. Given the budget and prize structure, a larger scale has the benefit of applying the sweepstakes promotion to a greater number of purchase occasions and products. This means more consumers are attracted by the sweepstakes to purchase the company's products. Conversely, a larger base does imply a smaller winning probability and hence a lower value of promotion. To search for the optimal scale that maximizes promotion outcomes, marketers need first to calibrate the probability weighting functions empirically.

Principle 3: Harness Embedding Social Relations

There are two types of social relations that affect incentive designs. One type of social relation naturally exists in consumers' social networks. The use of incentives can change the strength of ties and the structure of networks. A discount on a cellular phone service contract can encourage people to talk to their friends more often. The increased communications may further strengthen their ties. The dynamics of a social relationship, particularly reciprocity, lead to the need for companies to find unique ways to assess the effectiveness of consumer incentives. Another type of social relation is created artificially by the incentives. When airlines offer multi-tier loyalty programs, consumers are placed into different tiers, each associated with certain status. Companies need to properly design the path to achieving status in order to create continued motivation.

Social Relations and Sales Promotion for Phone Services

People communicate with others in their personal communication networks. To further increase consumer service usage and the adoption of new services, service providers often offer promotions just like their supermarket counterparts. But companies need to evaluate the return of promotions very differently. More specifically, one has to track the entire social network in order to accurately evaluate the return. Imagine a triad social network consisting of three consumers: John, David, and Erick. When a promotion targeting John prompts John to call David more, there will be at least three implications. First, although John is paying less for his own calls, David might be paying the full fares for incoming calls. If David is also a customer of the same company, then the return of the promotion targeting John should include increased revenue from David, too. Thus, any assessment and hence design of the promotion should be conducted at the level of social networks, not at the level of individuals. Second, now that John initiates more calls to

David, their tie is strengthened and very likely in the future David will call John more often, too. This type of reciprocity effect is engrained deeply in our culture. Third, the changes in the communication pattern between John and David may affect their respective communications with Erick, too. The direction of changes will depend on the nature of their relationship. Overall, not accounting for these ripple effects over social networks can cause a significant underestimation of the promotion effect.

Social Relation and Incentives for Customer Referrals

Referrals typically take place along social ties. People can be intrinsically motivated to make referrals. Referrals may help with an individual's self-esteem by creating a feeling of expertise or satisfaction in helping friends find the right products. A common measure for people's tendency to make referrals is the Opinion Leadership scale. The opinion leaders are those people who often make referrals and are often sought for advice. Opinion Leadership is category specific; that is, a person can be an opinion leader on automobiles, but not an opinion leader on the internet. In recent years, many companies have started incentive programs targeting these opinion leaders. For example, some pharmaceutical companies paid senior experts to influence opinions regarding new drugs, and cellular telephone manufacturers provided free phones to influential bloggers and encouraged them to blog. Would the incentives increase referrals from opinion leaders? What about the effect on non-opinion leaders?

These questions were investigated in a large field study in which participants were asked to refer a new website.[5] Results show that the referral rate increased significantly when offered a chance to win a sweepstakes. Interestingly, opinion leaders responded to the monetary incentives much more strongly than the non-opinion leaders. When people make referrals to help others, they often do so for the purpose of accumulating social capital, a valuable relationship-based capital. Social capital is deposited when intrinsically-motivated referrals are made. Social capital is withdrawn when people use social relations to make monetary gains. When no money is attached, it is certain to the receiver that referrals were motivated intrinsically. However, when money is rewarded, the true motive behind the referrals becomes ambiguous. The receivers have to infer whether the referral was motivated intrinsically or extrinsically. The opinion leaders have established the reputation of making intrinsically motivated referrals. In contrast, non-opinion leaders do not have that reputation. Referral receivers would naturally infer the non-opinion leaders as motivated by extrinsic rewards. Such referrals would thus be deemed as exploiting and reduce social capital. This negative effect could deter some non-opinion leaders from profiting from referrals. But the opinion leaders are shielded by their past reputation, and expect little loss of social capital. Despite the monetary rewards, the opinion leaders could be regarded as making intrinsically motivated referrals and earn social capital rather than withdrawing. This is why one would expect the established opinion leaders to be more responsive to referrals incentives.

Social Relations and Group Incentives

Marketers are increasingly using social media to promote their products or services. One prominent form is group-buying mechanism. Promoting services and events through group-buying mechanism has a long history. Artists have used Street Performer Protocol (SPP) to promote their work and events. SPP dictates that an event will not take place unless enough purchases and commitments have been pledged. Renowned musicians like Wolfgang Amadeus Mozart used SPP for his concerts. When e-commerce took off in the early 1990s, many websites like Mercata.com and Mobshop.com emerged to offer deep discounts for products conditional on enough people committed to purchases. More recently, similar business models launched by Groupon.com and LivingSocial.com have gained much media attention. Group-buying models have also been successfully launched in non-profit sectors. Many artists and non-profit organizations solicit funding for their projects through a crowd funding model that asks people to pledge their commitments to support the projects collectively. Websites like Kickstarter.com provide platforms for many projects to be posted simultaneously. This funding concept is similar with villagers gathering together monetary supports for public projects like road construction and bridge repair. What distinguish these online group-buying models are more formalized ideas, execution, and wider reach to potential donors.

A major deterrent from committing to participation is the risk of not having enough participants or not reaching sufficient funds. People would incur transaction costs in making a financial commitment, including registering for a deal, losing the opportunity of using the money for other purposes, concerns for not getting the money back on time if the deal is off, and so on. If a consumer does not believe enough people will sign up for a deal to succeed, then he or she will not sign up. Even if enough people find a deal or project valuable, the deal may not occur without a proper mechanism to facilitate the co-ordination between these potential participants. Thus, it is crucial to design proper participation mechanisms to alleviate the coordination problem. One important aspect of group-buying mechanism design concerns the information on the number of sign-ups. Like in auctions where auctioneers can choose either to disclose or seal all the ongoing bids, in group-buying mechanisms the sponsors can choose either to post or conceal the number of sign-ups. The choice does not appear to be straightforward because the sponsors are uncertain about the number of sign-ups in different stages of the deal. If the number of sign-ups in the early stage happens to be high, posting the sign-up numbers can boost the confidence of late arrivals in deal success and thus encourage late arrivals to participate in the deal. However, if the number of sign-ups in the early stage turns out to be low, posting the number of sign-ups can discourage the late arrivals from participating in the deal. Since the number of interested consumers arriving earlier in the deal is uncertain at the beginning of the deal, it is not obvious whether posting the sign-up numbers is the better design.

Research shows that posting the cumulative number of sign-ups can increase the success rate of group-buying deals. The intuition behind this result becomes much more clear if one views the deal from a backwards perspective. Such a perspective requires one to view the sign-up process backwards, starting from the last stage, and then going back to the first stage. First, for late arrivals of consumers, knowing the cumulative number of sign-ups and hence the progress towards the goal can enhance their confidence in the deal and consequently increase the expected number of sign-ups. At the late stage, as long as enough people are interested in the deal, the deal will succeed. In contrast, if the number of sign-ups is not posted, even if enough people are interested in the deal, they may not participate to unlock the deal. In essence, disclosing the sign-up numbers improves the deal success by eliminating the uncertainties. Second, knowing that late arrivals are more likely to sign up to the deal, the early arrivals become more confident in the success of the deal. As a result, those consumers who arrive at the deal earlier are more likely to sign up, too. This would further increase the sign-up numbers and deal success rate. Research also shows that a shorter sign-up period can improve the deal success rate. Otherwise, consumers arriving at the deal earlier would be less likely to commit to the deal. Fewer sign-ups earlier will subsequently dampen the interest of late arrivals.[6]

Status and Social Relations Created by Incentives

Many loyalty programs, including FFPs, artificially create ladders of social status. The elite members enjoy exclusive access to airport lounge services, priority check-in, and priority luggage services. The status rewards are social because they are visible to others: airport lounges are located in departure areas; when elite members board the planes, all other passengers have to wait patiently for them; and when passengers pick up their luggage, bags belonging to elite members appear first on luggage carousels with visible priority labels. Like social status, status rewards are earned through continued efforts. An elite member can lose the elite status if he or she did not fly enough segments in the past year. These members are not required to exchange miles for the use of any status services. Status rewards also exist in many other industries: rental car companies have separate lines for elite members, and credit card companies use different colours of cards and different phone numbers to service customers.

Social value for these status rewards can be substantial. Moreover, the value of status rewards created by loyalty programs increases as the status becomes scarce. A few years ago, an airline identified a large number of its regular members who often flew with other airlines. To attract these customers, the airline offered them one-year elite memberships. Soon the number of visitors to their airport lounges increased substantially in some large cities and complaints from existing elite members increased significantly. When a program has multiple tiers, those members on the top tier find the status more valuable when they see more levels below them. Tradeoffs clearly exist as scarcity implies a higher threshold required for top-level elite members. A given structure of status rewards may motivate some business travellers to consolidate their travels with the focal airline to maintain their privilege, but this may alienate others.[7]

Principle 4: Manage Psychological Perceptions

The value of consumer incentives is often subject to consumers' psychological perceptions. The perceived value of consumer incentives depends on the perceived value of rewards and perceived acquisition cost. Incentive features that can induce illusion of control and manipulate perceived progress can enhance the perceived value of rewards and reduce perceived cost.

Manage Perceptions in Sweepstakes Promotions

The attractiveness of sweepstakes promotions can be attributed to the consumer's tendency to over-weigh the odds of winning prizes. The heuristics people use in processing the winning probabilities are often subject to perceptions affected by marketing activities. State lottery organizations frequently run TV commercials featuring the winning stories, but exclude people who had won nothing despite persistent participation throughout their entire lives. Sweepstakes are perceived as more valuable when consumers are subject to illusions of control. Illusions of control can be achieved through some trivial activities required to reveal the outcome. The most common design is to let consumers scratch and reveal the outcome. In the Tim Hortons Roll Up the Rim sweepstakes held every year in Canada, the roll-up rim feature has generated great enthusiasm in the sweepstakes. Social media are full of stories about people inventing their own unique way of rolling up the coffee cups, in the same way that sports fans are superstitious about their rituals and teams winning. Similarly, McDonald's Monopoly game contest asked consumers to make online investment choices before revealing the random outcome. When sweepstakes are run during an extensive period of time in a frequently purchased category such as fast food and coffee, reasonable winning chances should be provided through small prizes. TV commercials should continue featuring the winners and stores should display the winning outcomes. Otherwise, the illusion of control may dissipate after repeated failures.

Manage Perceptions in Loyalty Programs

In customer loyalty programs, creating the sense of progress is critical in engaging consumers. When a consumer perceives the goal as being out of reach, the loyalty program no longer has an effect on the consumer. There are many ways a company can design loyalty programs to manage perceived progress. A program may have multiple levels of rewards so that consumers with different levels of usage have their own reachable goals. In most frequent flyer programs, while business travellers aspire to the elite status, leisure travellers set a goal of earning free tickets. Most network programs offer catalogues of rewards, requiring a different number of points for redemption. A nonlinear value structure is needed so that higher marginal value is offered for more expensive rewards. This is necessary to encourage consumers to continue to climb up the ladders and accumulate more points. Otherwise, continuity would break down once enough points have been accumulated. For example, a loyalty card offered by a coffee shop may give a free cup of coffee for every ten cups of drinks purchased. Once a consumer has accumulated ten purchases and redeems the free coffee, the past purchases no longer have any effect on the consumer's next purchase. In contrast, in the movie *Up in the Air*, Ryan Bingham (George Clooney), having earned elite status, continues his pursuit to fulfill his personal ambition of earning ten million frequent flyer miles with American Airlines.

Another way to manipulate the perceived progress towards goals is by creating additional layers of measurements, an idea similar to "Medium Maximization" discussed in chapter 6 of this book. To illustrate, consider a loyalty program that requires 1,000 points to earn a reward. In addition to handing out points to consumers for their purchases, if the program also gives out one voucher for every 100 points earned, then the consumer would perceive greater progress and feel closer to the goals. Consequently, the loyalty program would have a stronger effect in pulling the consumer to the company's products.[8]

A loyalty program can also create continued progress through alliance programs. Alliance programs like Air Miles allow members to accumulate points from a network of retailers. The enhanced opportunities to earn points make the goals more accessible. Network loyalty programs also enhance perceived progress by enabling frequent contacts. Most members of Aeroplan (Air Canada's frequent flier program) are leisure travellers who fly only a few times a year. The alliance of Aeroplan with Esso gas stations allows these members to accumulate Aeroplan miles with their regular gasoline purchases. Research has shown that loyalty programs become much more effective when consumers perceive shorter distances to their goals. As the members progress closer to the goals, they accelerate the pace towards the goal.[9] In contrast, when members face longer distances from their goals, their perceived progress tends to be much smaller. Offering members some starting points to reduce the gap can help to stimulate effort by reducing perceived difficulty. For example, Mileage Plus, the frequent flyer program of United Airlines, offered 5,000 free miles to each new member who joined the program through the referral of current members.

Summary

We have drawn four design principles for consumer incentive programs based on a series of research conducted in the past decade. An incentive program should start with clearly defined objectives in the context of customer relationship management. Objectives not only dictate the design of incentive programs, but also define the measurement for program effectiveness. An incentive program should explore and leverage the benefit of program scale internally. When the internal scale is limited, marketers should seek alliances with other companies to create a sufficient scale for competitive advantage. An incentive program should harness the social relations that have become increasingly visible in the internet age. The ripple effect of consumer promotions through social networks can be substantial. Status rewards artificially created through marketing programs and social media can be both effective and efficient in shaping consumer behaviour. Finally, an incentive program should manage psychological perceptions associated with benefits of consumer incentives and acquisition costs. Understanding the heuristics behind consumer decision-making is critical in achieving favourable attitudes towards the brand and promotion programs.

A Prescription for Designing Effective Consumer Incentive Programs
In an era of hypercompetition and information abundance, incentives have an even greater role to play. To design effective incentive programs, managers should:

- ALIGN the program to specific objectives. Design distinct incentive programs for customer acquisition and retention.
- CREATE and leverage size advantages. Use the size of an incentive program as a competitive advantage and develop size internally across divisions or externally through alliances.
- HARNESS embedded social relations. Embed the incentive programs in consumers' social networks and create social status to enhance value of incentives.
- MANAGE psychological perceptions. Increase the perceived value of incentives and reduce the perceived acquisition cost.

REFERENCES

1 A. Kalra and M. Shi, "Customer Value-maximizing Sweepstakes & Contests: A Theoretical and Experimental Investigation," *Journal of Marketing Research* (2010): 287–300.

2 B. Kim, M. Shi, and K. Srinivasan, "Reward Programs and Tacit Price Collusion," *Marketing Science* 20, no. 2 (2001): 99–120.

3 B. Kim, M. Shi, and K. Srinivasan, "Managing Capacity through Reward Programs," *Management Science* 50, no. 4 (2004): 503–20.

4 A. Pazgal and David A. Soberman, "Behavior-Based Discrimination: Is It a Winning Play and If So When?" *Marketing Science* 27, no. 6 (2008): 977–94.

5 M. Shi and A. C. Wojnicki, "Intrinsic and Extrinsic Incentives for Online Referrals: A Field Study," working paper, Rotman School of Management, University of Toronto, 2009.

6 M. Hu, M. Shi, and J. Wu, "Sequential versus Simultaneous Group Buying Mechanisms," working paper, Rotman School of Management, University of Toronto, 2012.

7 J. Nunes and X. Dreze, "Feeling Superior: The Impact of Loyalty Program Structure on Consumers' Perception of Status," *Journal of Consumer Research* 35, no. 6 (2009): 890–905.

8 X. Li, M. Shi, and D. Soman, "Multi-medium Reward Programs," working paper, Rotman School of Management, University of Toronto, 2008.

9 R. Kievt, O. Urminsky, and Z. Zheng, "The Goal-gradient Hypothesis Resurrected: Purchase Acceleration, Illusionary Goal Progress, and Customer Retention," *Journal of Marketing Research* (2006): 39–58.

12 Hang On: The Psychology of Time and Implications for Designing Queues

DILIP SOMAN

"How much of human life is lost in waiting!"

– Ralph Waldo Emerson

While Ralph Waldo Emerson made this proclamation in a metaphorical and philosophical sense, the modern-day consumer will appreciate the literal truth in the quote above. Queues are a ubiquitous consumer experience. We routinely queue up to take a bus to work, to use an ATM, to check into a flight, to send a parcel at the post office, to purchase groceries, or to speak to a telephone ticketing agent. There are queues for consumers to get a medical operation, and there are virtual queues that one gets into when one calls a customer service number and has to wait for the next available agent. Given their ubiquity, a rich literature in the field of *queuing theory* has studied efficiency in queuing using mathematical modelling.[1]

Queues have an important functional role to play – they determine the sequence in which, as well as the speed with which – customers arriving at a service location get served. As a result, much of the research in queuing theory has the explicit goal of maximizing the efficiency of the system on observable variables like throughput (number of people served per unit of time), average wait times, and the length of the queue. However, waiting in queues has a number of psychological and customer choice implications. Customers report feeling frustrated in queues, and the level of frustration often has very little to do with the actual duration of the wait. And the waiting experience often plays a significant role in the customer's evaluation of service quality and their decision to return or to recommend it. Behavioural researchers in marketing have therefore become interested in understanding the psychological costs that consumers expend while waiting for service, and in offering prescriptions on how to reduce these costs.[2]

While a lot of the research on the psychology of waiting has focused on the retrospective evaluation of the service experience measured at the conclusion of the service, relatively less attention has been given to the experiences and decision-making of consumers who are waiting in queues. As Meyer argued in a 1994 article, consumers "are not mindless passengers in a human line," but can make decisions, and their affective states are also open to environmental influence.[3] In particular, consumers can decide to leave a queue to return to it later, or to completely give up on doing business with the service provider and go elsewhere. These decisions are driven by their perception of how long they have waited and by social influences in the queue.

In this chapter, I first outline some of the key issues in psychological research on queuing and their implications. There are two broad sets of psychological phenomena: the first deals with the divergence between objective and perceived time, and the second relates to the social effects of waiting in queues. I then describe various queue disciplines and conclude with a set of prescriptions from this research for more effective service management.

Waiting for products and services has an obvious downside – consumers get frustrated and impatient. Consequently, a large number of studies have documented the fact that increasing the waiting time decreases the level of satisfaction with the product or service, and reduces the quality of the overall experience. Researchers and practitioners in marketing have therefore embarked on the mission of trying to create systems that reduce wait times.

The University of Chicago economist Gary Becker first developed an economic approach to the valuation of time.[4] In his approach, consumers behave as if there is a real economic consequence of waiting, and the magnitude of this cost is a function of the amount of time spent waiting. The "cost of time" is the weighted wage rate – the opportunity cost of wages that might have been earned had the consumer spent an hour working instead of, say, waiting in queue. In this traditional approach to studying waiting times, the actual length of the wait determines the cost of (and therefore the negative consequences of) waiting. However, researchers in marketing have subsequently argued that it is not the actual duration of the time spent waiting, but rather the perceived duration that should influence the cost of waiting.[5] Past research on queuing has shown that consumers retrospectively overestimate the duration of waiting time, resulting in a reduction in service evaluation. Researchers have also attempted to uncover strategies for reducing the negative effects of the perception of time. For instance, Katz and his colleagues found that distractions during the waiting period (e.g., a newsboard or television) made the wait more palatable and improved service evaluation.[6]

A rich literature in psychology and marketing has studied the divergence between objective time and perceived subjective time.

Perceived Time

Research suggests that consumers do not have a good sense of how to estimate objective durations of time. When consumers are made to wait in the absence of any gadgets that can tell the time, they are quite inaccurate in estimating how long they had waited. In their research on the memory of past experiences, Fredrickson and Kahneman[7] found that salient features of an affective experience (e.g., the highlights of the experience, the rate of change of the experience, and the end state) seem to influence memory of the experience more than its objective duration, and called this phenomena "duration neglect."[8] Clearly, right at the end of the experience, the salient features of the experience are immediately available as an input into judgment, while an "evaluation that incorporates duration must be constructed more laboriously."[9]

Another stream of research has focused almost exclusively on how consumers judge the duration of experiences.[10] There are two common themes in this research. First, the work suggests the existence of an internal timer to mark the passage of time. In essence, the human body has an internal timing mechanism, but this mechanism does not correspond to actual objective time durations. This internal clock is affected by physiological factors like arousal and pulse rates. Second, duration judgment is often flexible and inaccurate, and influenced by multiple factors like emotions, mental engagement, novelty, and variety in activity, among others. Consequently, time seems to move faster when the consumer is distracted from the wait, and hence we have the simple prescription from past research to use newsboards, TV screens, and other means of distraction.

In recent research, I collaborated with Hee-Kyung Ahn and Maggie Liu to develop a model of how people recall past experiences, and in particular how they estimate the duration of those experiences.[11] The basic setup of the model is best illustrated with a simple story. Imagine that last year Laurel and Hardy each went on an identical trip with family. Laurel took photographs of every family member he met and every event he participated in. Hardy did not take as many photographs. Several months later, when both men were asked to recall this otherwise unremarkable trip, they each went back to their digital photo albums marked "family trip" and viewed their trip pictures as a slideshow. After viewing his 100 photographs, Laurel seemed to believe that he had a longer and more eventful trip than did Hardy who had viewed his twenty photographs. Interestingly, though, during the trip, Laurel might have felt as if time were passing by quickly since he had so many different activities in which he and his family were engaged. Put differently, experiences that might seem short at the time because of distractions may actually seem very long in retrospect.

This story captures the basic intuition underlying our *memory marker* model. The following elements of the story are key variables in our model: (a) photographs that served as memory markers were taken by the two men during their trip, (b) the photographs were all stored in an album tagged with the name of the experience, and (c) the number of photographs was used as a cue to judge duration. These correspond to the three stages of the memory marker model: the encoding of markers, filing them in appropriate memory bins, and retrieving them after a delay. Encoding refers to the process by which certain slices or moments of the experience are recorded for later retrieval, typically when the environment changes. Not all changes in our cognitive and sensory environment result in a marker. In the filing stage, the encoded memory markers are categorized and stacked in memory bins, a process consistent with Wyer and Srull's bin model of memory.[12] This model conceptualizes memory as bins, or storehouses of individual pieces of information about people, objects, and events. The output of information processing is transmitted to and stored in a relevant bin as a separate information representation, in the order it is generated. During the retrieving stage, the memory markers stored in memory bins are reviewed and used to make judgments. Given that a larger number of markers would result in greater time needed to review them, we expect that the number of memory markers will serve as a cue to infer the duration of the recalled experience. Note, however, that when an experience is rich in cognitive and sensory changes, time might have flown by faster.[13] Such an experience will result in a greater number of memory markers, and as a result, it will be remembered as a long experience. This prediction of the memory marker model is consistent with the paradox noted by William James that "in general, a time filled with varied and interesting experiences seems short in passing, but long as we look back. On the other hand, a tract of time empty of experiences seems long in passing, but in retrospect short."[14]

This research, as well as similar research done by Gal Zauberman and colleagues,[15] points to the need for using caution with distraction as a queue-management strategy. While distraction might improve the perceptions of the wait during the fact, it may backfire when the consumer is making choices about which service provider to visit on a subsequent purchase occasion. The ideal queue is one in which the consumer does not feel frustrated during the wait, but where the distractions are not so vivid that they increase the remembered duration of the wait.

A second set of ideas that plays a role in the waiting environment is the manner in which consumers budget and mentally account for waits.[16] A health care facility that offered ongoing therapy and rehabilitation services for its patients had succeeded in cutting down wait times at some of their clinics by about forty-five minutes to an hour. However, the management was surprised and disappointed to learn that these process improvements had no effect on patients' reported satisfaction with the experience. The explanation was simple – given the nature of their treatments, most patients budgeted their time and had therefore psychologically adapted to be away at the facility for a day or half a day. In the context of this budget, the forty-five-minute time saving did not really matter!

Mental accounting research has also shown that consumers are risk-averse in the domain of losses. Consequently, a wait becomes more palatable when they know how long they are going to wait with relative certainty.

The Queue as a Social System

Queues represent an ad hoc collection of people, typically with the same goal (of consuming the target product or service, or accomplishing a task). These people often talk with each other, use others as reference points in assessing how fast the queue has been moving, get annoyed with each other for slowing down the queue or jumping it, and sometimes also develop camaraderie through their shared suffering. In a sense, queues represent temporary social systems, and as such, a lot of the behaviours studied by cognitive and social psychologists can be found in queues. In particular, I outline three sets of behaviours that I have done a fair bit of research on: (a) the need to experience progress, (b) the tendency to make social comparisons, and (c) the desire for social justice.

The Importance of Making Progress

Imagine that you need to take a business trip from Denver to Toronto. There are no direct flights, so your travel agent gives you two options at the same price. One, you could fly to Chicago and connect to a flight to Toronto. Two, you could fly to Phoenix and then connect to a flight to Toronto. Further imagine that under both options, it would take the same time for the entire journey from start to end. It would then appear that most people should be indifferent between the two itineraries. However, my research done in collaboration with Mengze Shi shows that when they make a choice, most people strongly prefer the first itinerary.[17]

Our prediction is based on a theory that we refer to as *virtual progress*. While we have an elaborate model to explain this theory, the idea is pretty intuitive and is based on two simple principles. First, whenever people undertake journeys that transport them from one place to another over a period of time, the speed and direction of travel contributes to a sense of progress they make towards their final destination – their goal. Travel directly towards their goal results in positive progress; travel away results in negative progress. The speed of travel relative to the average also matters. Travelling at speeds higher than average causes positive progress; speeds lower than average cause negative progress. Second, events that happen closer to the time of choice influence the choice more than events that are further away.

Applying this to the business traveller in Denver, we see that the second itinerary starts off with a negative progress situation, and hence this routing will be seen as particularly unpalatable. In the second route, there is also negative progress, but that happens at a later point in time and hence does not influence choice as much. Note that the actual progress – the distance covered divided by the time taken – is the same in both cases; however, one route seems to make more progress, and hence the term virtual progress.

Our research on virtual progress suggests the following rules of thumb for designers of waiting environments (and for route planners) in order to maximize consumer choice and experience.

1 Queues (routes) without stops are typically better than queues (routes) that stall for a large period of time. Put differently, a queue system that has the consumer making steady progress is better than another where there are periods of rapid progress interspersed with periods of no progress at all.
2 Avoid any components of reverse progress, such as movement in directions opposite to the goal. In many queuing environments, the line snakes back and forth such that during some parts, the consumer actually walks away from the end goal. Interviews with consumers in such queues confirmed our theorizing that these segments feel irksome to the consumer.
3 Should reverse travel and/or stops be necessary, the later they are in the route the better they are. In our theorizing, impediments to progress early in the wait have a greater likelihood of deterring consumers from joining the queue or causing reneging early on.

This theory of virtual progress is not restricted to queues and travel planning. Think about two groups of people training to be athletes that will run a cross-country 10 kilometre race at a competition. They trained on two separate courses. In one course, there were posts planted along the route at every kilometre indicating the distance covered; in the second course, these posts were planted every two kilometres. Interestingly, the athletes on the first course typically finished the distance sooner than athletes in the second race. That is because they received feedback on their progress more frequently and hence were motivated to try harder. In general, the more progress people think they have made, the more motivated they are to continue a task!

How do consumers estimate their rate of progress? In a straight queue, for example, the consumer can visually scan the length of the line and locate themselves in the context of the whole line. Alternately, consumers could be provided feedback. In many government offices in Asia – and in theme parks (both places where long queues are common) – consumers typically see signs informing them of the expected wait from that point onwards. And in many online and telephone queues, it is common to hear a message informing the caller about how many people are ahead of them.

Interestingly, we note that perceptions of progress (or, in our earlier words, virtual progress) are formed by data that may have nothing to do with actual progress. As an example, I gave a group of students thirty pages of text to proofread. Each page had either a short paragraph with fifteen lines of text, a medium paragraph with thirty lines of text, or a long paragraph with forty-five lines of text in it. Some students first had ten pages with short paragraphs, then ten medium paragraphs, and finally ten long paragraphs. A second set of students had the exact opposite sequence. All students flipped through the entire booklet before they started the task. When they were asked at the end of ten pages how much progress they thought they had made, the typical response was – incorrectly – one-third. More interestingly, students in both groups reported experiencing the same progress even though it was evident that in the first group, the actual progress was much less than one-third, and in the second group it was much more than one-third. While their motivation to continue the tasks would be about the same, those who had finished the long paragraphs should have been more motivated to continue.

All of this has interesting implications for how to structure long and complex tasks. Every so often we find ourselves doing tasks like writing a report, preparing a presentation, playing a limited overs cricket innings, learning a new computer program, or trying to lose weight. It is easy to be motivated in the beginning (after all, it is a new and exciting task) and in the end (after all, the end is in sight). It's the middle that often poses the problem. And that's when virtual progress can come in handy. By leaving the small paragraphs, the easy tasks, and the frequent signposts for the middle, we can ensure that we can signal enough progress to keep us motivated and engaged throughout.

These findings provide additional prescriptions for queue management. In particular, I find that consumers are more likely to stay in long queues when they see visible signs of progress. Thus, queues in which people physically move (rather than sit), where the physical environment changes with time (e.g., in Disneyland, different parts of the queue are coloured differently, have different photographs, or have different widths so that people have to walk faster as they get closer to their destination), and where people get feedback on how much progress they have made (e.g., in government offices in Hong Kong, signs posted along the queue inform the people waiting, "You are about 10 minutes away from the head of the queue") are more indicative of progress and hence more likely to retain consumers. The key again is to signal that progress is being made.

A corollary of the need for progress is the idea that consumers want to make progress not just in moving along in a queue, but also feel like they are making progress in the actual task. Consider consumers at a consulate office issuing visas. The process of receiving a visa after the application has been made has three parts: the physical submission of travel documents, the payment of fees, and the stamping of the visa. In research with Min Zhao and Leonard Lee,[18] we compared two queuing disciplines that both involved the same total waiting time. In one discipline, the visa applicant waits for (say) sixty minutes before they are called to a counter to get the entire visa processing done. In a second discipline, the three parts of the application process were separated, and each had a twenty-minute wait associated with it. We found that applicants found the palatability of the wait and overall experience in the second discipline to be significantly better. Why? In the second queue discipline, consumers interacted with a service provider after twenty minutes, while in the first case, they did so only after sixty minutes. In the second queue discipline, consumers were "in the system" sooner and hence were more committed to the task.

This idea of bringing people "in the system" sooner can manifest itself in many ways. In work I have done with a provider of specialty health care services, this principle has been used effectively to manage the anxiety of patients who have been referred to the facility. Patients traditionally had to wait for about thirty or forty days to get an appointment with a specialist, a period that is highly stress- and anxiety-provoking. This facility made a simple change in procedure to make the wait more palatable. As soon as they received a new referral, a nurse from the facility would call the patient, collect some basic medical information, and offer to answer any questions. By making the patient feel that they were now in the system, this procedural change resulted in a significant increase in satisfaction with the experience.

In a completely different domain, Eldar Shafir and Sendhil Mullainathan used the "bring consumers in the system sooner" principle to get more low-income consumers to open bank accounts. Low-income unbanked consumers in a soup kitchen in the United States attended an education seminar on the benefits of opening a bank account. While seminar attendees reported a good comprehension of these benefits, only a small proportion (11 per cent) went on to open an account. However, in a slight change of procedure, a bank representative was present at this seminar and collected the first of several required forms prior to attendees departing the seminar. These consumers now felt that they were "in the system" and were therefore more likely to follow through and complete the application process. Indeed, results showed that after this change in procedure, as many as 63 per cent of attendees opened accounts!

Social Comparisons

An extensive body of research in social psychology talks about a universal human tendency to learn about and improve oneself through comparison with others.[19] Social comparisons occur on an ongoing basis and have been described as spontaneous, effortless, and relatively automatic, but are especially likely in situations where there is uncertainty, novelty, evaluation, or change.

Consumers waiting in queues are good candidates for making social comparisons. The waiting situation is unusual – it is oriented towards meeting a personal goal and yet is social in that other individuals are also attempting to attain the same goal. It promotes evaluations, especially when consumers are contemplating reneging and even attempting to regulate their own affective state. And physical proximity to others can foster easy comparisons. One interesting consequence of this tendency to make social comparisons is the result that I find in research with Rongrong Zhou, that consumers are more willing to wait in line if there is a larger number of people behind them.[20] This finding is puzzling from a rational standpoint – after all, the only thing that should matter is the number of people ahead and the service rate, as these two data are suggestive of how long the consumer would need to continue waiting. However, in a generally unpleasant waiting environment, seeing people behind is somewhat comforting since the consumer may think, "There are people worse off than me."

The term *counterfactual thinking* refers to a set of cognitions involving the simulation of alternatives to past or present factual events or circumstances. In queues, the arrival of a number of people behind the consumer can potentially lead to counterfactual thinking about the consequences of a possible delay. An example of such a counterfactual thought is, "If I had arrived fifteen minutes late, I would be a long way behind the queue as compared to where I am now." This causes a sense of relief, positive emotion, and a greater commitment to wait in queue.

The Desire for Social Justice

The principle of social justice simply posits that consumers waiting in queues want to be treated fairly relative to other consumers in the waiting environment. Social justice in queues has been traditionally defined as and measured by the adherence to the principle of first in and first out (FIFO) queuing systems, in which consumers are served in their order of arrival.[21] Violations of the FIFO principle occur for a number of reasons. Intrusions of people into the queue violates social justice, as do certain designs of the queue system. For example, compared to a single-line system with guaranteed first-come, first-served queue discipline, a multi-line system often engenders situations of social injustice; that is, latecomers may get served earlier because they joined a faster queue. In addition, sometimes efforts made by service providers to speed up the service (e.g., opening up new service counters) may also lead to social injustice (e.g., when the latecomers rush to the front of the new counters and become the first to get served). While queue intrusions often elicit negative responses towards the intruder, social injustice that can be attributed to service providers (e.g., opening up new service counters) tends to result in negative reactions towards the service provider and lower customer satisfaction.

In research with Rongrong Zhou,[22] we refer to the FIFO principle as first-order justice. We further outline another dimension of social justice: people expect that everyone in the queue should spend an approximately equal amount of time waiting, and this concern is referred to as second-order justice. Even if everyone is served on a FIFO basis, many factors may contribute to a difference in how long people in a queue wait. For example, the arrival rate may change over time either systematically (e.g., there are high-traffic vs. low-traffic hours in a day) or due to random fluctuations. Imagine a scenario where a consumer happens to enter the queue after a big group of people; she then may have to wait for a period of time longer than average. Alternatively, fluctuations in departure rate may also lead to difference in waiting time. For instance, imagine that a consumer at a restaurant waited for a table for half an hour and the line had not been moving. Several tables then cleared up all around the same time. As a result, she and many others behind her in the line got seated at the same time. Compared to those behind, her waiting time could be much longer. Different waiting duration may also be caused by the service providers themselves. For example, upon seeing a long line, a restaurant may decide to open a new sitting area that was not put to use before. As a result, people who had waited longer (ahead in the queue) may get served at the same time as those who just arrived. Note that in none of the above scenarios was the FIFO principle being violated. Everyone got seated according to the order of arrival. However, it is conceivable that people who have waited longer may still feel that it is not fair and thus respond more negatively to the waiting situation.

Consumers need to make two decisions: first, whether or not to join a queue, and second, having joined a queue, whether or not to continue waiting. The extent to which each of these behaviours plays a role in any queuing system will depend on the type of queuing system used. In the parlance of operations managers, the algorithm used to determine how a queuing system works is called the queue discipline. Further, given a particular queue discipline, there are a number of ways in which the discipline can be executed.

Designing Queuing Systems

There are four basic types of queue disciplines created by combining two factors: the number of servers and the number of lines.[23] This results in four types of queues.

Single line and single server: This is not only the simplest form of queuing, but probably also the most prevalent. Consumers get priority as a function of when they arrive, and there is only one rank ordering across all consumers (as a function of arrival time). If enforced properly, the degree of social injustice is low, and the ability to make social comparisons is high, especially in situations in which the queue is a physical line of consumers (as in a bus stop). In cases where there is a physical line, it is also relatively easy for a consumer to evaluate the progress he/she is making over time. As a result, these queues are recommended for services where the rate of service is high, and there is not much variability in this rate.

Multiple lines and multiple servers: This is another fairly common queue discipline. There are multiple servers, and each server has a separate line of consumers. Supermarket check-out queues and tollbooths on highways often follow this discipline – consumers arrive, join one of the lines, and then wait till they advance towards the front of their selected queue. Consumers in this regime need to make many more decisions. When they arrive, they face two decisions: whether or not to join a queue, and if yes, which of the queues to join. And after joining a queue, they need to decide not only whether or not to stay in line, but if they decide to leave, whether they should join another line (and if so, which one) or leave altogether. In addition to the psychological phenomena discussed earlier, another powerful driver of consumer behaviour is regret. In particular, consumers joining one queue may regret their choice on seeing another queue move faster, and may therefore switch queues to their own detriment.

Single line and multiple servers: In this situation, consumers queue up in the order of their arrival. However, instead of being attended to by one server, there are multiple servers, and the person at the head of the line is called by the next available server. Such disciplines are commonly found in airline check-in areas, where passengers waiting to check into a flight follow one long queue, and the person at the head of the queue is called by the next available agent.

Multiple line and single server: Perhaps the only example of this queue discipline I have come across is when I drove my car aboard a ferry. There were three separate queues that cars got into for paying the fare and filling out registration details. But once they reached the head of the queue, only one car at a time could drive aboard the ferry and were directed to do so by an agent who waved them on.

Sometimes there are combinations of the above basic queue types:

- At San Francisco International Airport, all arriving passengers joined one common queue for passport and immigration control. However, once they got to the head of the queue, they had to decide which of multiple lines leading to multiple servers to join.
- At a consulate in Hong Kong issuing visas, incoming applicants joined one of multiple queues leading to multiple servers that checked visa applications and accepted them. However, once accepted, all applications got pooled into one queue for the next stage of processing. Finally, the total pile of passports was divided up among a number of immigration officers who processed their as-   . signed stack much like a multiple-server-multiple-line queue.

Comparing across the Different Queue Disciplines

1 *Consumer Decisions*: Queues with a single line involve simplified decision-making on the part of the consumer – they simply have to decide whether or not to join the line, and then whether or not to continue waiting. In the multiple line scenarios, however, consumer decision-making is more complicated as discussed earlier.
2 *Social Justice*: In a one-line system, the level of social justice is very high. Given that the line is formed in the order of arrival of the consumers, this discipline – almost by definition – serves consumers in

the order in which they arrived. There is, of course, the potential for "higher order" injustice. For instance, suppose the second consumer came ten minutes after the first, and the third came one minute after the second. However, it takes the same time to service each. The third consumer may feel some injustice since he will have to wait longer than the second one, provided that he knows when the second consumer arrived (perhaps they strolled in together). In a multiple line system, however, the potential for social injustice is high. Some consumers might be lucky to be in a line that is attended to by a more efficient server. In many such cases, one observes a fair degree of switching between lines such that consumers migrate to the faster line, which in turn creates a disincentive for that server to be more efficient. In situations where such switching is not possible (e.g. toll booth lanes on a highway that are separated by a divider) and yet the efficiency of the other line is visible, frustration and annoyance are expected to be very high. It is conceivable that people who came after you may be served sooner because they got a better server.

3 *Social Comparisons*: Consumers in single lines can make upward or downward comparisons. However, consumers in multiple line systems can also make lateral comparisons. As one example, consider two consumers who finish shopping at the same time and join different queues. One of these consumers keeps looking over to the other person who joined the other line at the same time as he joined this one to see if he is further ahead, at about the same place, or behind him. This lateral comparison can serve as a yardstick of whether he made the right decision in choosing this line. As another example, a consumer can look at people in other lines who are at about the same position as he/she is and see if they came at the same time, earlier than, or after he/she did.

While the queue discipline addresses the algorithm by which arriving consumers will be assigned to servers, managers need to make additional decisions regarding how the discipline will be operationalized. Here are some considerations:

1 *Physical Queue vs. Numerical Queue*: In a physical queue, consumers actually physically line up one after another (like passengers waiting for a bus). In a numerical queue, they are assigned a number or code name in the order of arrival, but are not physically restricted and can sit anywhere on the premises. The Cheesecake Factory in

Boston has a numerical queue: when you arrive at the restaurant, you are given a number and a beeper and told to stay within a certain distance of the restaurant. When you reach the head of this numerical queue, you get beeped. The immigration department in Hong Kong also uses a "take-a-number-and-wait" system. In terms of behavioural implications, it becomes much harder for consumers to keep track of progress, and social comparisons become difficult because it is not easy to keep track of who came when.

2 *Real Queue vs. Virtual Queue*: In a real queuing system, people or objects arrive at a service facility to participate in the queuing discipline. In a virtual queue, people participate remotely. One example is a consumer who calls a toll-free customer service number and is told to hold for the next available agent. In virtual queues, consumers still have to make decisions about whether to continue holding or not, but other social phenomena (such as comparisons or justice) are virtually non-existent.

Criteria in Choosing a Queuing System

We consider two decisions separately – the number of servers and the number of lines.

1 Cost and Volume (influences number of servers): Multiple server systems will indeed cost more than single server systems, but may be necessary depending on the volume of consumers needing to be serviced.

2 Consumer Perceptions (influence number of lines): Consumers arriving at a service facility and seeing one large queue may balk at the size of the queue and decide not to join it. Lines can be made to look less daunting by curving them back and forth so that they occupy a smaller space. However, once in the long queue, they may choose to stay if they experience progress, especially if there are a large number of people joining after them, which makes them feel good about their position. Remember that the potential for frustration and annoyance is greater in a multiple line system because the type of social comparisons could be greater, and because social injustice is more likely. More generally, unless there is a need to segment consumers into multiple lines (e.g., business class passengers in Line 1, economy in Line 2), a single line approach – if managed well – increases consumer happiness.

Once a decision has been made about the number of lines and the number of servers, the manager can identify specific constraints on both the operations management side and the psychology side, and use some of the executional tactics discussed earlier to overcome them.

Putting It All Together

The design of queuing systems is not easy. Money, volume, and operational issues are all important considerations. But as we move to a service-dominated society, consumer psychology will increasingly play an important role in designing better queues.

A Prescription for Reducing the Pain of Waiting and Creating Positive Experiences

Waiting is a ubiquitous consumer experience, but it does not have to be a negative one. Research on the psychology of time indicates that managers need to:

- USE distractions to reduce the pain of waiting.
- PROVIDE feedback to signal progress.
- START the service process sooner, and push the waits to later. The sooner people are in the service system, the happier they are.
- DESIGN fair processes to determine order of service.
- PROVIDE estimates of wait times; known waits are more palatable than unknown ones.

REFERENCES

1 N. Prabhu, *Foundations of Queuing Theory* (Boston: Kluwer, 1997).
2 M. Hui and D. Tse, "What to Tell Consumers in Waits of Different Lengths: An Integrative Model of Service Evaluation," *Journal of Marketing* 60 (1996): 81–90. See also S. Taylor, "Waiting for Service: The Relationship between Delays and Evaluations of Service," *Journal of Marketing* 58 (1994): 56–69.
3 T. Meyer, "Subjective Importance of Goal and Reactions to Waiting in Line," *The Journal of Social Psychology* 134 (1994): 819.
4 G.S. Becker, "A Theory of the Allocation of Time," *Economic Journal* 75 (1965): 493–517.
5 J. Hornik, "Subjective vs. Objective Time Measures: A Note on the Perception of Time in Consumer Behavior," *Journal of Consumer Research* 11 (1984): 615–18.

6 K. Katz, B. Larson, and R. Larson, "Prescriptions for the Waiting-in-Line Blues: Entertain, Enlighten and Engage," *Sloan Management Review* 32 (1991): 44–53.

7 B. Fredrickson and D. Kahneman, "Duration Neglect in Retrospective Evaluations of Affective Episodes," *Journal of Personality and Social Psychology* 65 (1993): 45–55.

8 See also D. Kahneman, B.L. Fredrickson, C.L. Schreiber, and D.A. Redelmeier, "When More Pain Is Preferred to Less: Adding a Better End," *Psychological Science* 4 (1993): 401–5; D.A. Redelmeier and D. Kahneman, "Patients' Memories of Painful Medical Treatments: Real-time and Retrospective Evaluations of Two Minimally Invasive Procedures," *Pain* 68 (1996): 3–8.

9 D. Ariely, D. Kahneman, and G. Loewenstein, "Joint Comment on 'When Does Duration Matter in Judgment and Decision Making?'" *Journal of Experimental Psychology: General* 129 (2000): 524–9.

10 See R.A. Block, "Models of Psychological Time," in R.A. Block, ed., *Cognitive Models of Psychological Time* (Hillsdale, NJ: Lawrence Erlbaum Associates, 1990), 1–30; J. Glicksohn, "Temporal Cognition and the Phenomenology of Time: A Multiplicative Function for Apparent Duration," *Consciousness and Cognition* 10 (2001): 1–25; M. Treisman, "Temporal Rhythms and Cerebral Rhythms," *Annals of the New York Academy of Sciences* 423 (1984): 542–65.

11 H. K, Ahn M. Liu, and D. Soman, "Memory Markers: How Consumers Remember Experiences," *Journal of Consumer Psychology* 19, no. 3 (2009): 508–16.

12 See R. S. Wyer and T.K. Srull, "Human Cognition and Its Social Context," *Psychological Review* 93 (1986): 322–59; R.S. Wyer and T.K. Srull, *Memory and Cognition in Its Social Context* (Hillsdale, NJ: Lawrence Erlbaum Associates, 1989).

13 This is consistent with the findings of J. Kellaris and R. Kent, "The Influence of Music on Consumers' Temporal Perceptions: Does Time Fly When You're Having Fun?" *Journal of Consumer Psychology* 1 (1992): 365–76.

14 W. James, *The Principles of Psychology*, vol. 1 (New York: Holt, 1890), chap. 15.

15 G. Zauberman, J. Levav, K. Diehl, and R. Bhargave, "1995 Feels so Close Yet so Far: The Effect of Event Markers on the Subjective Feeling of Elapsed Time," *Psychological Science* 21, no. 1 (2010): 133–9.

16 See D. Soman, "The Mental Accounting of Sunk Time Costs: Why Time is Not Like Money," *Journal of Behavioral Decision Making* 14 (2001): 169–85.

17 D. Soman and Mengze Shi, "Virtual Progress: The Effect of Path Character-
     istics on Perceptions of Progress and Choice Behavior," *Management Science*
     49, no. 9 (2003): 1229–50.

18 M. Zhao, L. Lee, and D. Soman, "The Effects of Virtual Boundaries on Task
     Commitment," working paper, Rotman School of Management, University
     of Toronto, 2011.

19 See L. Festinger, "A Theory of Social Comparison Processes," *Human Rela-
     tions* 7 (1954): 117–40; Paul Gilbert, John Price, and Steven Allan, "Social
     Comparison, Social Attractiveness and Evolution: How Might They Be
     Related?" *New Ideas in Psychology* 13 (1995): 149–65.

20 R. Zhou and D. Soman, "Looking Back: Exploring the Psychology of Queu-
     ing and the Effect of the Number of People Behind?" *Journal of Consumer
     Research* 29 (2003): 517–30.

21 R. Larson, "Perspectives on Queues: Social Justice and the Psychology of
     Queuing," *Operations Research* 35 (1987): 895–905.

22 R. Zhou and D. Soman, "Consumers Waiting in Queues: The Role of
     First and Second Order Justice," *Psychology and Marketing* 25, no. 3 (2008):
     262–79.

23 See N. Prabhu, *Foundations of Queuing Theory* (Boston: Kluwer, 1997), for
     alternative conceptualizations of queue discipline.

13 Brands as Humans: Relationship Norms and Anthropomorphism

PANKAJ AGGARWAL

When I worked as vice-president client-servicing in the New Delhi office of J. Walter Thompson Advertising, way back in the early nineties, one of the copywriters, Gene Hashmi, went to the country's movie capital – Mumbai (then Bombay) – to ensure that his script was faithfully translated into a thirty-second ad-film by the film producers we hired for the job. Gene returned a week later and proudly displayed a new tattoo adorning his somewhat hairy chest, right over where his heart would be. The tattoo was the logo of his favourite brand – the distinctive outline of the bitten-off apple, representing the Mac. While I was not surprised that a copywriter who was immersed in highlighting the virtues of a plethora of brands eighty hours a week would be especially fond of one, it did seem a bit extreme to allow your own body to be used as an advertising medium willingly and permanently. Of course, it did not surprise me to see that later in the year, when we were computerizing the creative department and installing new workstations for everyone, Gene led the informal office movement against IBM, demanding that the creative department be given Macs instead. To Gene Hashmi, Apple did not just mean a great computer. The brand meant a lot more. It represented a lot of things that Gene believed in personally and held in high regard – individuality, creativity, freedom, excellence, and success. Gene had a sort of relationship with Apple that most brands can only dream of: passionate, intimate, and bordering on the fanatical. Somehow, the team at Apple had figured out the right mix of brand ingredients to appeal to Gene and others like him, which we now know would continue to engender equally passionate and emotional bonding for the brand over twenty years later. What is it that Apple was able to put together that other brand managers may have overlooked? Can other brands too get Gene Hashmis to flaunt their logos next to their hearts?

This chapter examines the role of brands in the lives of consumers and the type of relationship that binds the two. Specifically, this research explores the broad framework of perceiving brands as people, and examines the appropriateness of applying this metaphor in better understanding consumer behaviour and their interaction with brands. This chapter examines the brands-as-people metaphor in two distinct ways. The first section examines the role of brands as relationship partners to consumers, much like interpersonal relationships between two people. The second section explores the relatively less studied but equally important idea of brand anthropomorphism; that is, when the brand more overtly takes on a human form. The interesting and somewhat unexpected ways in which brand anthropomorphism affects consumer behaviour will be discussed in this section. In addition to its theoretically rich contribution, the brand-as-person metaphor also offers some unique insights for brand managers who are constantly looking for practical ways to build deeper connections with their consumers, and to better understand the multi-faceted interactions that consumers have with brands.

Consumer–Brand Relationships and Norms of Behaviour

Even though marketing practitioners have long imbued brands with human traits with the objective of making brands more endearing, distinctive, and desirable, academic researchers who typically look at brands as passive, economically defined objects have only recently started perceiving brands as partners in socially construed relationships. Managers and academics have looked in some detail at the construct of brand personality, which refers to the set of human characteristics and traits that are associated with a brand. Research has typically focused on how a brand's personality helps consumers to relate better with the brand, since it is a means of self-expression and revealing the consumer's identity. The idea that consumers think of brands as relationship partners was first explored by Susan Fournier,[1] a professor at Boston University. Subsequent research has also emphasized the importance of understanding consumers' perspectives by examining different aspects of consumer–brand relationships.[2,3] My own research extends this stream of work by exploring a specific dimension of the complex consumer–brand relationship space. My research proposes a predictive framework by suggesting that when consumers form relationships with brands, they use norms of behaviour underlying these relationships as guides in their brand interactions.

Norms of Behaviour and Their Role in Social Interaction

Social relationships carry with them norms of behaviour that each relationship partner is expected to follow. Norms are typically not stated explicitly; they emerge from interactions with others and are acquired by people via the socialization process over long time periods.[4] As these norms become internalized, they serve as a guide for everyday behaviour, suggesting the right way for people to behave in novel situations. In addition, people also use these norms to judge behaviour: social norms form the basis of societal expectations of our behaviour, our expectations of others' behaviour, and our expectations of our own behaviour. A particular action may be an appropriate part of the norms of one relationship, while the same action may be seen as a serious violation of the norms of another relationship and perceived as improper For example, keeping a close tab on how much money one spends on a relationship partner may conform to the norms of a commercial relationship, but violate the norms of a relationship between family members. It is this adherence to or breach of the underlying relationship norms that informs our appraisals when we interact with our relationship partner.

The notion that relationship metaphors can help us understand consumer behaviour is based on the insight that when consumers see brands as relationship partners, they are in fact invoking norms that underlie a particular relationship. And depending upon the relationship that they perceive with the brand, the norms that are made salient would be different. These salient norms, then, serve as a lens to guide consumers on the "right" way to behave, as well as a way to evaluate the brand's actions. The main insight of my research on consumer–brand relationships is that the key to understanding consumer–brand interaction is a better appreciation of the norms that govern the particular brand relationship. My research has shown that relationship norms influence consumers' responses depending upon the extent to which the brand's actions are in violation of these norms[5] and are seen as unfair.[6] Further, relationship norms influence consumers' information processing,[7] their preference for self- versus other-chosen outcomes,[8] as well as their degree of loss aversion.[9]

In my research, I have relied on the distinction made in the literature between *exchange* relationships and *communal* relationships based on the norms of giving benefits to others.[10] Exchange relationships are those in which benefits to a partner are given with the specific expectation of receiving a comparable benefit in return. The receipt of a benefit incurs a debt or obligation to return a comparable benefit. People are concerned with how much they receive in exchange for how much they give. Such relationships involve a careful cost-benefit evaluation and the focus is on keeping track of inputs and outputs. Relationships between strangers and business partners are typical examples of this quid pro quo type of relationship. On the other hand, in communal relationships people give benefits to others to demonstrate a concern for that person and to express attention to their needs. They also expect others to demonstrate a similar concern for their own needs. Communal relationships focus on mutual support and cooperation, thus taking a perspective that transcends emphasis on self-interest alone. Most family relationships, romantic relationships, and friendships fall in this category. Although communal relationships are not completely bereft of a sense of reciprocity, the distinctive aspect of this relationship is that each individual interaction is not scrutinized for balance of the transaction. Prior work by Margaret Clark and her colleagues has identified the distinctive norms of these two relationships,[10,11,12] which have also been noted in my other work[5,13] and are summarized in Table 13.1.

Interestingly, these two relationship types are not mutually exclusive: it is possible to have a communal *and* an exchange relationship with someone simultaneously. For example, a business partnership with one's brother is likely to lead to the salience of communal and exchange norms concurrently. One reason why such relationships are difficult to manage in practice is that people may often be uncertain about which norms to use in specific situations. Given their commercial nature, arguably all consumer–brand relationships are inherently exchange-like. However, some marketers often endeavour to position their brand as being focused more on the well-being of the consumers than on maximizing their own profits. Take, for example, Virgin's claims to be "the consumer's champion," in contrast with incumbents that do not have the consumers' interest at heart (http://www.virgin atlantic.com/gb/en.html), as well as State Farm's endeavour to be "a good neighbor" (http://www.statefarm.com) or Nationwide's promise to be "on your side" (http://www.nationwide.com). Consequently, relationships with such brands may have an overlay of communal norms

Table 13.1 Norms of Exchange and Communal Relationships

Exchange Relationship	Communal Relationship
Prompt repayment for specific benefits received is expected.	Prompt repayment for specific benefits received is not expected.
Desirable to give "comparable" benefits in return for benefits received.	Less desirable to give "comparable" benefits in return for benefits received.
More likely to ask for repayments for benefits rendered.	Less likely to ask for repayments for benefits rendered.
More likely to keep track of individual inputs and outcomes in a joint task.	Less likely to keep track of individual inputs and outcomes in a joint task.
Less likely to keep track of others' needs.	More likely to keep track of others' needs.
Divide rewards according to each person's inputs and contributions.	Divide rewards according to each person's needs and requirements.
Helping others is less likely.	Helping others is more likely.
Requesting help from others is less likely.	Requesting help from others is more likely.
Accepting help with money is preferred to no payment.	Accepting help with no monetary payment is preferred.
Less responsive to others' emotional states.	More responsive to others' emotional states.

on top of the exchange norms that inform most commercial transactions. In my research, I have focused on the *relative* salience of exchange versus communal norms in a consumer–brand interaction. Further, in keeping with prior social psychology research, I have treated exchange and communal as two ends of a scale rather than two orthogonal dimensions. Next I describe two different projects that examine how relationship norms influence consumer behaviour. In the first project, I show how the type of relationship between a consumer and a brand – communal versus exchange – has its unique sets of norms of behaviour, and that the actions of the brand are judged through the lens of those relationship norms. If the actions violate the relationship norms, then the brand's evaluation is less positive; if the actions uphold and confirm the relationship norms, then the brand's evaluation is positive. The second project delves somewhat deeper into the underlying process and examines whether people examine information differently across different relationships. This project finds that consumers who form a communal relationship with a brand look at the brand in a more holistic manner and process information at a high level of abstraction.

On the other hand, consumers who form an exchange relationship with a brand focus on the nitty-gritty detailed pieces of information, processing the brand-related information at a lower level of abstraction. The six studies conducted for these two projects help us better understand some of the interesting ways in which norms of different relationship types influence consumer–brand interactions.

Case One: Relationship Norms as a Lens to Judge the Brand

This research, based on my doctoral dissertation, proposes that when consumers form a relationship with a brand, brands are evaluated as if they are members of a culture and need to conform to its norms: if the actions of the brand are in violation of the norms of a relationship, then the brand is evaluated negatively, but if the actions are in conformity with the norms of a relationship, then the evaluation is positive.[5] The theoretical framework proposes that the perceived violation of relationship norms mediates the effect of relationship type on consumers' attitudes and behaviour. For example, if consumers form a communal relationship with a brand such as the Apple iPhone, then they are likely to buy the brand because they "love" it and just want to have it, not for the specific features that it offers. On the other hand, they may have an exchange relationship with a brand like BlackBerry, which may make a lot of "sense" to buy, and is more likely to be evaluated on its features and the value it offers for the price it charges. In other words, it is the norms of the particular relationship that consumers form with the brand that guide them on what is the best way to interact with the brand. My dissertation work tests this premise by examining if, in fact, consumers who have a communal relationship with a brand versus those who have an exchange relationship with that brand respond differently when faced with an identical brand situation.

Three studies were conducted among student participant groups, each examining a different aspect of requests for help – a context chosen to highlight the exchange of benefits to the relationship partner. In this research I examined participants' reactions to being charged a fee or no fee for a "special" service rendered by a brand in response to a specific request made for that service by the consumer. The participants were first exposed to a description of a relationship between a consumer and a hypothetical bank aimed at triggering either communal or exchange norms. Next, the scenario described a consumer who sought help from the bank, requesting it to write a letter to their utility company that had not received some money, even though it had been cleared by the bank. The participants were then told that a week later, the bank informed them that the issue with the utility company had been resolved for no charge, or for a fee of $20. A demand for a fee by the bank in response to a request for help violates the norms of communal relationships, since the help is presumably being given for the fee rather than out of a concern for the consumer. This action, however, conforms to the norms of exchange relationships, since the fee highlights the quid pro quo nature of the relationship. Therefore, it was predicted that consumers' reactions to being charged would be different across the two relationship types. The results found support for the proposed hypothesis and indicated that, relative to exchange-oriented participants, communal participants evaluated the brand and its actions more positively when the action was in keeping with the communal norms but in violation of exchange norms (no fee was charged) than when the action was in violation of the communal but in keeping with the exchange norms (fee was charged).

This research also examined consumer responses to receiving a comparable or incomparable benefit back from the brand in response to some help rendered to a brand. Participants were first exposed to a brief description about a health club aimed at triggering norms of either a communal or an exchange relationship. Next, the health club requested that the consumer help them develop a website on healthy living by responding to a questionnaire requiring an hour of the consumer's time (non-monetary help) or by donating $15 for it (monetary help). In return, the brand promised the consumer either a one-hour-free coupon (comparable to the request for time but incomparable to the monetary help) or a $15 discount coupon (incomparable to the request for time but comparable to the monetary help). Results of study two suggest that the brand's action elicited different consumer evaluations depending upon whether the brand's actions violated or conformed to the norms of the underlying consumer–brand relationship. Since in an exchange relationship, benefits are given with an expectation of getting comparable benefits in return, any such offer, in cash or otherwise, would be seen to be in keeping with the relationship norms. Conversely, in a communal relationship, help is given to show concern for the partner's needs. A comparable benefit violates the underlying communal norms since it transforms the relationship into a tit-for-tat one, while an incomparable benefit would be in conformity with communal norms, since it de-links the benefit given from the benefit received.

Finally, to examine the mediating role of relationship norm violation overtly, a direct measure of participants' perceived norm violation was taken to see whether the brand evaluations were in fact influenced by the degree of norm violation experienced by the participants. This study examined whether the length of time between help given and help sought caused participants in different relationships to respond differently. If a request for help by a partner was immediately countered with a return request, the debt created by the original help is paid off right away – the return request being seen as a quid pro quo would be in keeping with the norms of exchange relationship. However, a return request that was delayed in time, being less likely to be connected to the original request, would be seen as a way to extract free help by the partner and hence be in violation of the exchange norms. On the other hand, an immediate return request was likely to be seen as a repayment for the original help and would thus be in violation of communal norms. Conversely, a delayed return request, being unconnected to the original request, was likely to be seen as an expression of a genuine need of the partner and hence be in keeping with the communal relationship norms. To test this, the participants read about a hypothetical coffee shop brand such that norms of either communal or exchange relationships were salient. Next, the participants read about a situation in which the brand asked the consumer to put up some promotional material on campus for them in response to the customer's request to make a fresh cup of coffee. This request was made either immediately afterwards or a week later. As expected, the results showed that exchange consumers evaluated the brand less positively in response to a delayed request but more positively in response to an immediate request as compared to the communal consumers. Further, the perceived level of norm violation completely mediated the effects on consumers' assessments of the brand and its actions.

Since communal relationships are likely to be more emotionally laden,[14] it was important to examine whether emotional attachment (rather than the relational norms) might had driven these results. To rule this out, measures of perceived affect were taken. In addition, the studies also ruled out uniqueness of monetary benefits and differences in quality perceptions across the two relationships as two supplemental alternative explanations. Overall, the results of this research supported the theory that a violation of or adherence to relationship norms influenced consumers' evaluation of the brand.

Case Two: Relationship Norms and Processing Brand Information

This project examines differences in consumers' strategies when they process brand-related information,[7] and suggests that norms of a communal relationship, relative to those of an exchange relationship, make individuals more likely to process brand information at a higher level of abstraction. Prior research suggests that people in an exchange relationship are more likely to keep track of their partner's inputs than their partner's needs.[12] In a consumer–brand context, we expected this focus on others' inputs in an exchange relationship to translate into attention to nitty-gritty details about the brand, enabling the consumers to track the balance of what they get for what they pay. In contrast, since consumers primed with communal norms do not look for immediate quid pro quo,[11] these consumers are more likely to evaluate brands holistically and attend to brand attributes at a higher level of abstraction. To illustrate, consumers in an exchange relationship with a brand such as Toyota Corolla may focus on the specific product features, such as gas mileage, resale price, engine capacity, and so on. Consumers who form a communal relationship with a brand such as Beetle Volkswagen may focus less on such detailed features and more on overall aspects, such as how appealing the car is to them.

This research tested the effect of relationship type on the level of abstraction of brand information, and used very different operationalizations of abstraction to provide strong converging evidence for the moderating role of relationship norms on consumers' information-processing strategies. First, the context of a near versus far product extension was used to examine the level of abstraction at which consumers process the proposed extension. It was argued that in a communal relationship, people process information at a higher level of abstraction, perceive the far extensions as being similar to the original product category, and evaluate these extensions relatively positively. Conversely, in an exchange relationship, people process brand information at a lower level of abstraction, perceive greater dissimilarities between the proposed far product extension and the original category, and are less likely than their communal counterparts to evaluate far product extensions positively. Scenario descriptions of a hypothetical relationship between two people were used to make communal and exchange relationship norms salient. In a presumably unrelated task, participants then evaluated a proposed extension for a product. Iced tea and toffee were the near and far extension for a cola product, but the far and near extension for a chewing gum product. The other pair of extensions was a calculator (near/far) and fashion accessories (far/near) for a pen/jean manufacturer. The extensions were evaluated on a four-item scale (dislike-like, bad-good, low quality–high quality, unpleasant-pleasant). Results showed that the norms of relationships moderated the degree to which far product extensions were seen as similar to the original product, as revealed by the differences in the evaluations of the product extensions: people evaluated the far extensions more positively when the norms of a communal rather than an exchange relationship were salient. These results supported the premise of differences in processing strategies adopted by consumers across the two relationship types.

Next, it was reasoned that if communal norms, more than exchange norms, make individuals process abstract brand information, then these encoding differences would be reflected in later memory measures. Accordingly, when presented with both abstract as well as specific (or concrete) brand information, individuals in a communal relationship would overwhelmingly encode the abstract information, whereas those in an exchange relationship condition would attend more to the concrete brand information. It was expected that consumers in an exchange relationship condition would be relatively more likely not only to recognize concrete brand information correctly, but also be able to detect inaccuracies. Further, it was expected that there would be no differences across the communal and exchange relationship groups for accurate recognition of abstract information, since communal participants would simply recall such information from memory, while the exchange participants would use their memory of concrete information to generate this information. However, because exchange-oriented consumers are assumed to rely on generating the abstract and plausible information, they would be slower than communal consumers at identifying this information as shown by the response latencies.

Participants were first presented with a relationship manipulation as before. Next, participants read a 450-word description about a hypothetical clothing store that contained both concrete and abstract brand information (e.g., "stores in 39 countries" vs. "it is an international brand"). Later, the participants completed a computer-based, multiple-choice recognition task. The results showed that, as expected, participants in the exchange condition had a higher likelihood of accepting correct concrete brand information and a lower likelihood of accepting incorrect concrete brand information relative to participants in the communal condition. Further, participants in the communal condition, relative to those in the exchange condition, had faster access to both correct abstract brand information and plausible inferences. Together, these findings supported the overall premise that brand-related information is processed at a higher level of abstraction in a communal relative to an exchange relationship.

Finally, the following premise was explored: if the type of consumer–brand relationship influences the level of abstraction at which the brand's features are processed, then differences in abstraction will be revealed in the way in which a consumer describes that brand to a third party. A scenario description was employed first to manipulate communal or exchange relationship with a hypothetical pen brand. Next, each participant was asked to describe the features of the pen to a friend. Two independent judges rated each feature for each participant on a seven-point concreteness-abstractness scale, with a higher score indicating a higher level of abstraction. For example, a feature like "color of the pen" or "ink flow" got a lower rating (1, 2, or 3), but a feature like "classy" or "stylish" received a higher rating (5, 6, or 7). Results showed that, as expected, participants in the communal condition listed brand features at a higher level of abstraction compared to those in the exchange condition. In sum, this research provided converging evidence in support of the hypothesis that communal norms lead consumers to process brand-related information at a higher level of abstraction compared to exchange norms. This research thus highlights the fact that relationship norms guide consumers and suggest to them the "right" way to conduct themselves in their interactions with the brand. Interestingly, the studies also show that the norms of relationships affect consumer behaviour even if they have been made salient in a context that is unrelated to the subsequent interaction with the brand.

Across these two cases I found that manipulating communal and exchange norms in a consumer–brand context was relatively effortless. These norms are quite well entrenched in us as part of our socialization process. Even subtle signals about these norms are easily deciphered by people and applied in their subsequent interactions with the brands. Oftentimes marketers understand this; however, at other times marketers use some of the cues about relationships not as adroitly, which then leads to the misapplication of relationship norms by the consumers. It is important that managers understand that when they try to become a friend to the consumer, the ability to take the consumers' mind off of the price tag comes along with the cost of having to do things for them as a matter of courtesy and "love."

Anthropomorphism, or When Brands Become Humanlike

Anthropomorphizing – that is, seeing the human in non-human forms and events – pervades human judgment.[15] People commonly see human features in natural formations, such as when they see faces in clouds, on the moon, or on the sides of mountains. They may attribute human goals, beliefs, and emotions to animals; for example, often people interpret the dynamics between two birds as reflecting the loving attention of newlyweds. As is perhaps more relevant to marketers, people see the human not just in nature but in artefacts as well. People sometimes see their cars as loyal companions, going so far as to name them. They argue with, cajole, and scold malfunctioning computers and engines.

The pervasiveness with which products are seen in at least partially human terms has long been noted by researchers. Products are seen as having consciousness or a soul;[16] an underlying defining essence, analogous to a genetic code;[17] personality;[18] the capacity for relationships;[1,5,19] and even features of their makers or owners that have been transferred during production or use.[20] In addition, research on uses and perceptions of technology has found that people often apply social norms of reciprocity in their interactions with computers,[21] such that a computer that is easy to use creates in us a warm feeling, and may be described as "friendly, faithful or obedient."[22] Further, marketers often encourage this tendency in consumers to anthropomorphize brands and products. In some cases, marketers design an anthropomorphized representation of the brand, such as Mr. Peanut, Tony the Tiger, and the Michelin Man. In other cases, marketers present the product itself in human terms, and may encourage consumers to think of their products as such by referring to them with the personal pronouns "he" or "she" instead of "it," by describing the product in first person instead of third, or by referring to their "product family" instead of their "product line." But whether or not consumers see the products as human may depend on the presence or absence of features that convey a sense of humanity. In fact, researchers and practitioners who study the area of corporate social responsibility suggest that one of the key reasons why corporations undertake socially responsible and desirable activities is to give their organizations a greater level of humanity – an entity that has a heart and a soul that goes well beyond the goal of profit maximization.

Although the tendency to anthropomorphize is pervasive, people do not anthropomorphize all objects, nor are they able to anthropomorphize different objects with equal ease. The literature suggests that the

Figure 13.1 Frowning Car

Figure 13.2 Smiling Car

ability to anthropomorphize may depend on the presence of specific features. For example, movement in an object can create the impression that it is alive.[23] Further, the timescale of this movement is important to the perception of humanity: things that dart about quickly may be seen as less human and more like insects, whereas things that move very slowly, such as clocks, may seem to lack humanity in this regard. Thus, the humanlike pace with which iRobot's Roomba vacuuming robot moves may be why some consumers dress it up in costumes and others have bought a second Roomba so that their first one would not be lonely! Further, objects that are shaped like people are more likely to be anthropomorphized.[24] Thus, the shape of a Coca-Cola bottle may be more easily anthropomorphized than a Coke can. Other features that signify humanness include facial features, sounds/voices, intentionality, imitation, and communication ability.[25]

Next, I give examples of research from two of my projects on anthropomorphism – one examining issues related to anthropomorphizing the physical product, and the other examining some unexpected effects of anthropomorphizing the brand rather than the physical product.

Case One: Smiling Cars and Beverage Families

The primary question addressed in this research[26] was whether an anthropomorphized presentation of a product affected its evaluation and, if so, how? Our central hypothesis was that when marketers encourage consumers to anthropomorphize a product, consumers bring to mind their schema for human beings, and the product is evaluated in part by how well its features fit that human schema.[27] Depending on the characteristics of the object, therefore, consumers may or may not be able to see the analogy suggested by the marketer to anthropomorphize products successfully. Thus, this research proposed schema congruity as a theoretical basis for examining the effectiveness of marketers' efforts to anthropomorphize their products. This overall hypothesis was examined in two laboratory studies. In these studies, a human or an object schema was first triggered by encouraging participants to think of the product as being like a person or an object. Next, a new product was presented to them with a feature that was more or less congruent with the human schema. Finally, the dependent variables were administered.

Study One used a car as the target product. We first primed a human schema by depicting the car as speaking in the first person so that it could be seen as its own spokesperson. By contrast, we primed the object schema by describing the car in third person. We also manipulated

Figure 13.3 Family of Bottles

the shape of the front grille of the car so that the edges pointed up or down to resemble a smile or a frown. Prior research suggests that a smile is more congruent with the general human schema than a frown: smiling faces are seen as more familiar.[28] Further, a pre-test indicated that smiles but not frowns were perceived to be congruent with the spokesperson schema. We expected that the "smiling" car would be a better fit with the spokesperson schema than the "frowning" car. The type of schema (spokesperson or object), the type of facial feature (smile or frown), and the type of car model (Lexus or Thunderbird) were all crossed and randomly shown to 120 undergraduate students. The results confirmed our hypotheses: participants shown the human schema were more likely to see the car as a person and evaluate it more positively when the target feature was more congruent (smiling) than less congruent (frowning) with the human schema. Further, the anthropomorphism score partially mediated the product evaluations.

In order to get deeper insights into the underlying mechanism and further validation of the schema congruity hypothesis, it was also decided to incorporate participants' thought protocols. Thus, we primed participants with a person or an object schema by telling them about the product "family" or the product "line" of a new beverage. The visual showed four bottles that were either identical in size, or they differed in size and were placed in such a way as to suggest different individuals (much like different members of a family). A pre-test confirmed that people expected members of a family to be of different sizes, suggesting different sizes of bottles to be congruent with the human schema. Ninety-two undergraduate students participated in this study and were shown a different schema (person or object) and bottle size (same or different). Results showed that participants in the person prime condition who saw differently sized bottles were more likely to perceive the beverage as a person and evaluate it more positively relative to the other conditions. Further, coding of the thought protocols showed that these participants made more schema-match related comments compared to the others. Finally, the anthropomorphism score partially mediated the product evaluation score. Also, since the bottle sizes (same vs. different) could not be mimicked, nor were they inherently better (or worse), this study ruled out product mimicry-led emotional contagion and contingent quality as two alternative explanations for the effects.

Results of this research also provided an additional nuance to our understanding by showing the two ways in which schema-based processing might influence consumers' evaluations of a product. Thus, we examined the influence of category affect and explored conditions in which greater perceived congruity with a human schema would not necessarily lead to more positive product evaluations. As such, we primed two different human schema, good twins and evil twins. We expected no difference in participants' ability to anthropomorphize the product across the positive (good twins) and negative (bad twins) schema conditions when presented with the congruent feature (i.e., same-sized bottles). However, we expected differences in the evaluation of the product depending on the affect associated with the schema. Findings for this study supported the view that the overall evaluation of the product may be influenced by schema congruity as well as by the "affective tag" associated with that schema. Hence, this study provided evidence of conditions in which anthropomorphizing the product did not lead to higher evaluations – participants evaluated the product that was anthropomorphized as "evil twins" less favourably than the product anthropomorphized as "twins." This result reinforces the cautionary point that anthropomorphizing a product may lead to more positive evaluations only when the type of person brought to mind is associated with positive feelings.

Our research offers a framework to better understand the phenomenon of product anthropomorphism. This research also provided support for schema-congruity theory as the underlying theoretical basis for explaining consumers' evaluations of anthropomorphized products. Our findings also offer marketing managers specific guidelines on how to ensure successful anthropomorphism of their products.

Case Two: Anthropomorphized Brands as Partners versus Servants

Research in social psychology has shown that automatic or unconscious behaviour may result from the activation of a social category. For example, it was noted that priming the concept of the "elderly" led to participants walking more slowly since the elderly are associated with the trait of being slow.[29] More recent research also found that participants exposed to the Apple brand behaved more creatively, and those exposed to the Disney brand responded more honestly to questions compared to control groups.[30] These results are interesting in that they show that effects previously observed for social constructs are replicated in the domain of brands.

In this research,[31] we argue that one reason for this effect may be that the iconic brands studied in earlier research[30] were perceived much like people. That is, respondents may have anthropomorphized those brands. If this argument is correct, it implies not that social effects extend to inanimate objects and brands, but that inanimate objects may sometimes extend into the social realm. That is, by anthropomorphizing brands, consumers open the door to "quasi-social influences" in which brands elicit effects previously seen for responses to people. We examine this possibility by considering differences in assimilation or contrast with traits associated with brands that have been anthropomorphized compared to those represented only as things. To inform our theory, we relied on prior research in social psychology, which shows that priming a social group triggers goals corresponding to people's desire for a successful social interaction. People show assimilative or contrastive behaviour to the extent that the corresponding behaviour achieves these interaction goals. Thus, priming "elderly" led participants who like the category to walk more slowly, but if they disliked the category they walked faster, presumably to get away.[32]

To test this framework, we proposed that brand priming will lead to assimilation or contrast with the behaviour implied by the anthropomorphized brand's image depending on consumers' beliefs about how best to achieve their social interaction goals. Two moderators were proposed: liking for the brand, and perceived role for the brand – as a partner or as a servant. Consumers would show assimilative behaviour with anthropomorphized brands perceived as partners if they liked them because in this case, assimilation – acting the same way as the brand – promotes getting along with and helping the partner. However, consumers show contrastive behaviour with traits associated with anthropomorphized partner brands if they disliked them because such behaviour pushes them away. Further, consumers show contrastive behaviour with traits associated with servant brands they liked because successful interaction involves letting the servant "take care of the work." Finally, consumers would show assimilative behaviour with anthropomorphized servant brands they disliked as a signal that the brand was not needed to be around. On the other hand, brands that were not anthropomorphized would not be affected by liking or role (partner or servant), because the goals of successful social interaction are not triggered for objects, making the relevance and impact of these social factors inconsequential.

We tested our proposed framework in three studies. In our first study, we considered two partner brands, Kellogg's and Krispy Kreme, near opposites on the healthy-unhealthy spectrum. Using an unrelated dependent variable that tapped into people's healthy (taking the stairs) or unhealthy (waiting for the elevator) behaviour, we found consumers to be more likely to show assimilative behaviour when they liked the anthropomorphized brand, and contrastive behaviour when they disliked it. By using opposing trait associations, we showed reversal of the overall effect within study one itself. In study two, we considered two servant brands: Volvo (associated with safety) and Discovery Channel (associated with knowledge). We expected consumers to be less likely to show assimilative behaviour when they liked the anthropomorphized brand, and more likely to show assimilative behaviour when they disliked it. For both brands, we found significant effects for unrelated tasks such as certainty equivalence for a risky gamble (Volvo) and responses to a set of SAT questions (Discovery Channel). In study three, we manipulated the perceived role of the brand, Volvo, under the pretext of testing two alternative advertising slogans that portrayed it either as a partner (works with you) or a servant (works for you). Results replicated the main effect in a more controlled environment.

This research is significant in its examination of an important yet very under-studied phenomenon in consumer behaviour: brand anthropomorphism. To our knowledge this is the first research that looks at the moderating effect of brand role on consumers' behaviour, highlighting the value of understanding how inanimate objects may extend into our social realm.

Conclusions

The four papers summarized here examine the "brands as people" metaphor in the context of consumer–brand interactions to get insights about different aspects of consumer behaviour. In this chapter I have described research examining two distinct aspects of the metaphor. The first section describes research that leans on the relationship metaphor using the interpersonal domain to get some unique insights into consumer–brand interactions. The second section describes the more general but eminently less studied area of anthropomorphism, or when brands and products more overtly take on a humanlike form. The key insight from these papers is that "brands as people" is an extremely useful and versatile metaphor to gain a deeper understanding of consumer behaviour. Our interactions with others in a social domain are so dominant that we often apply norms of social relationships to a brand context and we are very quick to "see" the human in products and brands. The (mis)application of the human metaphor to brands is quite common, instantaneous, and almost automatic, resulting in some very interesting and unexpected effects.

Although the "brands as people" metaphor is a useful tool for understanding and making predictions about consumer behaviour, clearly the research described here has merely scratched the surface. There remain many important questions that are still unanswered. How might norms get created in the first place? Why might some consumers form a communal while others form an exchange relationship with the same brand? How might one transition from one relationship type to the other? Thinking back to chapter 3 by Sridhar Moorthy, how might the type of relationship that consumers form with brands influence the expectations and the eventual success of a brand extension? As highlighted by David Dunne in chapter 2 on the changes brought about by the internet, consumers are now able to wield more control over marketers, clearly emphasizing that the role of relationships between brands and consumers becomes all the more critical. Consumers can no longer be seen as passive players in this relationship – they are equal and active partners and will not hesitate to let their partner brand and the rest of the world know how much they love their brands and also how much they hate them.

Similarly, there are important questions that one might ask relating to issues of product and brand anthropomorphism. Are service brands as easily anthropomorphized as product brands? What might be the potential downsides to anthropomorphizing a product or a brand? When brands are anthropomorphized in a certain way, are the brand extensions their natural siblings? What might be cross-cultural ramifications of brand anthropomorphism – are people from certain cultures more or less likely to anthropomorphize? Can brand anthropomorphism lead to gender stereotyping? While Claire Tsai has highlighted a number of factors that influence people's happiness, is the type of relationship that people form with humanized avatars of their brands in part driven by the degree of happiness they eventually want to experience from their consumption experiences? In short, what are the different person, product, and context-specific factors that result in particular consumer–brand relationships and the ease with which brands may be anthropomorphized? The full power of the "brands as person" metaphor to give insights into consumer behaviour is only limited by future researchers' imagination.

In addition to the way in which the brand is positioned in the marketplace, the dynamic and repeated interactions pursued by managers in the form of product design, ads, interactive media, direct mail, and telemarketing, as well as the use of brand mascots and spokespersons, are all potent tools to imbue brands with life, making them humanlike – our friends and partners, our servants and helpers. My research highlights to the managers some of the unique ways in which the relationships between consumers and brands influence how consumers behave, as well as the somewhat surprising downstream effects of endowing their brands more overtly with humanlike characteristics. I am not sure anymore whether Gene Hashmi, my copywriter friend from the J. Walter Thompson days, was a really creative copywriter who loved Apple, or whether his love for Apple made him a really creative copywriter!

A Prescription for Humanizing Consumer–Product Relationships
Consumers form relationships with brands. Communal relationships focus on mutual care; exchange relationships are based on quid pro quo. To better leverage these "relationships," managers need to:

- MATCH actions with consumer expectations of the relationship.
- HUMANIZE brands by matching product features with humanlike schema to anthropomorphize products and improve evaluation.
- If a brand is seen as a SERVANT, consumers behave in such a way as to distinguish themselves from the brand's personality.
- If a brand is a PARTNER brand, consumers behave consistently with the brand's personality.

REFERENCES

1 Susan Fournier, "Consumers and Their Brands: Developing Relationship Theory in Consumer Research," *Journal of Consumer Research* 24, no. 4 (1998): 343–73.
2 Jennifer L. Aaker, Susan Fournier, and S. Adam Brasel, "When Good Brands Do Bad," *Journal of Consumer Research* 31, no. 1 (2004): 1–16.
3 Vanitha Swaminathan, Karen L. Page, and Zeynep Gurhan-Canli, "'My' Brand or 'Our' Brand: The Effects of Brand Relationship Dimensions and Self-Construal on Brand Evaluations," *Journal of Consumer Research* 34, no. 2 (2007): 248–59.
4 Robert B. Cialdini and Melanie R. Trost, "Social Influence: Social Norms, Conformity and Compliance," in Daniel T. Gilbert and Susan T. Fiske, eds., *The Handbook of Social Psychology*, vol. 2, 4th ed. (New York: McGraw-Hill, 1998), 151–92.
5 Pankaj Aggarwal, "The Effects of Brand Relationship Norms on Consumer Attitudes and Behavior," *Journal of Consumer Research* 31, no. 1 (2004): 87–101.
6 Pankaj Aggarwal and Richard P. Larrick, "When Consumers Care about Being Treated Fairly: The Interaction of Relationship Norms and Fairness Norms," *Journal of Consumer Psychology* 22, no. 1 (2012): 114–27.
7 Pankaj Aggarwal and Sharmistha Law, "Role of Relationship Norms in Processing Brand Information," *Journal of Consumer Research* 32, no. 5 (2005): 453–64.
8 Pankaj Aggarwal, Simona Botti, and Ann L. McGill, "To Choose or Let Choose? Relationship Norms and Satisfaction with Customer- versus Provider-Chosen Outcome," working paper, Rotman School of Management, University of Toronto, 2011.
9 Pankaj Aggarwal and Meng Zhang, "The Moderating Effect of Relationship Norm Salience on Consumers' Loss Aversion," *Journal of Consumer Research* 33, no. 3 (2006): 413–19.
10 Margaret S. Clark and Judson Mills, "Interpersonal Attraction in Exchange and Communal Relationships," *Journal of Personality and Social Psychology* 37, no. 1 (1979): 12–24.
11 Margaret S. Clark, "Noncomparability of Benefits Given and Received: A Cue to the Existence of Friendship," *Social Psychology Quarterly* 44, no. 4 (1981): 375–81.
12 Margaret S. Clark, "Record Keeping in Two Types of Relationships," *Journal of Personality and Social Psychology* 47, no. 3 (1984): 549–57.

13 Pankaj Aggarwal, "Using Relationship Norms to Understand Consumer–Brand Interactions," in Deborah J. MacInnis, C. Whan Park, and Joseph W. Priester, eds., *Handbook of Brand Relationships* (New York: M.E. Sharpe, 2009), 25–42.

14 C. Whan Park, Joseph R. Priester, Deborah J. MacInnis, and Zhong Wan, "The Connection-Prominence Attachment Model (CPAM): A Conceptual and Methodological Exploration of Brand Attachment," in Deborah J. MacInnis, C. Whan Park, and Joseph W. Priester, eds., *Handbook of Brand Relationships* (New York: M.E. Sharpe, 2009), 327–41.

15 Stewart Guthrie, *Faces in the Clouds: A New Theory of Religion* (New York: Oxford, 1993).

16 George W. Gilmore, *Animism or Thought Currents of Primitive Peoples* (Boston: Jones, 1919).

17 Ann L. McGill, "Relative Use of Necessity and Sufficiency Information in Causal Judgments about Natural Categories," *Journal of Personality and Social Psychology* 75, no. 1 (1998): 70–81.

18 Jennifer L. Aaker, "Dimensions of Brand Personality," *Journal of Marketing Research* 34, no. 3 (1997): 347–56.

19 Albert M. Muniz Jr. and Thomas C. O'Guinn, "Brand Community," *Journal of Consumer Research* 27, no. 4 (2001): 412–32.

20 Paul Rozin and Carol Nemeroff, "Sympathetic Magical Thinking: The Contagion and Similarity 'Heuristics,'" in Thomas Gilovich, Dale Griffin, and Daniel Kahneman, eds., *Heuristics and Biases: The Psychology of Intuitive Judgment* (New York: Cambridge University Press, 2002), 201–16.

21 Youngme Moon, "Intimate Exchanges: Using Computers to Elicit Self-Disclosure from Consumers," *Journal of Consumer Research* 26, no. 4 (2000): 323–39.

22 Lewis M. Branscomb, "The Human Side of the Computer" (paper presented at the Symposium on Computer, Man, and Society, Haifa, Israel, 1979), 1–18.

23 Patrice D. Tremoulet and Jacob Feldman, "Perception of Animacy from the Motion of a Single Object," *Perception* 29, no. 8 (2000): 943–51.

24 Susan A. Graham and Diane Poulin-Dubois, "Infants' Reliance on Shape to Generalize Novel Labels to Animate and Inanimate Objects," *Journal of Child Language* 26, no. 2 (1999): 295–320.

25 Daniel C. Dennet, *Kinds of Minds: Towards an Understanding of Consciousness,* The Science Masters Series (New York: Basic Books, 1996).

26 Pankaj Aggarwal and Ann L. McGill, "Is That Car Smiling at Me? Schema Congruity as a Basis for Evaluating Anthropomorphized Products," *Journal of Consumer Research* 34, no. 4 (2007): 468–79.

27 Joan Meyers-Levy and Alice M. Tybout, "Schema Congruity as a Basis for Product Evaluation," *Journal of Consumer Research* 16, no. 1 (1989): 39–54.

28 Jean-Yves Baudouin, Daniel Gilbert, Stephane Sansone and Guy Tiberghien, "When the Smile Is a Cue to Familiarity," *Memory* 8, no. 5 (2000): 285–92.

29 John A. Bargh, Mark Chen, and Lara Burrows, "Automaticity of Social Behavior: Direct Effects of Trait Construct and Stereotype Activation on Action," *Journal of Personality and Social Psychology* 71, no. 2 (1996): 230–44.

30 Grainne M. Fitzsimons, Tanya L. Chartrand, and Gavan J. Fitzsimons, "Automatic Effects of Brand Exposure on Motivated Behavior: How Apple Makes You 'Think Different,'" *Journal of Consumer Research* 35, no. 1 (2008): 21–35.

31 Pankaj Aggarwal and Ann L. McGill, "When Brands Seem Human, Do Humans Act Like Brands? Automatic Behavioral Priming Effects of Brand Anthropomorphism," *Journal of Consumer Research* 39, no. 2 (2012): 307–23.

32 Joseph Cesario, Jason E. Plaks, and E. Tory Higgins, "Automatic Social Behavior as Motivated Preparation to Interact," *Journal of Personality and Social Psychology* 90, no. 6 (2006): 893–910.

14 The Psychology of Giving: Small Interventions That Make a Difference

APARNA A. LABROO

In 2010, an impressive $300 billion, or an average of $700 per person, was raised for charity in North America (the United States and Canada). Remarkably, 80 per cent of this money, or four of every five philanthropic dollars, was contributed by individuals rather than trusts and corporations.[1,2] In addition to cash, people made non-cash contributions such as stocks, real estate, art and collectibles, air miles, vehicles, food, clothing, and time. People were generous despite tough economic conditions. This level of giving is good news for charities, but raising money from individuals poses considerable challenges. First, the amount that different individuals donate as a percentage of their total income varies a good deal. Wealthier populations donate a lesser proportion of their income relative to poorer populations.[3] Second, the 2010 total of $300 billion works out to only $375,000 on average per charity, because over 800,000 charities compete for these philanthropic dollars.[4] Third, the kinds of charities that draw the maximum dollar vary.[2] More than half of the money that was raised in 2010 went to faith-based charities as well as to colleges, universities, and educational institutions. Money going to environmental causes and animal welfare issues was barely 2 per cent of the total money raised. In addition, the amount going to social and human charities actually dropped from previous years. Fifth, charitable giving is centred on events that draw maximum media attention. Vivid images of suffering draw the highest degrees of responsiveness from large numbers of people making smaller contributions. As an example, the Haiti disaster attracted over $1.3 billion within a six-month period.[5] This amount is nearly one-fifth of North America's entire annual contribution to all environmental and animal welfare charities combined.

Individual charities can meet the challenge of getting people to contribute more money by recognizing that different individuals have different motivations for giving, ranging from seeking recognition to feeling virtuous. For example, bundling frivolous products with charitable donations not only helps the charity but can also increase sales of the frivolous product because the charity aspect allows people to better justify their frivolous spending.[6] Charities should also improve the scope of their communication activities, make the plight of victims vivid, and make it easy for people to get involved with the cause. For example, charities can leverage new media such as texting. The Red Cross did so when it asked donors to text "GIVE" to "2HELP," which would donate $5.00 to help California fire victims. The charge appeared on the customer's monthly mobile phone bill. AT&T similarly raised funds to help 12.4 million children at risk of hunger in America by asking people to text in their donations, additionally offering to match every dollar raised. Social media can also be employed to raise awareness of causes and to connect with possible donors. When Stanford graduate Sameer Bhatia was diagnosed with leukemia, his friends managed to leverage social media to spread the word that he needed a bone marrow donor and drew a response from over 20,000 potential targeted donors. Within only a few months, all of them tested for a possible marrow match.[7] The power of social media for organizing volunteers, for instance by using Twitter or by getting large numbers of small donors engaged, was also demonstrated in the successful fund-raising by the Obama campaign in 2008.[7] The stories behind of all of these causes were vivid, donating was easy, and social media allowed opportunities for "emotional contagion" – donors felt more involved in the cause because they could relate to the cause not just by donating but also by spreading the information about the cause to other potential donors, thereby causing ripple effects. With the multitude of donation requests people encounter,[4] charities need to connect with potential donors at this emotional level.

Keeping with the theme of this book on flux in the marketplace, this chapter focuses on the challenges associated with charitable giving, and in particular on recent insights from consumer psychology that can help understand the motivational, situational, and emotional influences underlying charitable giving. In this chapter, "marketplace" is defined broadly as society while "social good" is defined as getting people to engage in pro-social actions that benefit society (see also chapter 10 by Nina Mazar) and to engage more with their favourite causes. This marketplace has seen rapid change and flux in recent years – social media has transformed and continues to transform this marketplace by allowing people to connect more rapidly and at a deeper level with their favourite causes, providing them opportunities to feel recognized, to communicate with others, and to achieve a sense of self-worth. These opportunities and challenges are likely to increase in coming years as consumers become savvier and better connected to each other, to marketers, and to their favourite causes through social media. In this chapter, I will elaborate on the reasons people behave altruistically and then suggest a set of strategies and interventions that can get people to give more. These insights are geared to help charities in soliciting donations, but companies in general can also employ cause marketing as a point of differentiation against competitors and a strategy to connect at a deeper level with consumers who are likely to see charity as an increasingly important reflection of their identity.

Why People Give: Extrinsic versus Intrinsic Reasons

People want to be happy (see chapter 6), but what makes people happy? Religions claim that giving one's wealth to others can make the giver happy, but scientists in general and economists in particular have stated that the act of giving wealth away to strangers is an act of irrationality.[8] Economists have argued that self-interest should guide rational human actions; people should be interested in accumulating resources for their own use and engage only in those actions that benefit them the most. Without the promise of reciprocity, the simple act of giving is unreasonable. Instead, studies have shown that people often act outside of pure self-interest and spontaneously choose to be more generous than the situation dictates, and that they tend to punish others who behave in purely selfish ways even when generosity would be costly. For instance, in "ultimatum game" experiments in which one of two participants must split a sum of money between himself and the other participant, the only condition being that the opponent must accept the proposed split for either participant to keep the money, givers were generally fair and split the money in half, with almost everyone giving more than one cent. Economists had proposed that the rational giver should offer a minimum of one cent as that amount would make the receiver strictly better off than before, meaning that he/she would be willing to accept it. However, receivers who were assigned less-than-fair amounts generally tended to reject the offers, with one-cent offers being rejected nearly 100 per cent of the time, even though accepting such an offer would have resulted in the receivers procuring more resources for themselves than before.[11] Economists prescribed this finding to the irrationality of human nature. Similar views can be found in psychology. Basic theories of human motivation also presumed that humans seek to maximize their pleasure and minimize their pain, and therefore the frequency and consistency with which people actively respond to the pain of others, even when doing so was costly to the self, seemed puzzling. More recent findings, however, have suggested that people derive basic value or "utility" via a feel-good factor when they act altruistically, and that this utility is what prompts altruism.[2,9,10] People also have just-world beliefs that lead them to give to others even when doing so is costly to the giver themselves. Social norms also encourage altruism and people give when being selfish would draw social criticism.[11,12]

These reasons for giving can be classified into two categories – extrinsic or intrinsic – both of which guide most human actions.[12] The first category represents the desire to attain extrinsic or external rewards or to avoid social censure or punishment, and this motivates many people. In the context of charity, extrinsic or external motivations could include the promise of recognition, the opportunity to be seen in a certain setting, or the prospect of getting tax deductions. For example, educational institutions and hospitals often attract large donors by promising recognition in terms of the naming of buildings and institutions, which might account for the large amount of money given to such organizations. Named bricks in the wall of an organization or even something as simple as a mention of the donor in a brochure or annual report also serve a similar purpose. Fundraisers provide such opportunities for extrinsic recognition or external reward as well. For instance, in his 2008 presidential run, Barack Obama offered a lottery in which two people who donated to his campaign would be chosen to attend a fundraising banquet that Obama himself would also be attending. Not surprisingly, the Obama campaign was one of the most successful in motivating large numbers of small, individual donations. The promise of avoiding social sanctions and censure might also motivate extrinsically oriented people, therefore leading them to abide by social norms. Some funding of religious charities may be driven by such motivations as well as social or peer pressures. The second category of motivation for engaging in any task is intrinsic, based on the inherent joy of doing the task. In the context of giving, intrinsically oriented people may choose to give because they find the act of giving inherently joyful or valuable and attain self-worth from doing so. Such people might prefer to donate anonymously because the lack of any external recognition, award, or pressure allows them to infer that they are involved in the cause because it is personal and that they care about the cause for its own sake. The act of giving is also a source of joy and can make the donor feel good in general and about himself/herself in particular.

For example, a classic study showed that spending money on others rather than on oneself could make people happier.[3] Researchers polled a national sample of 632 people, asking them to indicate how happy they were and what kinds of things they spent their income on. The activities people reported were classified into personal spending and prosocial spending, and the researchers found that whereas general happiness was uncorrelated with personal spending, it was positively correlated with prosocial spending. But because such a finding does not establish causality (in other words, happier people might tend to give more money to others because they are *already* happy), the researchers then approached a Boston firm for data. In this field study, the researchers first surveyed the general happiness levels among the firm's employees. The researchers took these measures just before the employees received their annual bonuses. After six to eight weeks, they again surveyed the same employees. This time, the researchers asked about their general levels of happiness and also what proportion of their bonuses they spent on themselves versus others. The researchers found that people who spent larger proportions on others had greater increases in their general happiness levels from the earlier baseline levels as compared to people who spent most of the bonus on themselves. The researchers also ran an additional study in a lab. They invited students on campus at the University of British Columbia to participate in an experiment. When students arrived to the experiment, experimenters assigned them to one of four conditions at random: (1) $20 cash and instructions to spend the money on themselves; (2) $20 cash and instructions to spend the money on someone else; (3) $5 cash and instructions to spend the money on themselves; and (4) $5 cash and instructions to spend the money on someone else. Participants returned in the evening to complete a survey in which they reported their current levels of happiness. The researchers found that students who had engaged in prosocial spending that day were significantly happier than those who had spent the money on themselves, and additionally that the amount of prosocial spending did not matter. Those who spent $20 on others were not happier than those who spent $5 on others. Thus, spending on others – even little acts of kindness towards others – can make a person happier.

While designing a program, managers should do more to let people know that altruistic actions result in greater happiness than selfish ones, and to encourage them to imagine how these actions will make them feel. Knowing this fact does not take away from people's happiness from giving; instead, it adds to it. It may be particularly important to remind people facing donor fatigue of such happiness, rather than just recounting reasons why the charitable donation is important. Fatigue leads to general cognitive depletion, and at such times emotional appeals are particularly effective. Small doses of happiness can also help counter fatigue and depletion. Furthermore, because the pleasure of donating to the same charity could wear out over time, charities will benefit by making it easy for consumers to make donations, for instance by providing opportunities for regular paycheck deductions. Managers should further consider the two distinct fundamental motivations (extrinsic and intrinsic) that underlie giving and sort different subgroups of populations for their different primary motivations. Recognizing whether the primary motivation of a target donor is intrinsic or extrinsic will help charities better refine their strategies by promising suitable rewards of recognition or by preserving their donors' anonymity. Importantly, even if a charity does not know the primary motivation of its target audience, small interventions can make people believe they are of one type and behave as if they have one or the other motivation in any situation.

For instance, in a lab study,[12] undergraduate students received a survey comprised of a battery of demographic questions presumably designed to better understand their motivations. Eight statements that either nudged participants to endorse statements that they are extrinsically motivated (e.g., "I work for recognition") or as intrinsically motivated ("I work for the inherent joy of doing") were embedded in the battery of questions. The authors designed this task based on the realization that in most situations, people's thinking reflects contextual environmental effects and tends to be very fluid.[13,14,15] Participants were then thanked and instructed to go to another experiment across the hallway if they wished to complete another study; all participants agreed to do the second study. In it, all participants again completed a second battery of tasks for twenty minutes, after which they received some materials pertaining to their university's annual efforts to raise money for a local food kitchen. Participants could look at the materials and make a donation (with their own money) if they wished to do so. Materials for one-third of the participants said the contribution would be recognized in the annual brochure; materials for another third said the contribution would be anonymous; and materials for the remaining third not only said the donation would be anonymous but also that they could spend a few minutes writing an anonymous card to the recipients of the contribution. Participants who had endorsed extrinsic reasons for generally doing things were more likely to donate to the recognized appeal, whereas those who had endorsed intrinsic reasons were most likely to donate to the anonymous appeals, regardless of whether they had to put in the additional effort of writing a card. Importantly, participants contributed real money – their own money – despite that they did not expect to part with money when they arrived at the lab. Notably, these motivations had been induced randomly among participants over the twenty minutes prior to the donation decision. Such a simple intervention as statement endorsement was thus able to override a person's chronic motivation and impact their giving.

Getting People to Commit: Identifying the Victim

Among uncommitted donors, making the plight of a victim salient can grab attention and get them to donate more. Among committed donors, this strategy of identifying a single victim can backfire – committed donors tend to already empathize with the victim at a deeper level and so highlighting plight of a victim can make them feel conflicted; also, highlighting a single victim makes such donors feel as if they are not doing enough to help a broader set of victims.

Numerous studies in experimental settings have shown that people who were not otherwise committed to a cause and were previously unaware of it tend to donate more to the cause when a single victim is identified. Stories of specific victims of a tragedy draw more attention compared to general information about the suffering of many, and this focus on a single identifiable victim helps raise more money than stories about diffuse, unidentifiable victims. For example, Lowenstein describes the case of eighteen-month-old Jessica McClure ("Baby Jessica") who drew worldwide media attention in 1987 when she was trapped in a well, resulting in over $700,000 pouring in to help her rescue efforts.[16] But numerous unidentified babies of that age die all over the world from starvation and disease, and that sum of money could have helped save several thousands of them rather than a single child.

Lowenstein and colleagues describe several reasons why identifiable victims garner greater support from a general public than the thousands of victims who remain nameless statistics.[17,18,19] First, stories of identified victims are more vivid than those of statistical victims,[20] making the cause more attention-grabbing, salient, and relatable, especially among people who would not otherwise relate with or attend to the cause. Individual victims also express emotions that can sway donors.[21] Second, losses faced by identifiable victims appear more real while those of unidentified victims appear less real, and people respond to this greater sense of reality.[22] Third, blame is easier to assign for the tragedy of an identifiable victim, less so for an unidentifiable one,[23] and simply assigning blame makes the loss from tragedy loom larger because it makes it seem preventable. Fourth, people also feel a greater concern towards victims who are part of a smaller rather than larger reference group. For example, a disease that kills 100 in a town of 100 people is viewed as a greater tragedy than a disease that kills 100 people across the country.[24] Identifiability makes the set of victims look like a set of one. Fifth, identifiable people appear similar to one's own reference group, which makes the tragedy seem worse and more personal. As an example of this, people contribute more to a charity when the recipient has been determined and selected from a list rather than when the recipient remains to be selected.[18] Teaching people about this anomaly (overweighting information pertaining to identified rather than unidentified victims) has an unfortunate and ironic effect of reducing donations to identified victims but not increasing donations to unidentified victims.[25] Highlighting the plight of a victim could also make people feel bad, and this negative mood could increase prosocial behaviour because donations and helping others provide mood-repairing opportunities. Thus managers should highlight the plight of a victim to encourage donations from people who might otherwise not relate to the cause.

However, among donors who are committed to a cause and already relate to it, highlighting the plight of a single victim can backfire by overwhelming the donor with extreme negative emotion and making him/her feel bad for a victim with whom he/she already strongly identifies.[26] For example, researchers found that people who cared about a natural disaster and read a general appeal about the disaster without being asked to imagine helping a specific victim were more likely to help the cause than were participants who were asked to consider a specific victim's plight. The cause was already dear to the potential donor's heart, and in this situation, reading about a specific victim (a) made the tragedy seem too close for comfort and increased emotional conflict and (b) made helping appear inadequate and as if it was only directed to one recipient. As a result, the potential donor emotionally distanced him/herself from the appeal and disengaged from the cause, which reduced the money he/she donated to the charity. These findings imply that appeals using identified victims will succeed with un-committed donors by getting them to attend to the cause but will fail with committed donors; for them, the plight of a single victim will create emotional turmoil by making the tragedy seem "too close for comfort," and helping what seems like only one person will simply not feel like it is enough.

Strengthening the Bond: Encouraging Effort to Make a Cause Seem Worthy

Charities should make it easy for uncommitted donors to get involved with the cause, but ironically, committed donors get value from the sense that they are investing effort to help their cause.[27,28,29,30] Contrary to economists' and psychologists' expectations that people shun pain because it reduces utility, to committed donors, the pain of exerting effort makes them see value in and become more committed to their cause. The reason for this anomaly is that when people are committed to any cause, they believe that exerting effort will result in a better outcome, which it usually does. The more valuable an outcome, the more effort people expect they will invest. As a consequence, effort holds symbolic value to most people. But people sometimes confuse the sense of effort with value and ironically end up liking hard-to-deliver outcomes simply because they are hard to deliver.[27,28] As a consequence, they come to view outcomes associated with symbolic effort as more valuable than those without similar effort, even when the effort does not ensure a better outcome. Charity is no exception. Not only is charity associated with the suffering of others, but people believe that effort is necessary to alleviate suffering, and this belief is stronger among people committed to the charity. As a consequence, making such people exert symbolic effort can increase the probability, and even the amount, that they will donate.

In a first demonstration of this phenomenon, Labroo and Kim[29] showed that people who are highly committed to helping a charity – for instance, people on a charity hotlist who have donated for many years or those who are personally vested in a cause because it directly impacts their lives – will be more likely to support the charity when symbolic effort is associated with their help. The reason is that people who are the most vested in a cause are those who usually invest the most effort into helping it, but because investing effort is so strongly ingrained in their minds as part of helping the cause, any sense of token effort, even when it does not really help the charity, can increase their commitment. In other words, not only do people who are committed to a charity exert more effort to help it, but the sense of token effort makes them infer greater commitment to the charity by making the charity appear more instrumental to fulfilling their charitable goals (e.g., the "Instrumentality" Heuristic).[29] To show that a token effort that does not help a charity can nonetheless increase commitment and donation among the most committed donors, these researchers created two versions of an advertisement for Kids In Danger, a Chicago-based charity that promotes safety of children's products. The parents of "Baby Danny" started the charity after their son was crushed by a defective crib in his daycare. One version of the charity appeal employed clear black text. The other version employed the same ad but in grey text that was readable but did involve a sense of effort, as participants had to furrow their brows and narrow their eyes to read the words (see Figure 14.1). Once respondents arrived at the lab, half of them were put through a "priming" procedure, which made them infer that they were highly committed to charity and that being a good person was important to them; the remainder of the respondents completed a neutral task. Researchers then presented one of the two versions of the charity materials to participants and provided them the opportunity to use their own money to make an anonymous donation. Notably, participants had come to the experiment to complete studies for which they thought they would be paid and did not expect to instead face a situation in which they had to part with their money. Uncommitted donors who had done the neutral scramble donated more money when the ad was clear and involved little effort rather than when it was blurry and they had to strain their eyes ($0.53 vs. $0.26). But respondents who were primed to feel committed tended to donate more of their money when they had to exert effort to read the ad compared to when the ad was clear. In fact, such individuals donated, on average, more than twice the money after reading the visually difficult rather than the easy-to-read appeal ($0.70 vs. $0.30).

Figure 14.1 Kids In Danger Sample Materials from Labroo & Kim[29]

"Kids in Danger" was established following the death of baby Danny, here in Chicago, in his daycare. Baby Danny awoke after a nap and as he stood up in his crib, it collapsed killing him. The company was aware of a defect in the manufacture of the crib and had recalled the product from its stores, but had not alerted consumers to the dangers of this product.

"Kids in Danger" was established following the death of baby Danny, here in Chicago, in his daycare. Baby Danny awoke after a nap and as he stood up in his crib, it collapsed killing him. The company was aware of a defect in the manufacture of the crib and had recalled the product from its stores, but had not alerted consumers to the dangers of this product.

In a follow-up study,[28] these researchers replicated this experiment in another context, using real but pointless token effort (instead of a subjective sense of effort from font in an ad). Once undergraduate students at the University of Chicago arrived at the lab, the experimenters thanked them and said they were glad to see them either because they were among the first to participate or because they were among the last to participate. The experimenters had previously tested this subtle manipulation and found that it changed people's inferences regarding the extent to which they might be able to impact the fate of the charity: those who were told they were among the first inferred they would set standards for future success of the charity and were more committed to its success; those who were told they were among the last felt they had little influence on the fate of the charity and were less committed to it. After this manipulation, the easy-to-read version of the materials for Kids In Danger was given to all participants, but for some of the participants, the donation box was right next to them; for others, it was about four feet away and would require the participant to stand up and stretch to make a donation. Thus, in this experiment, effort was real but truly pointless because everyone received the same information and distance to the box did not imply anything about the quality of the charity. Replicating their previous experiment, the authors again found that uncommitted donors were more likely to make a donation and donate higher amounts when the donation box was close rather than far. In contrast, committed donors were more likely to make a donation and donate higher amounts when the box was far rather than close. Thus highly committed donors inferred value from token effort while uncommitted donors were turned off by token effort. Other research showed that asking committed donors first whether they would donate time to a cause and then asking them to donate money increased donations relative to directly asking such people to donate money (the "Time-Ask" Effect).[31] Time is associated with an emotional commitment, whereas money is associated with economic and utilitarian concerns. Making people think about time makes them infer a commitment of effort to the cause and increases their intention to support the charity.

It is simple to associate effort or ease with the appeal or the act of making a donation. For example, in an online appeal, instead of clicking once to make a donation, a person could have to click twice. Instead of directly inserting a cheque in an envelope, a donor could have to first fold it in half. It is also simple to nudge people into thinking that they are either committed or uncommitted to a cause. For example, perceived commitment of a donor to a charitable cause can be increased by implying that a person is among the first (a pioneer) to help the cause, or by making them consider why the charity is personally important, or by making them think of volunteering time for the charity. Moreover, most charities already have hotlists with highly committed donors and cold lists with uncommitted donors. Thus, charities can and should match the effort a donor will need to invest to donor types. One precaution that charities employing token effort should take is to en-sure that, for repeated donations, effort on an earlier occasion does not make donors feel they are licensed to ignore a later appeal (see chapter 10). This objective could be accomplished with a message as simple as reminding donors of their commitment to the cause and how integral their support is to the cause. Such a message reminding donors of their commitment could further strengthen the effectiveness of symbolic ef-fort.

The Emotional Donor

Managers can also increase the probability that people will donate by tapping into the donors' emotions. A donor's feelings can be altered by simple interventions, and once altered these free-floating feelings can become attached to whatever information is subsequently presented. Feelings can combine with donors' beliefs about emotion transience and how being charitable can manage their moods.[32] Feelings can also become associated with a donor's personal goals to be a good person and can strengthen or weaken those goals, thereby impacting the do-nor's personal desire to be charitable.

In my research I propose that donation depends on whether people infer a need to manage their momentary feelings and the extent to which they believe attending to an appeal will be emotionally costly.[32] Although the act of donating makes a person feel better, attending to information about the disturbing plight of others is unsettling for most people. People who are cued with happy thoughts (or are feeling happy in the moment) and who believe emotion is fleeting avoid the pain of looking at charity materials or making a donation because they per-ceive the appeals as emotionally costly and likely to undo their positive feelings. However, happy people who believe emotion is lasting are more likely to make donations because they infer that the appeal can-not hurt their current positive feelings. Similarly, people cued with un-happy thoughts (or who are already feeling unhappy) and who believe that emotion is fleeting will attend to the charity and make a dona-tion because they infer no danger in doing so; the immediate negativ-ity will pass on its own. Unhappy people who think emotion is stable, on the other hand, avoid the appeal because looking at it could make their negative state even worse. Simple interventions can cue happy or unhappy thoughts and simple interventions can alter people's beliefs about the transience of emotion.

For example, in one experiment, participants who came to a lab were asked either to think of and write down words that made them feel happy or to think of and write down words that made them feel unhappy. In what was pitched as a second and unrelated study, participants completed word-scramble sentences in which they made coherent four-word sentences from sets of five words. These sentences reminded participants either that emotions can be fleeting or that they can be lasting. Once this task was over, experimenters thanked participants and then asked them to look at materials pertaining to Kids In Danger and to make a donation if they wished to do so. The materials, adapted from the charity's website (http://www.kidsindanger.com), were upsetting and comprised stories of young children who had lost their lives to defective products. Experimenters measured how long the respondents looked at the disturbing materials and also how much of their own money they donated. Experimenters found that respondents who wrote happy (vs. unhappy) words spent less time looking at the disturbing appeal when they believed that emotion is fleeting, but more time looking at the materials when they believed that emotion is lasting. Donation amounts mapped onto how much time respondents spent looking at the materials. In a follow-up study, the researchers found similar effects when they first provided respondents with a story claiming either that emotions are fleeting or that emotions are lasting, and then showed participants an advertisement for a charity, Save the Children. The appeal was either positive, urging respondents to put a smile on the face of devastated children and to share their happiness; or negative, urging respondents to experience the victims' misery. When people considered a gain-framed ad message advocating "putting a smile on the face of children," donations were higher among those who believed emotion is lasting rather than fleeting. However, when people considered a loss-framed ad message advocating "removing the victims' misery," donations were lower among people who believed emotion is lasting rather than fleeting. Thus, fitting people's momentary feelings with beliefs about transience of emotion can increase donation. Feelings and beliefs can be altered by simple interventions, including an advertisement appeal's characteristics – be they asking people to put a glow on the face of a recipient or to remove their misery – and by an accompanying cue that makes people consider emotions as fleeting or lasting. The decision to donate to charity depends on whether people believe they need to manage their feelings or not and whether attending to the appeal will be emotionally costly or not.

Managers should also consider a second set of findings showing that people's current feelings can change their commitment to being good.[33] In my research, I found that people who feel happy and are reminded of being committed to charity are likely to donate more than those in a neutral mood or who are not reminded of such commitment. Instead, people who feel unhappy and are asked to consider commitment to being a charitable person are less likely to engage in charitable acts than are those in a neutral mood or those not reminded of commitment. Positive mood allows people to recognize opportunities; therefore, people feeling happy become more committed to their goals of being a good person. Negative mood makes people sensitive to threat; therefore, unhappiness undermines people's commitment to their goals, including those of being charitable. As discussed, subtle cues in an advertisement that remind people of reasons to be happy or reasons to be unhappy may be sufficient to induce such momentary good or bad feelings. Subtle reminders of a person's commitment to charity can further enhance the probability and amount that someone who feels happy – but not someone who feels unhappy – will donate. As discussed, feelings are easy to induce via specific aspects of an advertising appeal. Expressing the right message after inducing such feelings can help maximize the probability that people will make a donation and in higher amounts than otherwise.

Conclusions

There is a growing importance in consumer psychology for research that can inform not-for-profit organizations and public policy on ways to encourage people to act in the greater social good in favour of their own personal interest. The findings detailed in this chapter highlight some reasons people act altruistically and suggest subtle interventions that can further encourage giving behaviours. The chapter began by providing a framework by which people's motivations to act altruistically can be classified either as extrinsic and therefore motivated by external rewards; or as intrinsic and therefore motivated by an inherent value and joy of giving. It then suggests several interventions and strategies that can increase altruism. The strategies can be classified into three categories: (1) information-based strategies advocating that charities highlight the plight of a single victim; (2) motivation-based strategies suggesting that people who are committed to a charity have an inherent need to exert effort and feel pain in order to sense they are making a worthwhile contribution; and (3) emotion-based strategies that focus on the role charity can play in making people feel better and also how people's current feelings can impact their need to help a charity. I suggested simple interventions to alter information, motivation, or emotion in a charity appeal, and ways that different groups of donors – committed ones such as those on a hotlist or uncommitted ones such as those on a cold list – might react to these interventions. Based on the evidence reviewed, one can argue that understanding aspects of information salience, donor motivation, and donor emotion is fundamental to promoting greater levels of altruism. The fact that some of the interventions described in this chapter are subtle should not be taken to mean that they cannot have a measurable impact in the field. In fact, it is their subtlety that will ensure their effectiveness in the field because they will likely fly below the radar among donors and yet powerfully nudge them to donate. Their subtlety should be maintained while running the appeal, because when the manipulations are made blatant, they tend to have the opposite effect in potential donors.[29]

Each of the studies reported in this chapter has specific practical implications, as discussed above. They also help illustrate key aspects of donor psychology that relate to the types of information people attend to, as well as their motivations and their emotions when faced with the prospect of helping a charity. But many of the reported studies have thus far only been tested in the lab, so extending them meaningfully to the field will benefit both science and charity – and the individual.

A Prescription to Encourage Consumers to Engage in Prosocial Behaviours
Asking consumers to contribute to a cause isn't just about making the cause seem worthy. Marketers need to:

- INCREASE the happiness of donors by asking them to imagine how they would feel.
- HIGHLIGHT the plight of the individual victim at an emotional (but not graphic) level.
- SEGMENT donors by whether their motives are intrinsic or extrinsic and design separate appeals for them.
- ENGAGE donors by making donation easy for uncommitted donors but mildly effortful for committed ones.

REFERENCES

1 Leave a Legacy, "Statistics on Giving," 2011, accessed 1 July 2011 from http://www.leavealegacy.ca/program/who/.

2 Giving USA Foundation, "Annual Report on Philanthropy 2009," 2010, accessed 1 July 2011 from http://www.nps.gov/partnerships/fundraising_individuals_statistics.htm.

3 Elizabeth W. Dunn, Lara B. Aknin, and Michael L. Norton, "Spending Money on Others Promotes Happiness," *Science* 319 (2008): 1687–8.

4 Lori A. West, "Non-profits Face Funding Pressures," *Journal of Accountancy* 198: 1–2.

5 "Haiti Donations: $1.3 Billion," *CNN Money*, 9 July 2010, accessed 1 July 2011from http://money.cnn.com/2010/07/09/news/international/haiti_donation/index.htm.

6 Michal Strahilevitz and John G. Myers, "Donations to Charity as Purchase Incentives: How Well They Work May Depend on What You Are Trying to Sell," *Journal of Consumer Research* 24 (1998): 434–46.

7 Jennifer Aaker and Adam Smith, *The Dragonfly Effect: Quick, Effective, and Powerful Ways to Use Social Media to Drive Social Change*, 1st ed. (San Francisco: Jossey-Bass, 2010).

8 Roland Benabou and Jean Tirole, "Pre-adaptation and the Puzzles and Properties of Pleasure," in Daniel Kahneman, Ed Deiner, and Norbert Schwarz, eds., *Wellbeing: The Foundations of Hedonic Psychology* (New York: Russell Sage, 2006), 109–13.

9 Sonja Lyubomirsky, Kennon M. Sheldon, and David Schkade, "Pursuing Happiness: The Architecture of Sustainable Change," *Review of General Psychology* 9 (2005): 111–31.

10 Tonya P. Williams and Angela Y. Lee, "Me and Benjamin: Transaction versus Relationship Wealth in Subjective Well-Being," working paper, Kellogg School of Management, Northwestern University, 2007.

11 Ernst Fehr and Urs Fischbacher, "The Nature of Human Altruism," *Nature* 425 (2003): 785–91.

12 Aparna A. Labroo and Michal Herzenstein, "Giving What One Values and Feeling Happy," working paper, University of Toronto, 2011.

13 Thomas Gilovich, *How We Know What Isn't So: The Fallibility of Human Reason in Everyday Life* (New York: Free Press, 1993).

14 Aparna A. Labroo, Ravi Dhar, and Norbert Schwarz, "Of Frowning Watches and Frog Wines: Semantic Priming, Perceptual Fluency, and Brand Evaluation," *Journal of Consumer Research* 34, no. 6 (2008): 819–31.

15 Thomas K. Srull and Robert S. Wyer, "The Role of Category Accessibility in the Interpretation of Information about Persons: Some Determinants and Implications," *Journal of Personality and Social Psychology* 37, no. 10 (1979): 1660–72.

16 "TV Reviews – Network: Everybody's Baby," *Variety*, 31 May 1989.

17 Karen Jenni and George Loewenstein, "Explaining the Identifiable Victim Effect," *Journal of Risk and Uncertainty* 14 (1997): 235–57.

18 Deborah A. Small and George Loewenstein, "Helping 'A' Victim or Helping 'THE' Victim: Altruism and Identifiability," *Journal of Risk and Uncertainty* 26, no. 1 (2003): 5–16.

19 Deborah Small and Uri Simohnson, "Friends of Victims: Personal Experience and Prosocial Behavior," *Journal of Consumer Research* 35 (2008): 532–42.

20 Richard E. Nisbett and Lee Ross, *Human Inference: Strategies and Shortcomings of Social Judgment* (Englewood Cliffs, NJ: Prentice-Hall, 1980).

21 Deborah Small and Nicole Verocchi, "The Face of Need: Facial Emotion Expression on Charity Advertisements," *Journal of Marketing Research* 46 (2009): 777–87.

22 Daniel Kahneman and Amos Tversky, "Prospect Theory: An Analysis of Decision under Risk," *Econometrica* 47, no. 2 (1979): 263–91.

23 Mary Douglas, *Risk and Blame: Essays in Cultural Theory* (New York: Routledge, 1992).

24 Paul Slovic, Baruch Fischhoff, and Sarah Lichtenstein, "Facts and Fears: Understanding Perceived Risk," in Richard C. Schwing and Walther A. Albers, Jr., eds., *Societal Risk Assessment: How Safe Is Safe Enough?* (New York: Plenum Press, 1980).

25 Deborah Small, George Loewenstein, and Paul Slovic, "Sympathy and Callousness: The Impact of Deliberative Thought on Donations to Identifiable and Statistical Victims," *Organizational Behavior and Human Decision Processes* 102, no. 2 (2007): 143–53.

26 Iris W. Hung and Robert S. Wyer, Jr., "Differences in Perspectives and the Influence of Charitable Appeals: When Imagining Oneself as the Victim is Not Always Beneficial," *Journal of Marketing Research* 46, no. 3 (2009): 421–34.

27 Sanford E. DeVoe and Jeffrey Pfeffer, "When Time Is Money: The Effect of Hourly Payment on the Evaluation of Time," *Organizational Behavior and Human Decision Processes* 104, no. 1 (2007): 1–13.

28 Sara Kim and Aparna A. Labroo, "From Inherent Value to Incentive Value: When and Why Pointless Effort Enhances Consumer Preference," *Journal of Consumer Research* 38, no. 4 (2011): 712–42.

29 Aparna A. Labroo and Sara Kim, "The 'Instrumentality' Heuristic: Why Metacognitive Difficulty is Desirable during Goal Pursuit," *Psychological Science* 20, no. 1 (2009): 127–34.

30 Christopher Y. Olivola and Eldar Shafir, "More Pain, More Gained: When the Prospect of Pain and Effort Increases Prosocial Contributions," working paper, Department of Psychology, Princeton University, 2007.

31 Wendy Liu and Jennifer Aaker, "The Happiness of Giving: The Time-Ask Effect," *Journal of Consumer Research* 35, no. 3 (2008): 543–57.

32 Aparna A. Labroo and Anirban Mukhopadhyay, "Lay Theories of Emotion Transience and the Search for Happiness: A Fresh Perspective on Affect Regulation," *Journal of Consumer Research* 36, no. 2 (2009): 242–54.

33 Ayelet Fishbach and Aparna A. Labroo, "Be Better or Be Merry? How Mood Influences Self-Control," *Journal of Personality and Social Psychology* 93, no. 2 (2007): 158–73.

15 Managing Brands by Leveraging Academic Research

DELAINE HAMPTON

In the last thirty years there have been several significant events that disrupted the practice of marketing. The advent of store-level checkout scanners and the development of people meters for TV ratings radically altered the world of market data, prompting a wave of academic research and new tools for marketers. Econometric models and single-source data (i.e., purchase and viewing data from the same household) changed the way marketers managed pricing, promotions, and media weights. The store-level data also started to shift the power between brand owners and retailers by putting more information under the retailers' control. Market research companies such as AC Nielsen and Information Resources Inc. developed many profitable new business divisions. Big changes in the marketing landscape accentuated the urgency for new practice and facilitated collaboration among academics, research companies, and marketing practitioners.

We are now facing another period of dramatic landscape change. Fragmented markets, social networking, instant information, online auctions, open-source development, global connectedness, and mobile platforms for commerce are among the many things changing the rules of engagement between brands, stores, and consumers. The changes are coming faster than new rules can be written down! This is another moment in the field of marketing when practitioners need to join forces with academics and market research experts to thrive and even to survive.

The first fourteen chapters of this book contain many important insights that have the potential to evolve marketing practice to meet the challenges of the times. There is a deep well of new knowledge explaining why people act as they do in the marketplace and in everyday life.

All of it can help managers connect better with their customers as well as help everyone make better choices and allocate resources more effectively. The question is, will it be put to use? Will the ideas and insights attract the attention of people who can act on them? Will managers understand how to use this information in their organizations?

What can we learn from patterns of past adoptions to seize the opportunities in front of us today?

My thirty-five years of experience at P&G say it is a difficult and often lengthy process to move new ideas from research into broad practice. Radically new scientific thinking faces many obstacles and challenges, which is why it has typically taken twenty years for broad adoption of a new idea to occur. Even less radical, but nonetheless beneficial, new thinking has a hard time being noticed by people who are immersed in the day-to-day throb of running a business.

P&G has benefited from past experience and is managing adoption of marketing innovations differently today. The cycle times for innovation in media and brand communications are becoming progressively shorter as new developments quickly emerge with social and digital media. The Connect and Develop Program in research and development (R&D) taps into the open-source movement to pose technology problems and find solutions anywhere in the world. Connect and Develop contributes to over 50 per cent of new of product innovation today (http://www.pg.com). This is paying huge dividends.

Another excellent way to shorten adoption time is to create closer ties between academics and practitioners. However, academic researchers and business practitioners do not naturally work together. They have very different goals and reward systems. Business people focus on spotting opportunities, solving problems, and making efficient use of resources. Marketing academics are trying to create a fundamental understanding of market behaviours that managers can use to deliberately design successful outcomes and engineer positive change. Business people are rewarded for growing sales and profits month by month while academics are rewarded for publishing and advancing the science step by step.

As a result, business people do not generally turn to academics to solve immediate problems and academics can rarely use the messy, pragmatic real world as their scientific laboratory.

This is a problem.

The goal of this final chapter of *Flux* is to use experience from past adoptions to speed up application of this latest wave of marketing science. I offer the case of simulated test-market adoption within P&G

as a template for the various stages required for new practice to occur inside large organizations. By clearly understanding the stages and the roles of various champions and experts along the way, we can accelerate the adoption of new practices and rewrite the role of the marketing manager for the modern age.

This chapter has three parts. Section one details the case of P&G's adoption of new marketing science; section two shows where to focus for faster adoption; and section three explores how the specific insights from this book might best be developed for application.

Section One. A Case Study from P&G: Adoption of Simulated Test Markets

Here is the story of P&G's adoption of simulated test markets for new item qualification. The business question was, "How could P&G better predict the sales of new products before investing in market introductions?" This story has all the typical features of the adoption of new marketing science in a large organization. In my career at P&G I participated in the adoption of half a dozen significant new business practices. Each time the same steps and stages emerged.

In 1989 I had been in my role as manager of the Market Research Department for P&G Canada for three years (having previously spent ten years in research and development and eighteen months as the Camay brand manager). At that time, P&G was beginning to experiment with two new research models (BASES and ASSESSOR).[3,4] They each promised to predict new item sales prior to their introduction to the test market. Bob Davis, one of the most experienced innovators in the Market Research Department, had championed the early experiments on the U.S. side of the business. He was developing an internal model based on the data from P&G U.S. introductions. I had persuaded him to help me predict sales for some new Canadian introductions and they had gone well. Based on this experience I was asked to lead the expansion for P&G International – in other words, anything outside the United States.

So, over the next five years we built an expert community of market research forecasters with representatives in all of P&G's geographic regions. Using the science of simulated test markets, the expertise of strategic partners, and the data from hundreds of P&G cases around the world, we created a new standard process for managing new product introductions. The company's success rate with new item introductions improved significantly and the return on investment was excellent.

Figure 15.1 The Journey from Knowledge to Belief (1)

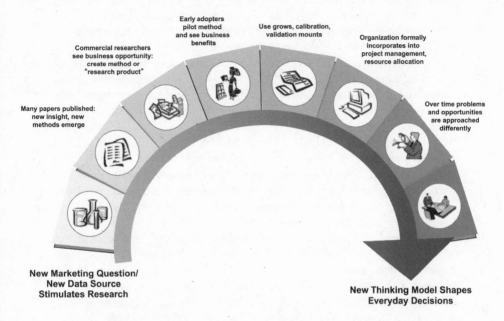

Early adopters
pilot method
and see business
benefits

Use grows, calibration,
validation mounts

Commercial researchers
see business opportunity:
create method or
"research product"

Organization formally
incorporates into
project management,
resource allocation

Many papers published:
new insight, new
methods emerge

Over time problems
and opportunities
are approached
differently

**New Marketing Question/
New Data Source
Stimulates Research**

**New Thinking Model Shapes
Everyday Decisions**

However, the five years of concentrated effort to create the new volume forecasting practice represents a relatively small part of the whole journey from published new science to full and secure adoption inside P&G. That complete process spanned about twenty years. I capture the stages and steps of that longer journey in the model below, which was shared at Informs and MSI conferences between 2004 and 2008. Practitioners and academics in many different areas of marketing agreed that these steps and the timelines were consistent with their experience introducing new marketing science into their organizations.

In the next few pages I will walk through the general model using the specific details of the simulated test marketing adoption. Then in section two I will highlight the core areas that need to be addressed to compress the process in the future.

Walking through the Model

The knowledge is first developed by academics researching new questions or working with new types of data. Academics were finding that real-world choices in many markets were not following expected patterns, especially when there was a large range of options. Simulated test markets were developed from new insights and theory explaining consumer choice behaviour. Advances by applied mathematician R. Duncan Luce in 1959 (Luce's Axiom of Choice) and by economist Daniel McFadden in 1970 (discrete choice application of Logit models) launched new research exploring various domains of consumer choice (transportation, careers, education, and so on). Many papers were published in the fields of psychology and economics that built on these fundamental insights.

In the next stage, scientific knowledge is transformed into a commercial product. By the mid-1970s at least two market research companies had developed new sales prediction tools for packaged-goods markets. The knowledge that "stated preferences in surveys" could be used to accurately estimate real-world choices sparked the development of new sales forecasting systems.

Urban and Silk developed the ASSESSOR model and fully documented it in 1978. Over the next seven years, they used it to estimate share for more than 200 new packaged goods products. Lynn Lin developed the BASES New Product Sales Forecasting system and co-founded the BASES Division in 1977 while at the consulting firm Booz Allen Hamilton. BASES and ASSESSOR each had proprietary forecasting models that used concept-and-use survey research along with the details of the planned marketing program to estimate the first year of sales/share for new products.

Both developers marketed their research systems to companies who frequently launched new products. The models promised to increase the odds of test-market success through reliable estimates of in-market results. (Over time and after many validations, each model was able to claim accuracy within 20 percent of market results in the majority of cases.)

For many companies the investment of $50,000 in a simulated test market was justified to increase the odds of success in a full test market, which typically cost $1,500,000.

The adoption process continues with companies agreeing to try out the new methods or services in their business. For a company to enter this stage of the process there must be a business incentive to experiment. P&G was not the first packaged-goods company to test these market simulations models. In the late 1970s and early 1980s, P&G's

own system was working well and they were not looking for a better way to estimate new product sales. There was not an urgent need or big problem to solve.

This is readily understood based on P&G's long and proud history of consumer research and product innovation. P&G is often credited with inventing modern market research. In 1924 they opened the first formal consumer research department. Doc Smelser, the founder, insisted that business managers "never forget the consumer is making the buying decision." According to the company archives, by 1934 P&G had thirty-four researchers talking to consumers in their homes, asking their opinions, and inspiring product improvements. The combined disciplines of consumer research and product research and development formed the foundation of the decision culture for new product management. During the 1930s and 1940s when overall economic conditions were difficult, P&G solidified its brands through product innovation based on disciplined consumer research. Products with meaningful benefits to consumers – like Dreft, the first synthetic detergent; Drene shampoo; and Crest toothpaste – were introduced before the end of the Second World War. (It became culturally ingrained that innovation is the key to brand growth, both in good times and in bad.)

So for P&G in the mid to late 1970s, there was no obvious incentive to experiment with new forecasting systems because big brand restages and new product introductions were still succeeding based on superior technical performance, excellent consumer understanding, and strong brand marketing. Well-loved brands like Tide, Ivory, Crest, Crisco, Downy, Mr. Clean, and Pampers built share and volume through a constant stream of new initiatives that kept them ahead of the competition in terms of consumer preference. New products or major upgrades were considered ready for market when they scored a five-point advantage in overall rating in a single product blind test versus an appropriate benchmark product. The P&G system of separate premarket testing of product and advertising followed by physical test marketing served the company well.

However, by the mid-1980s things began to change. P&G initiatives were not meeting profit and sales targets as reliably as before. National expansions were not replicating the gains of the test markets as closely as they had in the past. Maturing markets, more choices for consumers, and arguably less differentiation on basic product functions – all of this combined with heightened price sensitivity due to a recession – created very different market conditions. The long-standing P&G consensus on what produces share growth and profitable new brands needed re-examination.

This situation prompted P&G's Market Research Department (Bob Davis and Bill Farlow) to experiment with Burke International's BASES model and with Market Decision Systems' ASSESSOR model. Several brand initiative teams agreed to invest in these pre-test market research systems and share their results for corporate learning.

These experiments were much more than a technical qualification of a new research tool. In fact they created considerable anxiety and debate inside P&G because they disrupted important parts of the company's culture and beliefs. Many R&D managers held tightly to the principle that "product is king" and remained convinced that superior products would eventually rise to the top in the market over time. Others within marketing argued that brand advertising and pricing were equally important to the success of new products. R&D suspected that the reason some recent product introductions had fallen short of their expected targets was marketing's inability to persuasively communicate the full benefits to consumers.

So, on one level, test market simulations provided a way to resolve these debates using data on the effects of marketing communications and product experiences to estimate sales. (For an explanation of the research process, see reference note 2 below.) But the models were threatening on another level; neither brand managers nor product managers wanted to diminish the role of their expert judgment by deferring to a "black box" model.

Clearly the company needed to proceed carefully and create strong evidence of major business benefits before undertaking a dramatic change in its work processes and culture.

As use continues, the models are internally calibrated and validated. Experimentation with simulated test markets continued for several years, reinforced by good agreement between the model's forecast of sales and actual results in test markets. P&G in North America selected BASES as its preferred model. In Europe the P&G business teams were using a different forecasting system (also based on concept-and-use tests results) and tension remained over which method was better. By the late 1980s most senior managers were asking for "Concept and Use Purchase Intent" results before approving test markets. R&D and the Market Research Department (MRD) were each developing guidelines and training for good concept board development. Volume forecasts, using purchase intent as input, were optional but often persuasive in the financial forecasting process.

The organization formally incorporates the new system into its decision culture. Now convinced by accumulating data and a greater appreciation of the interdependence of product technology and marketing, the business teams were ready to entertain greater investment in these research models. MRD launched the Global Volume Forecasting Team to create a consistent global approach for approving the launch of new product introductions.[1] The team used the early Bob Davis models as a springboard to develop internal models suitable for other geographies. There were several benefits of internal proprietary models: (1) research costs were kept low during the development process while many iterations were explored; (2) small adjustments to the model could be made for special features of a particular P&G category; and (3) deeper knowledge of the building blocks of new item success was acquired by P&G managers. Even as the internal models got better and more accurate, the BASES model was retained as the final qualification just prior to launch as it was seen as more refined, more sophisticated, and more objective.

Over a four-year period, the Global Volume Forecasting Team rigorously validated internal forecasts, country by country, category by category. There was clear evidence that initiatives that had used MRD or BASES forecasts were far more likely to achieve their financial targets than initiatives that did not. By 1993, top company management decreed that all initiatives must have a forecast, sanctioned by MRD, before launch. *Simulated Test Marketing (or Initiative Volume Forecasting) had now become a formal part of the workflow at P&G.*

Over time, problems and opportunities are approached differently. The adoption was not, however, complete with the 1993 mandate. The practice was still vulnerable to resistance and de-adoption until it was fully ingrained in the decision culture. It took about five years of broad business team experience before the language and structure of the forecasting models became part of the mental models of P&G business managers. At that point, boardroom discussions and formal recommendations dealt with *trial volumes versus repeat volumes, concept norms, purchase frequencies, and consumption rates.* Along with BASES, MRD combed through the database of forecasts and published white papers on generalizations about what could be learned about (a) sampling effectiveness, (b) speed of trial, (c) the role of distribution, and (d) best selection of sizes in a brand line-up.

The true sign of acceptance came when managers realized that they could influence the size of the sales forecast by providing somewhat optimistic assumptions on the marketing plans for the new item. They learned that distribution levels and media weights had a direct influence on trial forecasts and nudged their estimates to the top end of expectations. To prevent "gaming of the system," submodels were developed to provide more rigour around the input estimates.

As managers became more expert at using models to guide their decisions and recommendations, they relaxed their early fears that their judgment would take a backseat to model forecasts. In practice, models were best used as "aids to judgment" and not replacements for judgment. This is because all models require the artful blend of domain knowledge with analytical prowess. The model output is greatly influenced by the choice of input values and boundary conditions. Brand managers and multifunctional teams debated which variables to emphasize, when to make sensible adjustments based on empirical evidence, and what to assume about general market conditions; for example, competitive response, strength of retail support, or category growth dynamics. All of this strengthened P&G's institutional knowledge on new item introductions.

As the business needs and the limitations of the early models were better understood, more knowledge from academic research found its way to application. For example, Andrew Ehrenberg's 1972 book, *Repeat Buying*, revealed many generalized patterns associated with category buying. With the help of Ehrenberg, MRD volume forecasters amended the internal models to incorporate his repeat-buying simulation processes. The accuracy in forecasting improved and fundamental understanding of category-buying patterns accelerated.

New "Thinking Models" shape everyday decisions. These models had benefits beyond improved financial results. By the late 1990s, managers were approaching their business challenges with a new set of thinking tools. They framed solutions around the drivers of growth embedded in the simulation models. Marketing, R&D, sales, and finance planned and managed product initiatives more co-operatively. Everyone had a better understanding of the interdependencies among all parts of the marketing plan. Adoption was now complete. New mental models had taken hold and influenced choices and decisions formally and informally at each stage of the new product process.

The revised picture of the model below includes the softer, more social and psychological stages of adoption. These aspects are as impor-

Figure 15.2 The Journey from Knowledge to Belief (2)

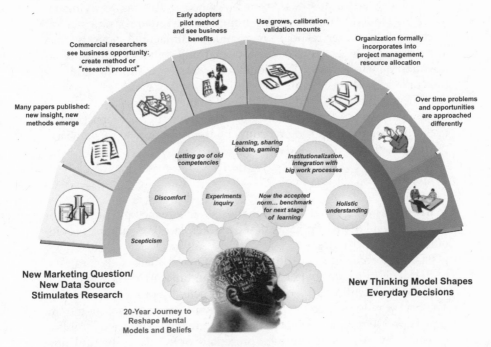

tant as the rational, logical steps. Champions of new knowledge need to anticipate and plan for the discomfort and human issues that go along with changes in business processes. Most people need to have direct experience with something new to develop an internal sense of how it fits into their situation. Old competencies are hard to relinquish or even modify. Any new behaviour has to link with many existing procedures and activities; otherwise it will not find a home.

Section Two. How to Accelerate Adoption of Academic Research

Marketing managers today deal with ever-increasing complexity as business models transform and consumers exert more power through information technology and social connection. Paradoxically, business requires both *deeper specialization* in many emerging areas and *greater simplification* of decision processes to move with agility and efficiency in this dynamic marketplace.

Disciplined research and rapid uptake are going to be matters of pure survival for many industries. Around us whole industries are dying because they failed to foresee or accommodate the impact of new market forces and consumer response (e.g., music, publishing, video rentals, and want ads). Not only do industries rearrange but acceleration of innovation demands faster abandonment or transformation of old business practices. This is threatening, inhibits progress, and is a key part of what needs to be managed in the overall change process.

So what can we learn specifically from the patterns of past adoptions? Below are four strong recommendations for how to seize the opportunities in front of us today.

1. Take a Solutions Orientation

Marketing is an applied science that exists to advance the practice for the good of all the participants in the marketplace: consumers, providers, and intermediaries.

Basic research into consumer behaviour and market dynamics is undertaken to inform better practice. It can only do so, however, if it attracts the attention of people who will actually put it into practice. The best way to engage practitioners is by presenting a solution to an urgent problem they have or a road map towards a business-building opportunity. Academic findings presented primarily as helpful new ways to think about consumers or markets are rarely applied quickly or directly. Many times, I heard people inside P&G say, "That is nice to know, but so what?"

Typical questions asked by business managers when shown really interesting (to me) research findings were:

- What do you want me to do differently?
- How does this insight help me?
- Why should I pay attention to this?
- Can you give me an example of how it built business somewhere else?

Note that I do not mean to imply that business managers are not imaginative enough to see the possibilities for themselves. I am simply saying that most of the time they are in a problem-solving mindset, are working at full capacity to meet the demands of daily business, and do not have the mind-space or time to sort through the huge amount of research being published or imagine how the insights might help in their specific situation.

I had many of these "nice to know" conversations in my role on P&G's Global Trends Team. Well-respected futurists would speak to executives about the big forces of change at work in the world. They would share radical new happenings on the fringe of society which would amaze and provoke the audience. However, back on the category teams the next day, people would scratch their heads and wonder what impact Burning Man or *Second Life* or biotech-enhanced humans might have on marketing shampoo or diapers. (Of course, it is possible to imagine connections, but this clearly wouldn't be the best way for a business team to invest time and energy.) The lesson for the Global Trends Team was clear. We needed to build the bridge between trends and the emerging needs and wants of P&G consumers. Managers welcomed our assistance in navigating the seemingly chaotic array of interesting future trends. Along with outside expert partners we created an organizing framework dubbed the Global Trends Wheel. It mapped significant socio-psychological trends to the concrete changes in the lives of target consumers. Now the business teams could see the importance of incorporating key trends information into their strategic plans and were motivated to imagine new opportunities. For example, growing mistrust of big institutions reinforced the importance of linking brands to strong values. The Pampers brand's partnership with UNICEF was very popular with moms because it meant they could personally contribute to baby welfare globally.

2. "Productize"

We need to think of the output of academic research as "idea products" to be marketed. The customers are organization leaders and managers with everyday brands to market and pressing problems to solve in the competitive and changing market landscape.

Marketers should ideally rely on sound science to guide their experiments towards productive and efficient outcomes, but they don't have the luxury of time to identify important findings. Academics are ready with new research on what really controls decisions and choices, but they don't have the opportunity to deal with the messy, nitty-gritty problems of everyday practice. We have a classic marketing challenge in front of us to bring needs and resources together. There are crucial roles for academics, practicing managers, and skilled intermediaries who can create markets and productize knowledge for application. This can take many different forms:

- Analytical models like simulated test markets or economic models
- Conceptual frameworks like the Brand Building Framework
- Integrating platforms like decision dashboards
- Case study examples like the "Value Sweet Spot"
- New processes like New Product Stage Gates
- New measurements like "clicks" or "views" or "touches"

DIFFUSION THEORY CASE

In the early 2000s, R&D argued that our forecasting models could not predict sales for radically different products. Swiffer (electrostatic floor cleaning and dusters), Dryel (home dry cleaning), and Fit (produce wash) were products so different that they required consumers to adopt new habits. At the time, I was leading an upstream methods development team in the Consumer Research Department, and we encountered Everett Roger's work on the diffusion of innovation. It contained great insight on how to market and forecast radical innovations.

The theory explains and quantifies recurring patterns in terms of key consumer segments. Diffusion begins when a small group of innovators (2.5 per cent) find the innovation and start to engage. The next group to join are deemed the early adopters (13.5 per cent) who, while typically more mainstream, are often opinion leaders for the next group of adopters, the early majority (34 per cent). Once an innovation has been adopted by 50 per cent of the population, the momentum has swung in favour of adoption and the late majority comes on board (34 per cent) – often due to social pressure. Finally, laggards (the remaining 16 per cent) join in as the previous products disappear or become dated.

Convinced of the soundness of this science, we partnered with corporate innovators in marketing and R&D and began a global P&G tour to share stories from Roger's research. A classic is the case of the adoption of hybrid seed by Iowa corn farmers. Knowing P&G managers would need evidence closer to home, we also developed (with the help of outside experts in benchmarking) a new set of cases from packaged-goods marketing . One simple example was the adoption of Maggi 2-Minute Noodles packets in India. In the mid-1980s it was very tough to persuade Indian moms to feed their families a pre-packaged food. They prided themselves on their cooking and tended to stick with family tradition and family culinary secrets. The breakthrough came with the insight that kids came home from school very hungry and moms needed a quick and nutritious snack to serve before dinnertime. A few innovative moms experimented with Maggi noodles and their kids loved them. These moms quickly told other moms. Even the kids would have acted as diffusion agents. A new snack food category had been launched. For Nestlé India, Maggi noodles became the successful launch point for strong brand development in noodles as well as soups, sauces, and ketchups.

Armed with new theory and great case studies, we imagined that new product teams could now design better introductory marketing plans. They would study innovators and partner with opinion leaders to build "word of mouth." These actions would prime the launch and make traditional marketing investments more effective.

But it turned out that the business teams required a lot more support than insightful stories and good advice. They needed concrete products to help them. Over the next few years we went further with the productization of our knowledge. We created new research tools to segment consumers according to their degree of innovativeness. We set up tracking systems for word-of-mouth activity (well before the internet was involved) to evaluate launch progress, and we funded many experiments on opinion-leadership marketing. These tools were precursors to the web-enhanced systems used by P&G today to foster social collaboration and consumer involvement in new product adoption.

3. Invest in Market Development

Markets for new products often have to be created. People did not know they needed microwave ovens or email accounts or Swiffer mops until the marketers of these products invested heavily in demonstrating how they could bring convenience and speed to routine tasks. Similarly, P&G didn't know that new product investment decisions could be made with greater accuracy and speed until academics teamed up with commercial partners to bring new research products to business clients. In many cases, the academics who developed the research-based forecasting models partnered with consulting firms and research houses to fully develop and market the products and service them along the way.

Market developers work with researchers to transform academic learning into useful tools or frameworks that adopting organizations can use to solve important problems or develop strategies. They must understand both the academic science and the needs of practising marketers. The best ways to find partners who will champion new decision science are to look for functional specialists inside large business organizations, or in product development departments of consultancy firms, or in market research companies, or even among business writers and publishers like Harvard Business Review. Without these intermediaries, the insightful ideas from emerging academic research rarely find their way into practice – at least, not within a reasonable time frame.

The relatively rapid adoption of conjoint analysis among academics and practitioners was due to the development work of Rich Johnson along with an extremely practical productization (via Sawtooth Software) of his ideas. He is a true "market maker" for new science, spending the bulk of his career at the interface between academic science and enabling practice. As a newly graduated PhD psychometrician, Johnson joined P&G in 1960 just as large-scale computing was emerging in corporations. He pioneered many applications of regression and factor analysis while also developing a strong interest in market research. This interest eventually led him to the big research firm Market Facts. There he was immersed in the practical problem of how to efficiently research progressive iterations of product designs. He teamed up with rigorous academics who were researching methods of conjoint research that might be useful in designing complex products that had multiple options for multiple attributes. This experience eventually resulted in Johnson's founding of Sawtooth Software – a complete design and analysis package for conjoint research. His tools were accessible to practitioners, commercial researchers, and academics alike. He credits his outstanding success with research invention to his intimate knowledge of the needs of both academics and practitioners.[5]

Marketing Science Institute (MSI) is an entire organization devoted to connecting academics and practitioners to advance the field of marketing. They provide a useful bridge by publishing research priorities that have been developed collaboratively with member companies. These priorities influence the funding of academic research and determine the topics for MSI conferences and other publications. They also facilitate the connection between companies who want to develop new insights for their particular business practice and academics who want to explore that area of market behaviour.

4. Consider the Fit with the Decision Culture

As illustrated in the simulated test-market adoption story, there will always be a natural resistance to changing current processes. Changes in standard activities are costly, disruptive, and confusing. Many careers and much mastery have been invested in the current way of doing things. Steve Knox, formerly the director of Tremor (a word-of-mouth marketing service company),[4] describes this resistance as the "Competency Trap." It is often the group most skilled in the current generation of business practice who is slowest to move to the next generation of practice. Consciously or subconsciously, managers don't want to lose the feeling and efficiency of their current mastery and so are slower to see the need for change.

In the case of simulated test marketing, P&G probably would have seen benefits of the new science earlier if they hadn't been so skilled for so long with basic product research and consumer understanding.

It can be relatively easy to introduce a new decision-support tool or method that is a simple replacement for one part of an existing process, costs about the same, and is owned by the same department. Straightforward replacements look much more familiar to people; they can imagine how to use them and see where they fit in the overall scheme of things.

But when a marketing innovation is incremental, adds costs, and brings new players into a decision process, it will meet with natural resistance. For example, it took many years and intense effort to move P&G's primary copy testing method from the standard metric of Day-After Recall (DAR) to a more predictive but complex pre/post-testing that measured persuasive power. The new method was based on sound academic research, published around 1990, that revealed DAR and sales did not correlate well. Yet it took several years of experimentation and debate with advertising agencies for the company to formally move to the more comprehensive communication testing. Eventually, because of the thorough adoption effort, both new thinking and new research methods became part of the corporate mental model and were well integrated into P&G's practices.

Even smaller innovations like new measures or new types of data face compatibility challenges. Many academic research findings deal with a small part of a large, complex decision matrix. If new metrics or types of data are not compatible with the overall decision ecosystem, they will be hard to use. Any new parts must fit nicely into the existing machinery.

Today, P&G is a successful frontrunner in the testing and development of digital advertising. The company's pace of innovation and adoption has accelerated. One might speculate that this is the result of digital advertising fitting more naturally within the existing research systems and overall thinking on communication effectiveness. Importantly, digital marketing was also publicly embraced as the way of the future by top marketing executives early on in the information technology revolution. High-level champions can be very effective at establishing the need for change.

It is easy to see why many good ideas do not get taken up. Organizations can only manage a few changes in their work processes at a time. The ones that are selected have to be very compelling and compete against many other ideas for improved business practice.

Section Three. How Will Marketers Put These Insights into Practice?

Practitioners would turn this question around and say, "How does the information in this book address my issues?" Whose responsibility is it to connect the ideas to new practice; the practitioner's, the researcher's, or a third party's? Practitioners are receptive to help from many different directions, including academic research, but they are searching for specific connections to their important questions (unlike a game of *Jeopardy!* where the answer is out there looking for a question). It stands to reason that marketing innovations presented as "solutions to pressing needs" or "compelling opportunities for gain" are more likely to meet receptive audiences than face general organizational resistance.

A) What Do Marketers Need?

I asked the marketers in my network for the big questions on their mind today. Here is what they said:

Subject	Marketing Question
Branding	What role will branding play in the future where radical transparency is the norm and consumers can make evidence-based decisions at the touch of an iPhone app?
Communication and New Media	How are we going to develop new communication models with unpredictable "new media" elements that are largely out of marketers' hands to manage?
	How would we create communication from the bottom up if we were not carrying the "ghosts of evolution" of traditional marketing? We continue to cram "mini ads" into web-based and handheld media. Would we do that if we'd never had TV-based advertising in the first place?

Subject	Marketing Question
	Could I establish a reward structure to drive word of mouth (WOM)?
	Are there insights that would yield just-in-time (closer to store-visiting or shopping time frame) awareness building? Are these digital or is there something else emerging?
Location/Context	How will we leverage location-based information to more effectively market to our targets? To create a better loyalty model?
	How do people respond (non-consciously) to contexts like the store . . . but also in front of their TV, online, using their smartphone?
Privacy	Is Google going to eventually know everything about us? Listening to our conversations on Android phones, reading our email, tracking our locations, seeing our bank account balances when using Google Chrome, deducing how we likely feel based on complex algorithms, and so on? Will we let Google do this? Will it make the world a better place?
Pricing	How can brands maintain necessary margins when economies are drifting in and out of recession and raw material prices are fluctuating wildly?
Stores	The grocery store of the future – what does it look like? How might technology improve or change the shopping experience?
	How do I improve the interaction between consumers and the shelf? There are many different sources of data here; how do I integrate these with existing data to improve sales and profitability?
	The majority of shampoo volume in India is sold in sachets without consumer visibility in the store for a large segment of channels. The consumer has to be aware of the product and ask for it by name in order to get it into their basket. What shopper knowledge is most relevant in these scenarios and how do we build awareness beyond the obvious traditional media?

Subject	Marketing Question
Product Innovation	Can I link the data from loyalty and WOM to the product development funnel in order to hone new areas of demands, new products, and new fast prototypes? Can I tie consumers to this database and use it as an ongoing dynamic laboratory?
	The majority of brands – including private-label brands – in beauty care and laundry have achieved levels of performance that are so far beyond sufficient that consumers see less and less differentiation on traditional performance vectors. This is true in both developing and developed regions. How can we help manufacturers determine the point of diminishing returns for a specific category in a specific country so that money can be redistributed once it has been hit?

Marketing Science Institute uses a more rigorous process than mine to determine the research priorities of their member companies. Their current set of published priorities hover around two big areas: (1) marketers want to create strategies that anticipate and respond to changing conditions; and (2) they want to advance marketing management and practice to meet the challenges of the evolving landscape (see http://www.msi.org).

No matter how you look at it, practitioners have questions on almost every aspect of marketing. There is lots of help to be gained from the research in this book; some of it is in the form of straightforward advice but other insights require further productization and partnership with expert market developers to make the connections clear. Here are my thoughts on the adoption potential of the specific insights in this book.

B) Ready Solutions

There are many intriguing ideas for consumer brand marketers that are relatively easy to work with right away. A few are highlighted below. (Readers who are experts in other fields like social policy, health care, government, or insurance might highlight other opportunities.)

BRANDING IDEAS

In chapter 13 of this volume, Pankaj Aggarwal offers thoughtful relationship advice for brands trying to connect more personally with their
consumers. Marketers need to be very aware of the kind of relationship
they are signalling since good efforts can backfire. Consumers will react
negatively to a brand that provides seemingly friendly help but then
turns around and charges for it (e.g., banks charging to sort out bill con-
fusion with a third party). The tone of the relationship also determines
how happy consumers are to help the brand by providing referrals or
testimonials.

Morality in consumer decisions affects almost every brand in some
way. Nina Mazar's research on the role of morality in chapter 10 offers
some very practical ways to manage the issues without offending good
customers. Her research is directly relevant for reducing online piracy
of digital products or curbing the "wardrobing" practice that plagues
fashion retailers. Insurance companies will find great ideas for promoting more honest reporting and less "fudging" of claims. Even consumer
goods products suffer losses from fraud when consumers knowingly
purchase counterfeit products. Her prescriptions for redirecting these
behaviours are quite provocative and straightforward. For example, insurance companies can move the "honour statement" to the top of their
reporting form to obtain more truthful data. Or how about people who
buy hybrid cars and then drive more, using up any CO_2 benefit to the
planet? Nina Mazar describes this as the licensing effect and ironically
recommends less patting hybrid owners on the back for their virtuous
purchase and more communication that "green" decisions are the norm
for everyone.

NEW MEDIA COMMUNICATIONS

Avi Goldfarb's "What Makes the Internet Different?" (chapter 4) has
"application-ready" advice especially for marketers launching into
mobile communications. The interplay between online and offline is
heightened on this platform, making it a far more attractive space for
businesses drawing local traffic (restaurants, community theatres, dog
grooming). Oddly enough, the investment in mobile apps and mobile
search rankings would pay out more for local merchants than for the
bigger mass-market players.

Here is another gem that seems obvious in hindsight: online marketing is particularly valuable for people who are different from others in
their local community. If there are lots of people with the same inter-

ests, demographics, and lifestyles, then there will be a ready supply of products and services to meet their needs in the local community. The people who most need online commerce and connection are the ones unlike their neighbours. Brands should invest in online marketing when their target consumers are geographically scattered or isolated (e.g., people who suffer from a fairly rare medical condition, participate in an unusual hobby, or enjoy obscure forms of music).

In chapter 2, David Dunne provides both cautionary tales and success stories to support a simple memorable marketing mantra for Web 2.0: Lose, Monitor, Engage. (Lose the illusion of control, monitor public conversation about your brand, and engage the consumer.)

His advice for dealing with rumours is a good example of pragmatic problem solving. First of all, brand managers need to know what is being said publicly and by whom. There are lots of popular rating sites like Tripadvisor.com or the more far-ranging Suck500.com to keep the marketer informed. When negative or false information is in circulation, marketers need to stay cool, not overreact or become defensive with bloggers and social networkers. Marketers who engage with an open mind and treat the exchange with respect often learn a lot about the collective impression of the brand formed by lots of consumer experiences and conversations. This helps build stronger, more relevant brand communications in partnership with the consumer. David Dunne has another great rule of thumb for dealing with rumours: only pursue those that are credible, severe, and salient. All in all, this chapter provides a new-age rulebook for updating many old chestnuts of marketing.

CUSTOMER EXPERIENCE

Anyone whose business requires consumers to wait in line will find terrific guidance in chapter 12, "Hang On: The Psychology of Time and Implications for Designing Queues." Dilip Soman has very concrete ideas for making lineups feel faster, pleasanter, and more productive for everyone involved. "Keep it moving and change the scenery" are good rules for preventing people from leaving the line in frustration. The chapter strikes a familiar chord with the discussion of social justice and lineups. We all know the feeling of outrage at queue jumpers or the irritation when a new line opens up and the latecomers rush in. Businesses can greatly improve consumers' perceptions of their fairness and speed of service by following the design principles in this chapter.

Beyond the obvious lineup situations (banks, grocery stores, and government offices), there are queues associated with many more businesses, for example with phone lines for customer service, technical support, or product information. The same principles apply for creating a positive interaction with the customer. As communication technologies advance so will the diversity of line-ups, virtual and real.

C) Productization Opportunities

There are many insights shared in this book that relate to the human psychology of choice and decision-making. In fact there are so many newly understood influences on consumer choices that practitioners will have trouble selecting the right ones to address their situation. There is a big need for situational interpretation and new navigational tools and methods.

APPLYING BEHAVIOURAL ECONOMICS
Chapter 6, "Hedonomics: Why People Do Not Buy What They Enjoy the Most," presents the hypothesis that marketers can increase consumer satisfaction with products without asking them to buy more of a product or upgrade to a product of better quality. The answer is to help more consumers buy the best product for their situation in the first place. Consumers are surprisingly poor at making the best choices, often because there are too many choices and too much information to process. Claire Tsai's research demonstrates that consumers' ultimate satisfaction with their choice is affected by the following:

- the level of arousal of the chooser – for example, if they are hungry, tired, anxious, celebratory, or excited
- whether the evaluation is made in isolation (take this item or nothing) or in comparison to something else (trip to Paris vs. Hawaii)
- whether or not the advantage will wear off over time and become the new norm (e.g., a salary increase that becomes the baseline over time)
- the presence of intermediary rewards like loyalty points or air miles
- the form and timing of payment (i.e., using cash causes the most pain on payment)
- the amount of hard evidence available for the most important attribute (e.g., the power of the stereo has more available data than richness of sound but is less important to long-term enjoyment)

There are many strategies that marketers can use to nudge their consumers towards happier choices. How will practitioners select the best ones for their products? Academics need to help marketers navigate this complex set of decisions by participating in the development of an application framework or decision aid.

VISUALIZATION AND NEW PRODUCTS

Web 2.0 and digital technology are rapidly expanding the use of visualization for all kinds of communications – both personal and commercial. Min Zhao's "Just Imagine: The Role of Visualization in New Product Evaluation" (chapter 9) provides very timely research on how to heighten interest in a new product and increase the accuracy of sales predictions. Yet marketers will have trouble using all of this research to design a good visualization because there are many questions to consider.

Suppose you are preparing to launch a new home appliance that extracts surface pesticides from fruits and vegetables without damaging the food or destroying nutrients. (This is a totally hypothetical product.) You know it is important to visualize the product in use, especially when it involves a habit change and a capital investment (for example, $50). According to Min Zhao's research, there are many different ways to design the visualization and each of these choices will impact the overall result. Do you focus on the process of using the new appliance or do you visualize the outcome of cleaner food without purchasing expensive organic produce? Do you emphasize the feelings of confidence and security associated with this new food preparation method or do you focus on the science and rational proof of contamination removal? Do you use visualization for early marketing efforts or just before purchase with live or video demos? Do you evoke past feelings of uncertainty and guilt over homemakers not feeding their families organic produce or do you focus on the new experience and satisfaction of doing good things?

It is very complicated to make all of these choices, yet each decision can affect the outcome. A navigation tool is needed: a clear step-by-step process for diagnosing the situation and setting the right objectives and strategies for visualization would be an essential aid to marketers. Academics can help create an application for this.

INCORPORATING NEW METRICS AND MODELS

Some of the insights in this book are aimed at intermediary experts, not front-line practitioners. This is the case with Andrew Ching's research on forward-thinking consumer behaviours (chapter 7). He points out that the current analytical models for evaluating marketing strategies and pricing policies fail to account for "forward-thinking" questions like: how much do consumers consider resale value when making a new item purchase? The resale market is growing, especially with digital products that do not physically deteriorate and can be resold until they are outdated. New versus used textbook purchase decisions frequently consider the books' resale potential. New car prices are directly influenced by used car prices and vice versa.

Andrew Ching's analytical approach for addressing forward thinking was presented to marketing scientists and modellers at the AMA Advanced Research Techniques conference in June 2011. Practitioners will benefit at a later stage when this research has been incorporated into new models and estimation tools that have been made commercially available.

D) Consideration of Fit for Adopting Organizations

This book contains sound, research-based advice for improving brand strategies and managing marketing resources more productively in the current context. Every marketing organization is trying to cope with rapid change and implement new approaches that work with their own distinct culture.

ADAPTING TO NEW CHALLENGES

Judging from the above list of their needs, marketers today are adjusting to simultaneous changes from many external directions. "The Challenge of Today's Marketing Environment" by David Soberman (chapter 1) reports that managers are also dealing with internal organizational tensions that get in the way of progress. For example:

1 Rapid change and instant information are causing mangers to focus on quick decisions and frequent plan adjustments. This distracts them from doing broader, more diverse explorations of longer-term strategies for thriving in new conditions.
2 The traditional focus on share and beating the competition has been built into many organizations' training and development programs. New values need to be instilled to avoid counterproductive, combative behaviours and balance share growth in existing categories with growth created through new market and category development.

3 Organizations need to encourage the transfer of knowledge from experienced managers to younger employees in order to benefit from
past organizational learning. Yet "old wisdom" can't be allowed to
crowd out the adaptive new learning that is occurring at all levels in
the organization.
4 Information is power, yet much of that power has been shifting
from marketing firms to retailers and directly to consumers. Managers need to continually revisit their information strategies to provide
the right business intelligence, then artfully integrate old and new
information sources into strategies and business plans.

Given my background in consumer and market information, I can
easily relate to the need for information sources and decision models to
keep pace with changing business strategies. When P&G moved from
brand management to category management, all the decision-support
systems and research models had to be upgraded to reflect total category activity. Market mix models and new-item forecasting models all
had to project total category sales and profits instead of estimates for
individual brands. This in turn demanded much deeper knowledge of
competitive reactions and strategies.

Today, the power of consumers to shape brand impressions through
social media and word of mouth is inflicting even more dramatic pressure to evolve information and research systems. Consumer-generated
communications must be monitored to understand brand identity and
nurture loyalty, yet these data don't look anything like information obtained in traditional survey research. Managers are learning new ways
to integrate diverse sources of information with traditional metrics and
decision models.

We are on the verge of a total reinvention of market research methods
and change is coming fast. Organizations will need the help of new information experts, traditional research experts, and academics to create
information systems that will uniquely support their business through
the next waves of change.

EVOLVING THE FOUR PS

All organizations have their own way of managing the four Ps of marketing: price, product, place, and promotion. This is based on their
collective wisdom drawn from past successes and disappointments.
Upgrades to marketing practice in any of these areas must simultaneously accommodate new realities and lessons from the past. Chapter

11, "Manage Customer Value through Incentives," does both. Mengze Shi re-examines tried and true incentives like sweepstakes and loyalty programs using the psychological bias of loss aversion to differentiate new users from current brand users. A new user takes a bigger gamble because they have to switch brands for a chance to win a big prize whereas the current user would probably have considered the brand anyway. To attract new users, sweepstakes should offer a big prize and lots of smaller prizes (like free coffee from coffee shops) to give more hope of winning something. "Winner takes all" sweepstakes are more suitable for retaining current users. Insights such as these are easily adopted to improve the success of familiar promotional vehicles.

Social networking, on the other hand, significantly changes the rules. For example, group buying programs like MobShop or Groupon or LivingSocial alter the whole pricing strategy for consumers. To take advantage of an offer, consumers have to commit funds and hope that enough people participate for the promotion to be executed. If the promotion fails, they have invested time and effort for nothing and have to get their money back. Research has shown that these promotions are more successful when progress with signups is transparent. The more participants who sign up early, the more likely it is that latecomers will sign up with confidence, and the more likely it is that the whole thing proceeds. (If no one knows the progress, this momentum does not have a chance to build.)

This is just one example of research that helps organizations manage new pricing structures without disrupting the fundamental pricing strategies for the mainstream distribution channels.

STRATEGIC CHOICE – NEW BRAND VS. LINE EXTENSION

In chapter 3, Sridhar Moorthy addresses the question of whether it is better to introduce a new product as a line extension or as a new brand. A simple framework is offered that condenses the learning from two different research streams. In essence, this framework suggests that the decision can be made based on the degree of fit between the new product and an existing brand's combined marketing identity (image, personality, familiarity) and product identity (observed and experienced attributes). If the new product is a good fit with an existing brand then the economics strongly favour the line extension choice.

This framework provides thoughtful guidance on some, but not all of the critical issues involved. The next steps would be to find practitioner partners to test the framework in the context of their organization's decision processes and category strategies. It would be instructive to both sides to see how and where academic research in this area can guide real-world strategies.

Having participated in many of these debates at P&G, I can attest to the complexity and intensity of these discussions. Large brands are the crown jewels of an organization and their image and equity need to be protected and defended with great care. Line extensions can present a risk to the parent product and are considered very carefully. This presumes that the product innovation comes first and the branding decision follows, but this isn't always the case. Sometimes a brand's growth strategy identifies the need for a line extension and specifies the desired product innovation. When brands have large shares in mature categories they often look to adjacent categories to meet their growth targets. In other cases, new forms or subcategories emerge to address new consumer needs; a big brand may choose to launch a line extension to participate in growth without disrupting current users.

Over the years, P&G's North American laundry detergent category wrestled with many of these issues. Throughout the 1980s and 1990s there was a significant rearrangement of brands and forms in P&G's laundry detergent portfolio. Over this period, Oxydol was sold and Dreft was restricted to U.S. distribution only. New technologies like enzymes and two-in-one detergent plus softener were introduced as upgrades to Bold, a smaller share brand that was less risky than Tide. A new brand, ERA, was launched as P&G's first liquid detergent for main wash use. Tide liquid came later when the subcategory was more mature. In the late 1980s, powder detergents were compacted to compete better with liquids, reduce environmental impact, and adapt to front-loading machines. Over time more new technologies were introduced as Tide line extensions, such as Tide with Bleach and Tide Free. Tide Ultra was introduced as a line extension and then quickly became the main format for Tide powder. More recently, Tide has been extended into the stain-release category with Tide to Go and Tide Stain Release. Early decisions favoured new brand introductions but over the years Tide has proved to be a very extendable brand, housing almost all P&G laundry cleaning innovations.

There is an evolving and dynamic interdependency between category strategy, brand strategy, and product innovation. It would be ideal for academics and practitioners to engage more directly in promoting the right research and applying the best learning.

In Summary

In publishing this book, the Rotman School of Management Marketing Faculty has taken an important step forward on the road to application. Beyond bringing current research to the attention of marketers, they are inviting conversation and ongoing dialogue. Readers are encouraged to contact the editors directly by email to comment, question, or share experiences Readers are also invited to participate in our blog to build understanding and strengthen communication. The best strategy for working better together is to invest in mutual understanding and rela-tionship building. Over time, all parties will see more ways to support each other and advance the practice of marketing in the process.

Here are my parting thoughts for each of the participants in this whole complex system.

Thoughts for Academics

Don't assume that new knowledge on its own will inspire ideas for new practice. Your role should not end with the publication of new insights; others need your help to figure out how to incorporate new thinking into their decisions and plans. Academics who do stay involved and help develop tools, models, and processes have a much greater chance of seeing their research applied.

This is a good model for academics who want to consult broadly and in-teract with leaders of different organizations. Development of decision-support products builds credibility and expands your network of po-tential business partners and research supporters. These partnerships often inspire future research that addresses real and pressing problems. They can open up new opportunities for financial support and data sharing.

Ongoing partnerships between model builders and model users also minimize the risk that the tools will be used inappropriately or beyond the ranges of their proven accuracy. We have seen financial models blow up when real-world events forced existing models into areas well outside the conditions for which they were built. Knowing and adher-ing to sensible boundary conditions is critical for model reliability and utility.

Teaching is another important channel for new knowledge transfer, especially in non-degree programs and corporate training workshops. It creates direct access to marketing leaders who want professional development and are receptive to fresh ideas for their organizations. These leaders may not be the ones who actually modify models and change decision metrics, but they will champion adoption inside their organizations if they see the potential to improve practice and boost the bottom line. Academics who bring their research forward in these forums will benefit from the perspective of practitioners, see new possibilities for application, and develop ideas for future research.

Teaching from your research also promotes application, because early exposure shortens the timeline to adoption. It is exciting that Rotman is offering courses in behavioural economics well ahead of the writing of standard textbooks or consensus among business schools that it should be a core subject. The students of these courses will be powerful envoys for new thinking wherever they choose to develop their careers.

Presenting your work at industry associations and general audience conferences also helps develop the market for the knowledge and forces a solutions orientation to its communication. Consider the power of white papers and overview research reports to reach adopters who do not read professional and scientific journals. They put research learning into a broader, more accessible context that invites application.

Thoughts for Executives

Professional development on a personal and organizational level is taking many forms in today's fast-paced market environment. Customized training sessions with academic institutions, as discussed above, can be a great and timely complement to sponsoring MBAs for emerging business leaders. Inviting academics to participate with in-house education programs is another good way to have a deeper exploration of emerging research through dialogue and idea exchange.

In a less direct fashion, you can nurture better bridging between academics and your business practice by enlisting help from strategic partners in communications agencies, research firms, and consulting companies. Ask them to investigate the possibility for your business in new areas of academic research. This is often an efficient way for an organization to screen the landscape of academic research. Your firm gets the new solutions and the strategic partner gets the benefit of developing a new set of services that can be used more broadly.

Whichever route you take, there are benefits to engaging early. By helping to develop better decision-support tools, you are able to shape them to the particular needs of your business. If you wait for others to lead the development, the resulting products are less likely to be well tuned to your needs. You also develop closer ties to the network of innovators in business practice and consumer knowledge. They will help you focus on important signals of change and opportunity in the years ahead.

Thoughts for Students

On almost any given day, you can open a newspaper and read an article challenging the relevance of business education, and MBAs in particular. Many argue that business learning is not experiential enough and that its core content has not been updated for the realities of today's business world. There is broad concern that the schools are not preparing the graduates to put their knowledge into practice.

While I do not agree with this overall assessment, I do see the criticism as cautionary for current students. You need to be aware that the future application of your knowledge is mostly in your own hands. Your agility, insight, and ingenuity, along with your power to persuade and influence, will determine how big a role you can play to move your organization forward in difficult and dynamic markets.

The ideas and research described in this book are part of the emerging knowledge that will shape future business practice and be part of your professional life in the years ahead. I encourage you to read and engage where you can with the people who are forging new ground. Even if there is just one area that grabs your interest – go with it.

Thoughts for Everyone

The divisions between research and practice, testing and expansion, designing and consuming, brand builders and brand consumers are breaking down, and new rules of engagement are developing at every interface. As citizens, consumers, and professionals, we stand to prosper by learning and growing together. One thing that clearly unites and fascinates us all is the mystery of human behaviour. Let the conversation continue.

REFERENCES

1 Initial members of the P&G Global Volume Forecasting Community, 1990–3: Bob Davis, Mitch Barns, Delaine Hampton, Joan Lewis, Marlon McCormick,

Thomas Methner, Phil Parker, Chris Hannaford, Joe Stagaman, Bob Alt, Kathy French, Rafael Corral, Jos De Winter, Seiki Imanishi, and John Cook.

2 The format of a BASES research project is as follows: the new product team provides the finished product, the communication concept, package graphics, and pricing information to the research supplier who then recruits a large sample of potential consumers to participate in the study. Respondents first read a concept board describing the new item – you can think of a concept board as a rough print ad with product, price, and size availability information. Respondents indicate their purchase interest and then take the finished product home to use it for a few weeks. They are contacted again by the research firm and asked about their purchase interest. Several other diagnostic measures are taken. These purchase intent measures are combined with information on the marketing plan to model the sales/share. (The BASES forecasting model grew to dominate the forecasting business and has since been acquired by AC Nielsen.)

3 ASSESSOR is Glenn Urban's forecasting model. It was first published in 1983 (see http://www.jstor.org/stable/25060493). The ASSESSOR research system is conceptually similar to BASES but involves different processes for estimating the share of choices for the new product among existing products.

4 Tremor is a marketing service company that was launched by P&G to develop word-of-mouth marketing programs among teens. It has helped launch several P&G initiatives and has been used by external companies as well.

5 Much of the description in this paragraph has been adapted from a series of articles honouring Rich Johnson in the *Journal of Marketing Research* 42, no. 3 (2005).

Contributors

Each of the contributors is a faculty member in the marketing area at the Rotman School of Management, University of Toronto. Collectively, this group has a wide range of academic and business expertise, and they have served in many leading roles in research, consulting, and advisory capacities in academic and business organizations alike. Brief biographies of each contributor appear below, and more details can be found on our website at http://www.rotman.utoronto.ca/marketing/. You can also contact the authors at flux@rotman.utoronto.ca.

Pankaj Aggarwal received his PhD and MBA from the Graduate School of Business, University of Chicago. His doctoral dissertation applied the interpersonal relationship metaphor to a consumer-brand context and won the Alden G. Clayton best dissertation award in 2000, given by the Marketing Science Institute. In his recent work, he adopts the brand-as-a-person metaphor to conduct some pioneering research in the area of product and brand anthropomorphism. His research has appeared in leading marketing and psychology journals. He serves on the editorial review board of the *Journal of Consumer Research* and the *Journal of Consumer Psychology*. In the past, he worked in the advertising industry for many years, last serving as the vice-president in the New Delhi office of Contract Advertising (J. Walter Thompson), India.

Ron N. Borkovsky received his PhD from the Kellogg School of Management, Northwestern University. His research interests include the computation and estimation of dynamic models of industry equilibrium. He has applied such models to study innovation, product development, and brand building.

Andrew T. Ching's research focuses on developing new empirical models and estimation methods to understand the choices of consumers and firms. His research has led to a new discrete choice model that outperforms the commonly used multinomial logit or nested multinomial logit models. He has also developed a new Bayesian estimation algorithm that reduces the computational burden of estimating dynamic programming discrete choice models, which are commonly used to capture forward-looking agents' behaviour. He has applied these models to study how credit/debit cards' rewards programs would affect consumer choice of payment methods, how word of mouth (WOM) affects consumer choice, and how firms decide their marketing mix when consumers need to learn about product qualities via WOM.

David Dunne is an adjunct professor of marketing. As a senior marketing executive with Unilever, he led a marketing division and was responsible for the success of several well-known brands. His interests include innovation and problem solving, particularly the application of design methodologies to business problems. He has been widely published in journals such as *Harvard Business Review* and *Academy of Management Learning & Education*. He teaches marketing, advertising, and strategic innovation to students and executives throughout the world, and has won many awards for his teaching, including the prestigious 3M National Fellowship and the University of Toronto President's Teaching Award. He consults to multinationals in consumer packaged goods, advertising, and pharmaceuticals and is regularly interviewed by the media on these and related issues.

Avi Goldfarb received his PhD in economics from Northwestern University. His research explores how information technology affects consumers, companies, and marketing strategies. Research support from Google, Bell University Labs, SSHRC, Industry Canada, and the Sloan Foundation has resulted in over thirty publications in a variety of fields including marketing, economics, law, and computer science.

Delaine Hampton is an executive in residence at Rotman. Over a thirty-five-year career (1974 to 2009) at Procter & Gamble, she held roles of increasing responsibility in product development, marketing, market research, and lastly in corporate innovation for consumer and market knowledge. She continues to contribute as an "emeritus" member of the North Star Fellowship, P&G's lifetime mastery community for consumer and market knowledge innovators. Delaine has added significantly to P&G's past and future growth by translating new theory and science into practical business application tools used for product innovation and strategy development. She continues to advise and consult with various organizations seeking innovations in marketing strategy, practices, and consumer understanding.

Aparna A. Labroo is a consumer psychologist and holds the Patricia C. Ellison Professorship of Marketing. She holds a PhD in marketing (with minors in statistics and psychology) from Cornell University. Her research studies the effect of consumers' feelings on their decisions, especially decisions pertaining to product purchases and brand evaluations, health-related choices, and charitable giving. She has written numerous articles in this area, including several articles in the *Journal of Consumer Research*, the *Journal of Marketing Research*, *Journal of Personality and Social Psychology*, *Marketing Science*, *Motivation and Emotion*, and *Psychological Science*.

Nina Mazar received her PhD from the Johannes-Gutenberg University Mainz. Her research and experimentation focuses on behavioural economics, social and moral acts in decision-making, as well as pricing, and has been featured in NYT bestsellers *Predictably Irrational* and *The Upside of Irrationality*.

Andrew A. Mitchell holds a PhD from the University of California at Berkeley, and has done pioneering research in the areas of goal-driven behaviour, memory, self-control processes, and non-conscious influences on consumer behaviour. He has published numerous articles in several leading journals and has received a number of research awards. In his spare time, he enjoys jazz, the opera, fine dining, and contemporary classical music.

Sridhar Moorthy serves as a senior consultant at CRA International in addition to his Rotman position, and until recently he was also the vice-president (education) for INFORMS Society for Marketing Science. His PhD is from Stanford University, and he has previously taught at University of Rochester, Yale, INSEAD, UCLA, Wharton, and Indian School of Business. Professor Moorthy's research uses the tools of economics to study marketing problems. He is co-editor-in-chief of *Quantitative Marketing and Economics*, associate editor of *Management Science*, and serves on the editorial board of *Journal of Marketing Research*. He is the co-author (with Philip Kotler and Gary Lilien) of the textbook *Marketing Models* (Prentice Hall).

Mengze Shi is an expert on incentive programs for marketing and sales management. His research draws on and synthesizes theories from economics, social psychology, and operations. He has worked on incentive designs with companies in many industries including airlines, catalogues, financial services, gasoline retail, and wireless services. In his leisure time, Professor Shi enjoys watching and reading about sports, both professional and at the youth level.

David Soberman holds the Canadian National Chair of Strategic Marketing and has previously served on the faculty at INSEAD. He is a licensed professional engineer (Ontario), holds a PhD (management) from the University of Toronto, and an MBA and a BSc in chemical engineering from Queen's University. Professor Soberman's research consists of using applied microeconomics and game theory to analyse marketing phenomena. He uses this approach to examine how the operation of markets is affected by the exchange of information between firms and customers, relationships within the distribution channel, and the introduction of innovations to markets. His research has appeared in *Marketing Science, Management Science,* the *Journal of Marketing Research,* the *Journal of Marketing,* and the *California Management Review.* He has held a number of positions in marketing management, sales, and engineering with Molson Breweries, Nabisco Brands Ltd., and Imperial Oil Ltd.

Dilip Soman studies interesting human behaviours and applies his findings to marketing, consumer welfare, and public policy. He has a PhD from the University of Chicago and an MBA from the Indian Institute of Management, and has previously taught at the University of Colorado, Hong Kong University of Science and Technology (both full-time), the Indian School of Business, and the National University of Singapore (as a visiting faculty member). His research in behavioural economics, marketing strategy, social media, CRM/data-driven marketing, pricing, customer engagement, and customer psychology is widely published and cited, and he is a sought-after executive trainer and consultant in these areas. He is also the co-author of *Managing Customer Value: One Stage at a Time* (World Scientific). When not working on any of these, he spends time on photography, watching Bollywood masala movies, and agonizing over successive Indian cricket teams.

Claire I. Tsai received her PhD in marketing (with minors in economics and behavioural science) from the Booth School of Business, University of Chicago. She also received an MBA from Booth and has worked in financial service in New York, Taipei, and Hong Kong. She adopts n behavioural economics approach in studying decision-making in such disparate areas as financial decisions, prosocial behaviour, and food consumption. She finds that in many situations, people ultimately choose products or make decisions that they enjoy less than the options they reject. Her work has appeared in leading marketing and psychology journals and often receives featured coverage in popular media. Outside of research, she enjoys spending time with family, classical music, golf, and visiting architecturally noteworthy buildings.

Min Zhao received her PhD in marketing from the University of North Carolina at Chapel Hill. Her primary research interests include choice over time, mental simulation, new product adoption, and consumers' affective experiences. Her research has appeared in marketing journals such as the *Journal of Marketing Research*, *Journal of Consumer Research*, *Journal of Consumer Psychology*, and *Journal of Product Innovation Management*.

Subject Index

Name Index